A REGIONAL HISTORY OF
THE RAILWAYS OF GREAT BRITAIN

General Editors
DAVID ST JOHN THOMAS AND J. ALLAN PATMORE

VOLUME XII
SOUTH WALES

OTHER TITLES IN THIS SERIES

A REGIONAL HISTORY OF
THE RAILWAYS OF GREAT BRITAIN

Volume XII

SOUTH WALES

by
D. S. M. Barrie, OBE, FCIT
Revised by Peter E. Baughan

WITH 60 PLATES
11 MAPS
AND FOLDING MAP

DAVID ST JOHN THOMAS PUBLISHER

an imprint of
*T*HOMAS & *L*OCHAR
PO Box 4, Nairn IV12 4HU

British Library Cataloguing in Publication Data

Regional history of the railways of
Great Britain. – Vol. 12: South Wales. – 2rev. ed
I. Barrie, D. S. M. II. Baughan, Peter E.
385.09429

ISBN 0-946537-69-0

First published 1980
Second edition 1994

Typeset by XL Publishing Services, Nairn
Printed and bound in Great Britain by
Butler & Tanner Ltd, Frome and London
for David St John Thomas Publisher
PO Box 4, Nairn IV12 4HU.

Contents

Note: For key to line ownerships in folding map at end,
also to area maps within text, see overleaf.

8

Area Maps
Regional Map is Inside Back Cover

Key to all Maps

———————	GW
———————	LNW
++++++++	Midland
— — — — —	Cambrian
—·—·—·—	Taff Vale
— — — —	Rhymney
—·—·—·—	Barry
+—+—+—+	Brecon & Merthyr
—ı—ı—ı—	Neath & Brecon
·— — —·—	Port Talbot
—·—··—	Cardiff
—···—···—	Rhondda & Swansea Bay
— — — — —	S. Wales Mineral
····················	Alexandra (Newport & S. Wales) Docks & Rly
(GV) +++++++++++++++++	Other Railways:–
GV	Gwendraeth Valley
BP&GV	Burry Port & Gwendraeth Valley
L&MM	Llanelly & Mynydd Mawr
S&M	Swansea & Mumbles
(GW & RR JT) ════════	Joint lines (as indicated)

In the maps, pre-Grouping company ownership is indicated as in 1921, except that in a few cases companies which retained their separate existences until the operation of the Railways Act 1921 are shown in the key of the company which worked them, eg the Penarth Harbour, Dock & Railway is shown as part of the Taff Vale Railway, and the Vale of Glamorgan as part of the Barry Railway.

Introduction

The geographical region with which this book is concerned embraces in railway historical terms the western or industrial part of the former county of Monmouthshire (now Gwent), the whole of Glamorganshire, the relevant parts of Brecknock (Breconshire, now Powys), and the three westerly former counties beyond the River Loughor. This reference to 'former' counties is necessary because in administrative terms the area was realigned by the Local Government Act, 1972. If, for instance, this book had been published prior to that Act, I should have perforce referred to the region as 'South Wales & Monmouthshire,' since most of my native county, although belonging in almost every other sense – and certainly in the railway sense – to South Wales, had for some 400 years been governmentally part of England. Now legislation has restored nearly all of it, together with the borough of Newport and some small pieces of Breconshire around Brynmawr and Crickhowell, to its old place in Wales under its old name of 'Gwent'.

Other relevant changes under the Local Government Act were the absorption of most of the administrative county of Brecon, together with Montgomeryshire and Radnorshire, to form a new county with the ancient title of Powys; the amalgamation of the three westerly counties (Carmarthenshire, Pembrokeshire and Cardiganshire) into 'Dyfed'; and the division of Glamorganshire into three new counties. Of these, South Glamorgan embraces Cardiff, Penarth, Barry and the coastal belt from St Mellons (formerly in Monmouthshire) to Cowbridge; Mid-Glamorgan comprises mainly Merthyr Tydfil, Aberdare, Rhondda and the mining valleys as far west as Bridgend and Maesteg, while West Glamorgan covers Neath, Port Talbot, Swansea and the Gower Peninsula. Where in this book it is necessary to refer to county names, the names used are those operable at the relevant period.

Even this principle is liable to difficulty of observance, however, since in at least one case, the GWR used two different spellings of the same place in the same time table!

Place Names
In Wales perhaps more than anywhere else this is a jungle or a morass in which geographer and historian can only tread most warily. The advent of industry and railways to South Wales contributed to the anglicisation or other alteration of many place names, whereby for example Pwll-cawl in one Parliamentary Act became Porthcawl in another, but applicable to the same line of railway. It would be wrong however wholly to blame the English for all these variances, since the historic Penydarren Tramroad is traceable as having at least three different versions of spelling, while much further west, there are at least four known variants of the Preseli Mountains and district, the latest local government version being Presaly! Then as late as 1966, the county borough of Llanelly obtained formal authority to alter the name of its town back to Llanelli; only a few miles away, Kidwelly remains in that spelling, yet to the north, Llandilo has become Llandeilo. And while the River Gwendraeth in Carmarthenshire had its name correctly adopted by the little Gwendraeth Valleys Railway, the neighbouring and larger Burry Port & Gwendreath *(sic)* Valley Railway seems to have used either the 'ae' or 'ea' spelling with cheerful impartiality, and even in an official light railway order is referred to as 'Gwendreath' . Again, words which occur fairly often must not be assumed to indicate location; a specific example is 'Merthyr' (meaning 'martyr') which does not necessarily refer to its best-known example of Merthyr Tydfil – a railway centre of formerly great importance which figures substantially in our story – but which may well apply to distant places such as Merthyr Mawr, near Bridgend, or to even more distant collieries like Graig Merthyr or Graigola Merthyr above Swansea, where the suffix 'Merthyr' related to ownership and not necessarily to location. And how do we grapple with refinements like Pontnewydd and Pontnewynydd, which were separate stations on the same route only a few miles apart? (Or distinguish between Pont-Nedd-Fechan (local spelling) and Pontneath Vaughan (railway spelling)?)

The answer is that one does one's best, and follows either the spelling most consistently used, or that which was used by the railway company concerned at the relevant time. As my uncle (like myself a Man of Gwent) once said when I asked him about the spelling of Cwmffrwd, 'What does it matter, boy, so long as you know where it is?'

If I have thereby been led astray, I am consoled in that I am not the first, nor likely to be the last; a Parliamentary draftsman once turned 'Talybont' into 'Jalybout', while a signal engineer from England produced a beautiful diagram and name board for a box which he had written down as 'Red Meadow', having evidently misheard or wrongly transcribed the instructions of his Welsh cicerone that the box was to be called 'Waenledr' . In a country where two separate railways, only a short distance apart, both bore the initials PC & N some funny things could happen. Fortunately, perhaps, nobody seems to have tried to Anglicise Cynwmllwynddu, except for adding the suffix 'Siding (Lower) ' .

Since this introduction was written, however, British Rail has introduced in the late 1970s bi-lingual spelling of station names and of places referred to in publicity literature, using a 'preferred' system for the Welsh equivalents, which differs in some instances from older versions in the native language.

Distances

Particularly in the mining valleys, where distances between junctions were often extremely short, there are many discrepancies in official publications. Generally, therefore, I have quoted distances to the nearest quarter-mile, referring to chainages only where specific very short distances are involved.

Closures

In order to avoid the complexity of numerous footnotes, dates which may be thought significant have been included in the relevant text. Whereas the dates of passenger closures are generally well documented, there is a special problem in respect of closures for freight traffic in industrial areas like South Wales; the dates of withdrawing public goods facilities often preceded by a considerable period closures of private sidings or connections to collieries or public utilities, where lines may be kept idle for some time after traffic ceases, against possible resumption for clearance of stocks, dismantling, or even re-opening. In such cases the formal date of closure may occur some years after the railway ceases to be used, as in one case quoted in Chapter VII, where formal closure took place five years after the last train ran.

Maps
For the readers' convenience, as has been adopted elsewhere in this Regional series, maps show the railways as at their maximum development, even though this may include a few instances of lines which had been closed by the time the last new ones on the same map had been opened. Dates of closures are quoted as being the first days on which there was no public service, ignoring Sundays because in some cases no Sunday services were run.

Wherever possible, factual references have been corrected to mid 1980. Railtours are generally omitted.

If this book gives the impression of being nostalgic and valetudinarian because of the emphasis laid upon past achievements, this is in no way intentional. These are railways which throughout their long, turbulent and distinguished history were and, with some difference of emphasis, still are orientated towards particular industries. But only the mountains are forever.

January 1980   D. S. M. Barrie

PREFACE TO SECOND EDITION

At the time of his death in 1989 Derek Barrie had started revising and extending the text of this book. When David St John Thomas asked me to take over, Derek Barrie's family generously passed to me his papers and correspondence relating to the book. I owe a debt to James Page of Machen for sorting the correspondence and for general advice, and to those who wrote to Derek Barrie with suggestions on the text: W. Batteson, R. Bond, Dr W.R. Bucknall, R.J. Caston, C. Chapman, R.W.N. Drummond, M. Hale, H. Morgan, E.R. Mountford, I.W. Prothero, J.W.P. Rowledge, W.J. Skillern, N.W. Sprinks, T. Wallis and others.

My thanks go to Tony Cooke for expanding on detail from his Atlas and Track Layout Diagrams of the GWR, to Terence Barry for invaluable further research, and to staff at the House of Lords Record Office, Public Record Office, National Library of Wales, and the County Record Office, Gwent.

May 1993   Peter E. Baughan

CHAPTER I

The South Wales Railway Scene

Historically, scenically, and in their engineering and traffic interest, the railways of South Wales challenge comparison for fascination and variety with any other regional group in the British Isles. Not for them is it necessary or sensible to claim that this corner of Great Britain was 'the birthplace of railways'; rather it is enough to demonstrate that South Wales made outstanding contributions to the advent and evolution of railways. Here in one of the many valleys we shall introduce in this book, a steam locomotive for the first time hauled a load on rails (1804); here too was inaugurated the regular conveyance of passengers by rail (1807). Here developed the most dense, and probably the most profitable coal traffic of its time in the world, while long after the railways of the North East and of Lancashire had become consolidated in the hands of a few big companies, there lingered in South Wales until the early 1920s a sturdily independent array of 'local' railway companies which for the greater part of a century had fought their bigger brethren, and each other, up and down the narrow valleys in a welter of competing projects, lawsuits, rate wars, complex junctions and even more complicated running powers. Their story of strife and rivalry, of contrasting wealth and poverty, forms one of the most exciting chapters of the Industrial Revolution which spawned them, and which then in turn they helped to develop in all its extremes of strife, squalor, riches, and of human arrogance, power and misery.

The country to which these railways belonged, and whose history they helped to forge in the painful transition from an agricultural to an industrial society, extends for some 140 miles from the west bank of the River Severn east of Newport through Cardiff, Bridgend, Port Talbot, Neath and Swansea to Carmarthen and thence west to Fishguard and Cardigan.

This is a country of strong and often painful contrasts. The principal cities and towns, having evolved largely through seaborne trade, lie naturally along the northern shore of the Bristol Channel, linked with each other and with London by the main line of the old South Wales Railway, later part of the GWR, but the hinterland in which industry laid its roots is divided up into the valleys carved by the rivers which rise in the Black Mountains of Gwent, in the outliers of the Brecon Beacons, and in the Blaenau Morganwg of Glamorgan, the whole forming a magnificent, serried massif of hills and mountains rising from 600ft to nearly 2,000ft above sea level.

Down from these mountains come the rivers whose names are landmarks in railway history: Sirhowy, Rhymney, Taff, Ely, Llynvi, Ogmore, Neath, Gwendraeth, Towy – all of which at one time or another gave their names to railway companies. In a country where so much of the space is occupied by upland, and where the habitations and products of man were squeezed into narrow valleys or along the seaboard strip, it was astonishing that in the great age of railways, one was never far from the sight or sound of a train, nor from pithead gear and heaps of spoil.

The coalfield itself is reputed to cover about 1,000 square miles, of which a fair proportion lies under the waters of Swansea Bay and beyond, and has never been exploited by undersea mining. Excluding also a small degree of past exploitation in the south-west corner of the former county of Pembrokeshire (Dyfed), the practicable extent of the field begins west of a line from Newport to Abergavenny, and terminates slightly north and west of Llanelli. Its horizontal boundaries are formed by the northern and southern outcrops, the former along a line roughly from Brynmawr through Merthyr to Ammanford, and the latter mostly just north of the GWR South Wales main line; only one colliery of any modern significance (Llanharan) has been sunk on the south side of this railway. Owing to the geological structure, the best steam coals were generally found in the lower coal measures, especially in the Rhondda and neighbouring valleys, and required improvements in mining technique for their exploitation. North and west of Swansea, the seams are mostly anthracite.

At the height of its prosperity in 1913, when South Wales had become the largest coal-producing area of the country, and when nearly 37 million tons of coal were shipped from her principal ports to some 500 ports and coaling stations all over the world, sixteen different public railway companies were working traffic in the industrial rectangle comprised within the eighty miles along the coast between Newport and Carmarthen, and the twenty to twenty-five miles inland to the mountain barriers that mark the northern limit of the coalfield. There were also in 1921 nine joint railways, involving six different companies, which as often as not in such joint ventures, were bedfellows *faute de mieux*.

These were railways of character, contrast and complexity such as at that time no other part of Britain could offer; the lordly expresses of the Great Western, spinning along the coastal levels trailing white banners of steam behind them, burnished side rods and copper boiler fittings agleam in the sun, or 300-plus trains a day shuffling through the Pontypridd junctions, or the little tank engines struggling with their loads up some of the most ferocious gradients in Britain.

The heart and core of those railways was in the valleys; in the deep clefts in the bare hills where road, weedy canal, blackened river and probably at least two railways competed for living space amid a muddle of winding shafts, colliery tips, foundries, shops, chapels and the terraced streets stretching up the mountainside – anything over a few hundred feet is reckoned a mountain in South Wales. Down into these streets came the mountain sheep, and down the valleys came the coal trains, buffered up against the locomotives, flanges squealing on the curves, every wagon with its white-painted blazon: *Cory, Powell Duffryn, Ocean, Nixon, Ynisarwed, Navigation, GCG.* (In my little school we ran a weekly sweep, each pupil drawing a wagon name, but the school and the names alike are gone now).

The eventual destination of these trains was usually the same: 'the docks', where drifting, dissolving black clouds of coal dust marked the rows of mechanical tips, and where the ultimate expression of the process was the black-hulled tramp, low-decked and tall-funnelled, edging deep-laden out into Severn's mouth.

But in these valleys there were many other trains: the local passengers (very busy on market days and on Saturdays), which enjoyed a smarter livery than the workmen's, for which latter brass checks were issued by the colliery company to each workman; the empties, which went up the valley a good deal faster than the coal trains came down; and the loaded ore trains from the docks to the steel works. The ore trains that I knew ran mostly at night, double-headed or with a banker in the rear, the twin exhausts deep, solemn, purposeful, slow. And a little boy in an upstairs bedroom would slip

to the window and catch a glimpse of the pulsating glow from an
open fire-door, illuminating momentarily the underside of the
billowing plume of steam as the train bore right-handed at the junction for Ebbw Vale, and surged up into the darkness of the adjoining
valley.

SUMMITS AND GRADIENTS

As a general rule in South Wales, the 'Up' line has always been that
leading up into the valleys from the seaboard. This is entirely
logical, seeing that the majority of these lines had to overcome a
difference in level of between 1,000ft and 1,300ft in not more than
twenty-five miles. Along the heads of the valleys between
Abergavenny and Merthyr, station altitudes ranged from 1,160ft at
Brynmawr to 1,250ft near Dowlais, while the branch line from
Brynmawr to Blaenavon got up to no less than 1,400ft above sea
level at Waenavon – at one time the highest station on any standard
gauge railway in Britain. Even higher altitudes were attained on
some of the earlier tramroads; the line to the Trevil Quarries which
in modern times formed part of the sixty miles or so industrial
railway network associated with the Ebbw Vale Steelworks, reached
1,600ft. Even with severely restricted loading, the working of industrial traffic on such lines required a hard, continuous uphill slog
and meticulously careful descent. In 1913, the Rhymney Railway
hauled 400,000 tons of iron ore to Dowlais furnaces over the seven-
mile ascent at between 1 in 40 and 1 in 49 of the Taff Bargoed Joint
Line, using three locomotives for a 20-wagon train and taking forty
minutes to get up. Another Seven Mile Bank (officially so named)
was that on the Brecon & Merthyr line southbound from Talybont
up Glyn Collwyn to the Summit Tunnel 1,313ft up at Torpantau,
including 6½ miles rising continuously at 1 in 38. Exposed to every
vice of winter wind and weather, the barren uplands that form the
outliers of the Black Mountains and Brecon Beacons demanded of
men and machines some of the toughest railway working in the
British Isles.

   On mineral branches down in the valleys we shall meet gradients
as steep as 1 in 18 worked by normal adhesion, while the steepest
over which passenger-carrying trains were run was 1 in 22. Into the
nationalisation period, cable-assisted steam locomotives were
employed on the 1 in 13 gradient of the Pwllyrhebog Incline of the
former Taff Vale Railway.

ENGINEERING FEATURES

As befitted a race of miners, the Welsh were great tunnellers in the Railway Age. Even before, in the era of the tramroads, tunnels were driven from one valley to another up to a maximum estimated length of 2,000yd. Excluding the Severn Tunnel, there were five tunnels over a mile in length on the South Wales railways, the longest being the Rhondda Tunnel, at 1m 1,683yd made by the Rhondda & Swansea Bay Railway to connect the Avon and Rhondda valleys. Sad to relate, not every Welsh tunnel saw the opposing head-ings meet with the miraculous accuracy loved of some railway histo-rians. One indeed has a noticeable kink in the middle, while enough water was struck in driving the Rhymney's tunnel (1m 181yd) under Caerphilly Mountain to supply water for the company's plant and locomotives in Cardiff.

Tunnels and bridges alike in this part of the world are liable to earth movement and mining subsidence, so in general the bridge builders also did their work massively and well. Two of I. K. Brunel's timber viaducts on the former Vale of Neath Railway near Aberdare were not pulled down until 1947, and T. W. Kennard's wrought-iron masterpiece spanning the Ebbw Valley at Crumlin outlasted even its own usefulness for traffic. So, too, have gone the great steel-on-masonry viaducts whereby the Barry Railway soared arrogantly over the heads of its rivals at Walnut Tree and Llanbradach, both built (and knocked down) in the present century. Other big bridges had curious histories: the massive steel structure carrying the Cardiff Railway across the River Taff at Treforest was used only once by a revenue-earning train, while Porthkerry Viaduct on the Vale of Glamorgan line suffered a partial collapse soon after its opening in 1897, and during rebuilding was replaced by a temporary 'shoo-fly' line for which Parliamentary powers were duly obtained – retrospec-tively!

PROSPERITY – AND POVERTY

The South Wales railways ran many other things besides railways: steamers, hotels, lighthouses, collieries, the largest geographical group of docks in the country (1923) and, in the far west of the region, a railway and harbour undertaking owned jointly with an Irish railway company. By contrast, between Penarth Dock and Penarth Harbour there was a subway, successor to a chain-ferry, through which the public could pass on foot on buying a *railway* ticket, price one (old, and real) penny. Despite the long prosperous summer of the steam coal trade, the railways were not universally successful financially. At one end of the scale, the Barry Railway paid an average dividend of 8½ per cent for twenty-eight years, and the Taff Vale's Ordinary dividend only once fell below 10 per cent between 1870 and 1888, touching 17½ per cent in one year. Some of the small lines like the Neath & Brecon and the Brecon & Merthyr knew the rigours of receivership, while the antecedent of the Llanelly & Mynydd Mawr was actually dismantled between 1844 and 1883. It was a fine country for the strong, but a hard one for the weak.

Through long decades of inter-company rivalry and strife, the South Wales companies took up much time on the part of Parliamentary committees, and solicitors, counsel and Parliamentary agents profited accordingly. An official return issued in 1901 showed that during the years 1892-98 inclusive, the aggregate expenses incurred by eleven South Wales undertakings in the promotion of and opposition to private Parliamentary bills amounted to more than £275,000:

Undertaking	*Expenditure* £
Cardiff Railway Company	83,760
Taff Vale	55,544
Rhymney	20,204
Barry	66,730
Port Talbot	27,370
Vale of Glamorgan	3,282
Alexandra (Newport)	10,059
Brecon & Merthyr	2,574
Burry Port	926
Fishguard & Rosslare	3,717
Mumbles Railway & Pier	1,776
Total	£275,942

The high level of these expenses reflected a correspondingly heavy volume of capital expenditure, especially by the railways serving West Monmouthshire and East Glamorganshire, including the ports of Newport, Cardiff, Penarth and Barry. In 1911 it was estimated that there were at least 75 miles of duplicate, competitive railways in this area; these could still earn reasonable returns in the boom years of the coal trade, but were to prove a heavy drain on the South Wales railway economy from the 1930s onwards.

A PANOPLY OF BADGES

The South Wales railway companies brought to railway 'heraldry' – though few if any of them were armorially authorised – a splendiferous panoply of badges and seals; however several did embody elements from the grants-of-arms of the boroughs they served, or of the families which had helped to sponsor them. Thus, the badge of the Rhondda & Swansea Bay Railway comprised not only the full armorial achievement of the Earl of Jersey (the first chairman), but also a sail-assisted steam vessel, and one of the earliest versions of the 0-6-2T locomotive wheel arrangement, built by Kitson's in 1885, three years after the company's incorporation. Welsh motifs were used by three of the largest companies. The oldest, the Taff Vale, started with the Prince of Wales' feathers and motto, but later adopted an ornate version of the Welsh Dragon, *y Ddraig goch*, the whole surmounted by a goat and the motto *Cymru a fu a Chymru a fydd* (Wales hath been and Wales shall be). The Red Dragon was also the main component of the Barry Railway's badge, the crest in this case however being the stag's head from the arms of the Earl of Plymouth, the first chairman.

Perhaps the most remarkable badge among the larger South Wales railways was that of the Cardiff Railway Company, the components embracing Welsh, English, French and Scottish origins! The company's title in English formed the circlet; the motto *Wrth ddwr a Than* (By water and fire) was in Welsh; the left-hand shield displayed the chevrons gules of the Norman family of de Clare, later adopted by the County of Glamorgan and at one time by the City of Cardiff, while the right-hand shield displayed the checky of the marquisate of Bute, of whom the second marquis was the founder of Cardiff Docks. The Cardiff Company's device is carved, one hopes for a long time to come, on the front of the docks offices at Cardiff Pier Head, this version also including a locomotive. Finally of these examples, the Rhymney Railway Company displayed the shields from the arms of Cardiff and Newport, surmounted by a sailing ship and an early (Egyptian type) iron furnace. The inclusion of the Newport shield is flattering but a shade optimistic – the RR unsuccessfully sought running powers to that port in 1861, but had to be content with handing-over its Newport traffic to other companies, with some financial compensation from the GWR.

STATION NAMES

South Wales also contributed picturesquely (if to the stranger some-times almost unpronounceably) to the varied nomenclature of British railway stations, halts, and junctions. There are or were Seven Sisters, two Six Bells, and a Nine Mile Point which was very sensibly given its name from the fact that it was nine miles from the start of the original tramway in Newport. Many railway places, as else where, took their names from adjacent hostelries, and others (Waterloo, Sebastopol) from battles long ago; Quakers' Yard was named (with three variations of spelling) after a nearby burial ground of the Society of Friends, while the second half of 'Panteg & Griffithstown' honoured Henry Griffiths, the first stationmaster at Pontypool (Newport Road), now Pontypool. Then there were Stormy and Stormstown, while the Welsh affection for flowers and trees reflected itself – sometimes in insalubrious surroundings – in Walnut Tree, Cherry Orchard, Mountain Ash, and others. Whiterose on the B & M Rhymney branch was spelt as one word until 1906, when the station finally became New Tredegar.

There was a string of 'saints', not all of whom are universally familiar – St Athan, St Bride's, St Clears, St Fagan's, St Mellons; the Cornish Saint Cenydd gave his name to the terminus of the Aber branch of the Rhymney Railway, but became translated into Senghenydd in the process. Golden Grove on the Llandilo-Carmarthen line was so named (to quote an obsequious article in the *GWR Magazine)* as being adjacent to 'the handsome and historic demesne of Lord Emlyn, Deputy Chairman of the GWR'. (But Mme Patti, the famous opera singer, had silver taps in her private toilet at Craig-y-Nos on the Neath & Brecon).

My favourite station name in the whole region was Fleur-de Lis, where the Brecon & Merthyr line from Newport ran parallel with the Rhymney Railway in the Rhymney valley. Like many things on the old B & M, the name was improbable and incongruous, since the little station afforded a good view of some coke ovens. But its origin was romantic and a trifle sad: a small colony of Huguenot refugees from France came there and called their place of exile Fleur-de- Lis. The old porter just called out 'Flower! Flower!', perhaps with greater scholarship than he would own to.

There were also some richly named signalboxes, like Rumney River Bridge Junction on the eastern edge of Cardiff, the location of which by a muddy creek for long indicated the legal boundary between England (Monmouthshire) and Wales (Glamorganshire);

like the particular boundary itself, this box is no more. For many years after the amalgamations of 1922-23 submerged the individual South Wales railways, the GWR commemorated them by the retention of signalbox names such as PC & N Junction at Pontypridd, or 'Rhondda & Swansea Bay Junction' at Treherbert; my father professed to recall an 'Upper Hengoed Lower Junction', but I have never been able to trace it.

The variety of station nomenclature was perhaps rivalled only by the diversity of their styles of architecture. There were stations like Port Talbot (Central), a wooden, single-platform passenger terminal contrasting with its nearby office block that could be mistaken for the town hall; there were extraordinary Swiss-chalet 'halts' and 'platforms' which dated from the steam railmotor era of the early 1900s. But full marks must go to the GWR which in the 1920s and 1930s rebuilt Newport, Cardiff and Swansea in a lavish style that betokened a firm confidence in the future of railways as Paddington foresaw it then... or Pontypridd with its curious little bays for railmotors, indented into the face of the long main platform faces ... or Bridgend's remarkable and comprehensive name boards:

```
┌─────────────────────────────────────────┐
│                                         │
│              BRIDGEND                   │
│                                         │
│        JUNCTION FOR LLYNVI              │
│                                         │
│      OGMORE & GARW BRANCHES            │
│                                         │
│    & VALE OF GLAMORGAN RAILWAY         │
│                                         │
└─────────────────────────────────────────┘
```

Now, this is just 'Bridgend'. There were stations and engine sheds which looked like chapels, and chapels which looked like either.

MEN OF STATURE

Lest it may seem that this introductory chapter to the South Wales railway scene is all about places and things without reference to people, let it be said that railways of this kind, in such country and under the conditions which prevailed during the formative and combative period, could only have been promoted, built and run by tough and able men. Some of their names have passed enduringly into railway history: I. K. Brunel, who planned both the first public railway of major commercial importance in South Wales (the Taff Vale), and engineered the South Wales Railway and some of its satellites; David Davies of Llandinam, the successful railway contractor who became a great coal-owner and fathered the Barry Railway to triumph; even the redoubtable Sir Edward Watkin, Demon King of many a railway pantomime, swept dramatically across the South Wales stage at the end of last century.

But most of the professionals came up the hard way and held on to the railways until the end of their working lives. Typical of these was Ammon Beasley, who came from the GWR in 1890 to be general manager of the Taff Vale, and retired from that post at the age of eighty to become deputy chairman, dying in 1924 at the age of 86. But even this Grand Old Man of the TVR must have seemed a child in arms to his neighbour and rival, Cornelius Lundie of the Rhymney Railway. The latter had come to Cardiff from Northumberland in 1862 to become traffic manager, engineer and later director of the RR, serving the company almost until his death in 1908, in his 94th year. Feudalism persisted well into this century. A former colleague of the author, who had been a junior in E. A. Prosser's office at Cardiff in the last pre-grouping days when Prosser was joint general manager of the Taff Vale, Rhymney, and Cardiff Railways, recalls the great man sounding his bell around five o'clock and (without looking up as he signed another letter) saying: 'Slip down to the platform, boy, and tell the guard of the Penarth train to wait a minute or two…'. And the general manager of the Taff Vale enjoyed not merely an inspection saloon, but an ancillary private 'dining carriage' which may have been unique in being wallpapered throughout.

These were among the giants of the hierarchy. But consider humbler men, not necessarily less dignified, who helped to make the South Wales railways what they became. William Lewis Meredith, founder of the Permanent Way Institution in 1884, was born in 1843 at Argoed in the Sirhowy Valley, being the grandson of a contractor who had helped maintain the track of the Sirhowy Tramroad. J. H. Read, a native of Chepstow, joined the railway in 1856 as a cleaner, became a driver at Newport, and drove the first train through the Severn Tunnel. He retired in 1906 as divisional locomotive superintendent at Newport. Henry Griffiths, also from a Chepstow family, whose father fought at Corunna and his uncle at Trafalgar, joined the GWR as a policeman (pointsman), became the first stationmaster at Pontypool Road and later assistant goods superintendent, South Wales, before joining the Ebbw Vale Iron & Steel Company as traffic manager, and living in retirement to the age of ninety.

Not all were so fortunate. Low pay and rigid, puritanical discipline, coupled with long hours and physical danger and discomfort, were for generations the lot of the working railwayman in South Wales. The 1856 rules of the TVR stipulated that staff should keep their hair cut, were not to sing or whistle on duty, and should attend a place of worship on Sunday, 'as it will be the means of promotion when vacancies occur'. And if you had a free pass, you had to ride 'in a sitting position on the floor of the fourth wagon from the rear of the train'. (Perhaps it was to offset the effects of this procedure that the TVR dispensed an indigestion medicine gratis to its staff until 1892, when presumably travel was more comfortable, or stomachs better nourished). But Frederick Harcombe, a TVR goods guard who gave damaging evidence before a Royal Commission on Railway Accidents, soon lost his job afterwards. Yet to the credit of the TVR, let it be remembered that in 1893 it set up a non-contributory pension fund which survived until recent years, and that the Taff Vale Railway Employees' Accident Fund was not closed until 30 December 1967 – 45 years after the company itself had ceased to exist.

Nor was the Taff Vale unmindful of the spiritual well-being of its clientele. If you had time to spare before your train, you could find in the waiting room a Bible inscribed in gold lettering on the cover with the name of the company and of the station, printed (of course) in Welsh, but with an English Translation of both Testaments also provided. To the credit of both successors, GWR and BR, these Bibles are still issued, but kept now, I understand, in the booking office. Yet it was the same TVR which in 1900–01 proved victorious in an outstanding legal case whereby the company was awarded £23,000 damages against the Amalgamated Society of Railway Servants, arising from a strike. (See Chapter XI).

In a country where both won their living the hard way, mainly from the same commodity, affinities of danger and the early struggles of trade unionism ran deep between railwaymen and miners. More than once railway locomotives were rushed into the Rhondda to help pump out flooded pits where men were trapped. In the great disaster at Universal Colliery, Senghenydd, in 1913, when more than 400 men and boys perished, twenty-seven railway ambulance workers were among the first volunteers for rescue work.

As with the collieries, but on a much smaller scale, the South Wales railways have not been without their own background of industrial strife, especially during the latent days of trade unionism. During periodical depressions, valley folk were not above putting soap on to rails and looting the wagons of the labouring trains to relieve their own desperate needs. But the railways in bygone days were regarded as a sort of public highway for pedestrians and sheep alike; some even regarded them as common property, like the five men who were fined 10s 0d. (50p) each at Bridgend in 1911 for breaking-up a signal cabin at Nantymoel and taking it away piecemeal.

'Which do you want to do, boy, the pit or the railway?' was the question sometimes asked by schools inspectors as a conversational gambit with pupils. But a cynical old collier put it this way: 'On the railway, mun, there is a collision, and there you are. But in an explosion down the pit, where are you?'

There is more to railway history than may be found in archives. These survive as dry bones; men were and are the lifeblood.

CHAPTER II

Evolution
of the System

The history of the South Wales railways, and to a relevant extent that of their forebears the tramroads, falls naturally into five fairly distinct phases:

First, from 1790 until the 1840s, the canal-and-tramroad phase.

Second, from the opening of the Llanelly Railway & Dock and the Taff Vale Railway in 1833-40, the gradual supersession of the tramroads by conventional railways, and the rapid growth of the latter.

Third, from mid-century until the end of World War I, the great era of prosperity of the South Wales industries and of most of the railways serving them.

Fourth, from 1922 onwards, the amalgamation of the independent railways with their larger neighbours under the 'grouping' system produced by the Railways Act, 1921.

Fifth, from 1948, nationalisation of the railways and docks (but with separate management of the latter) under the Transport Act, 1947.

This phasing of transport development follows closely that of patterns of industrial and social change, with qualifications that there were periods, first in the last century when rail and dock capacity seriously lagged behind industrial requirements, and again towards the middle of this century, when rail transport capacity clearly became excessive. Whereas for instance the production of coal in South Wales was initially used mainly for local consumption, with a secondary usage for landsale and shipment coastwise or short-sea, the opening up from about 1850 of the deep-level seams in the central part of the coalfield led to enormous growth in the world-wide use of Welsh steam coals. Then the translation from iron- to steel-making from the 1860s onwards brought further changes in the transport requirement, largely because of the importation of ore and the phasing-out of many of the early ironworks. The high peak of the traditional coal-based system came in 1913, and after the artificial stimulus of two World Wars the decline in the coal industry, the growth of road transport and changes in the distributive pattern of the consumer trades, helped to lop many branches off the railway tree while leaving the railways with a changed and expanding role in bulk transport by trainloads and in the service of fewer but larger industrial installations.

In the realm of social change, the canals and tramroads did little or nothing towards higher standards of living of the working population in a region which throughout the nineteenth century was sadly backward in wages, working conditions, and housing. But the railways did much to provide a substantial amount of employment, together with a better range of consumer goods for those who could afford it, and to offer recreational outlets from the valleys to the towns and to rail stimulated seaside resorts such as Penarth, Barry Island, Porthcawl and Tenby. Movement up and down the valleys was also stimulated by railways, but it was left largely to the bus and the private car to revolutionise lateral communication between one valley and its neighbours across the mountains on either side and eventually to erode – and in some important instances to destroy – the local railway passenger services.

INDUSTRIAL BEGINNINGS

What were to become the two basic industries of South Wales, the winning of coal and the smelting of iron, had been carried on in a small way for centuries before the railway era. Operations were mainly confined to the working of outcrops, levels or drifts sunk into the mountain sides, while the lack of inland transport facilities helped to concentrate activities fairly close to the sea- board. From the sixteenth century onwards there was a growing if still limited trade in sea-coal across the Bristol Channel to Devon, Cornwall, and Northern France, and coastwise to Southern England and the Thames. Sailing ships, often no larger than the famous Severn 'trows', loaded mainly at small 'pills' or mud creeks near the river mouths, or (as initially at Swansea) in the open roadstead. The trade was distributed not only among those places which in due course were to become major ports, but also at smaller sites like Sully and Aberthaw.

Iron manufacture, which had progressed slowly in South Wales during the sixteenth and seventeenth centuries, and which had suffered a set-back after the Civil War, burst into violent activity during the latter half of the eighteenth century. This was basically due to the greatly increased demand for iron arising from the Industrial Revolution, but specifically also from the discovery that coal and coke were effective substitutes for the diminishing availability of charcoal, due to the restrictions placed on the cutting-down of forests elsewhere in the country. Not only were there still ample and scarcely touched areas of woodland in South Wales, but the co-existence of limestone and coal, together with large deposits of argillaceous ore, made the northern areas of Monmouthshire and Glamorganshire a custom-built region for the rapid development of the iron industry. Nor was there any lack of entrepreneurs and of skilled labour to exploit the situation; men from Sussex, the Midlands and even from Scotland came in large numbers to help develop the expanding industry. (This admixture was to persist for generations: my grandfather, a 'free-sinker' mining engineer, came from Staffordshire to prospect coal in Monmouthshire; my father came from the Steel Company of Scotland to work at Ebbw Vale).

Since the essential basic ingredients were mostly found together along the Northern Outcrop of the coalfield, it was around the valley heads or *blaenau* that a vast array of ironworks erupted into flame from about 1757 onwards: the beacons of a new industrial age now glowed on the mountains as the beacons had flamed out for the Spanish Armada two hundred years before. From Hirwaun through Merthyr and Dowlais, past Rhymney, Sirhowy, Tredegar, Beaufort, Nantyglo and Ebbw Vale, a great chain of ironworks was established between 1750 and 1800, their prosperity largely undiminished until the introduction of the Bessemer and other steel-making processes brought about a substantial re-orientation during the second half of the following century.

TRANSPORT PIONEERS

The men who launched and guided these enterprises became important in the sphere of transport as well as being notable iron-

masters. Anthony Bacon, who established the Cyfarthfa Ironworks
at Merthyr in 1765; Richard Hill of the Plymouth works, Merthyr;
Francis Homfray of Penydarren, (also at Merthyr), the Crawshays of
a later generation at Cyfarthfa, and the Harfords at Ebbw Vale – they
and their successors were contributors to the later development of
rail transport, not merely as builders and promoters of railways or
tramroads, but also as manufacturers of cast-iron, wrought-iron and
later of rolled rails, originally for their own local systems, then for
the Liverpool & Manchester Railway (1830), and eventually for railways in many parts of the world. In the second generation, (Sir)
John Josiah Guest, son of the John Guest who had come from the
Midlands to manage Dowlais in 1760, became chairman of the Taff
Vale Railway and a notable figure in the railway world, while Dowlais
was to roll its first steel rails by the Bessemer process.

One essential ingredient was missing from the late eighteenth-
century 'mix' of the South Wales iron industry: effective transport.
This requirement was necessary for three separate reasons; the
movement of raw materials from source to the works (the limestone
quarries, for instance, were mostly on the high ground to the north
of the furnaces) the movement of pig-iron between one works and
another and, predominantly and of progressively increasing importance, the need for trunk outlets to the developing ports on the
Bristol Channel. With this object in view, Anthony Bacon of
Cyfarthfa as early as 1767 had persuaded his fellow ironmasters to
join him in raising funds for the making of a trunk road from
Merthyr Tydfil to Cardiff Town Quay and so improve upon the
limited capacity and slow movement of the pack horse routes, which
wherever possible followed the hill-tops in order to avoid the
marshy ground lower down. But the future lay initially with the
canals and tramroads.

CANALS AND TRAMROADS

This book does not pretend to be a history of either canals or tramroads, both of which have been the subjects of specialist works of
much greater authority than mine. But the rail transport system of
the Welsh valleys owed so much to these progenitors, and railway
evolution derived so much from their location and physical pattern,
that some general consideration of their origins is essential.

Railed transport in a primitive form actually preceded the canals.
The first recorded instance in South Wales appeared about 1695 as

a 'new road or wagon-way' laid down by Sir Humphrey Mackworth to connect his copper-works and coal mines with the waterside at Neath. There were undoubtedly other instances of primitive tramroads or wagonways used domestically in ironworks and limestone quarries well before the end of the eighteenth century, but it was the ironworks developments from this period onwards that led to their rapid expansion, substantially in conjunction with canals.

Even prior to the incorporation of the principal canal companies, ie the Glamorganshire (1790), the Neath (1791), the Monmouthshire (1792), the Brecknock & Abergavenny (1793) and the Swansea (1794), there is estimated to have been around 100 miles of tramroads in use. Although these canals were eventually all superseded by railways (and, with the exception of the Glamorganshire, all bought-up by the GWR), several of them included in their Acts of Incorporation powers to construct railways, tramroads or wagonways as feeders to and from ironworks, collieries or quarries, within specified distances from the canal, with alternate powers for industrialists to make such tramroads if the canal companies did not do so. In the context of this book, the definition 'tramroad' is used empirically and conveniently as applicable generally to such lines whether laid with edge-rails for use by wagons with flanged wheels, or with L-shaped plates suitable for the flangeless wheels of tram wagons or even ordinary carts; the customary practice in early days was for the edge-rail lines to be described as 'railways' and the plateways as 'tramroads'. Although the edged rail and flanged wheel combination was eventually to become standard practice in the railway era proper, it proved unpopular at the outset due to the heavier type of wagon requiring greater horse-power, but when steam locomotives were introduced, these in turn broke up the cast-iron plates, and the wrought-iron (later still, of course, steel) edge-rail evolved as standard.

Because so many of the early tramroads were extensions of internal lines domestic to works, quarries and mines, a wide variety of gauges was manifested, ranging from 3ft 2in to 4ft 4in. Stone sleeper blocks were almost universal. The tramroads added words and phrases to our vocabulary which became carried down into railway usage. The word 'tram' itself has been the subject of much learned debate, as to whether it derives from Norse or German origin, from Benjamin Outram, the engineer who influenced considerably the growth and techniques of the South Wales tramroad system, or simply from the Welsh word *dram*, meaning 'tram'.

The terms 'dram road' or 'dram way' occur in early legislation refer-ring to South Wales railways or tramroads. It must be admitted that it had earlier currency elsewhere, but on purely Welsh emotional grounds, rather than logic, I am all for the third alternative. In my own youth in South Wales, any mine or works railway was simply referred to as 'the tram'. Another word of tramroad origin is 'parting', used in colliery practice in modern times to denote points or a loop, while most English and Scottish railways referred to 'crossing loops' on single lines; the Taff Vale for example named one of its signalboxes on its Ynysybwl Branch 'Windsor Passing Siding'.

TRAMROAD OPERATION

The working of these early tramroads was often casual and some-times exciting. Many of them were toll roads, open to anybody who was prepared to pay for hauling traffic with his own teams or by contract, not excluding the gigs and chaises of the gentry, for whose benefit few highways worthy of the name then existed. Quite early on, some sort of rules had to be laid down for regulating the traffic, the most common being the allocation of different periods of the day or night for the movement of 'Up' and 'Down' traffic respec-tively. As late as 1855 the Traffic Superintendent of the Llynvi Valley Railway had to direct that: 'the Servants of the Company are autho-rised to remove from the line on to the siding or convenient place, all Trams or Trains obstructing the regular traffic, and all persons causing such obstruction... will render themselves liable to Heavy Penalties'. Local folk-lore of this particular district recalled that when two trains of trams met between passing places, precedence was often decided by the teamsters delegating their boy assistants to fight it out, the loser having to back down. Because of the heavy gradients up into the valleys, change of horses had to be effected at fairly short intervals; at such places, rows of cottages were sometimes provided wherein the teamsters and their families lived in the upper storey, with the horses stabled on the ground floor. One such row of buildings was still in existence on the former Monmouthshire Railway & Canal Company's line below my grandfather's house at Risca, Monmouthshire, at least until 1930.

The early years of the nineteenth century witnessed the incorpo-ration of several tramroads which were significant as extending the South Wales network independently of the canals. These included notably the Sirhowy Tramroad Company (1802), the Carmarthenshire Railway Company of the same year, which later became the Llanelly & Mynydd Mawr Railway, and the Oystermouth Railway or Tramroad Company (1804), which became the Swansea & Mumbles, and was the first railway to provide a regular passenger service.

At its peak, before being largely overtaken by railways proper, the total tramroad mileage was probably not less than 400. The late Bertram Baxter recorded over 120 separate tramroads as having existed in the region, of which thirty-seven were in Monmouthshire, fifty in Glamorgan, seventeen in Brecknock, twenty in Carmarthenshire, and three in Pembrokeshire. About three-quarters of this total were built specifically as canal feeders, not necessarily by the navigation companies, but mainly by the owners of works within reasonable (if not always strictly legal) distance of the waterways.

FATE OF THE CANALS

The fates of the two largest canal companies became strangely contrasted in the coming Railway Age.

The Monmouthshire Canal Navigation Company (which bought out the Brecknock & Abergavenny in 1865) was formed largely by ironmasters, coalowners and shippers; the Glamorganshire Company was almost entirely subscribed jointly by Merthyr and Dowlais ironmasters. Merthyr-Dowlais was growing so fast during the iron industry bonanza that its population for some time exceeded those of Newport, Cardiff and Swansea combined. By the Newport & Ponty Pool (sic) Railway Act 1845 the Monmouthshire was empowered to consolidate its tramways into railways proper; changing its name to Monmouthshire Railway & Canal Company by 1848 Act, and granting running powers to the GWR in 1875, it became the latter's backbone of operations in the Monmouthshire valleys. The Glamorganshire on the other hand had early difficulties through quarrels among its proprietors, leading to proposals in 1798 for a competitive 'dram road' between Cardiff, Merthyr and adjacent valleys. An attempt to obtain Parliamentary powers for this was abandoned in the following year but, led by Richard Hill of Plymouth, the Penydarren Tramroad was built without such powers; the Glamorganshire Canal Company's 'Four Mile Clause' was scarcely viable authority for the purpose, since the tramroad from

Penydarren to the canal-side at Navigation House (later known as
Abercynon) was 9½ miles long.

EVOLUTION

Engineered by George Overton, the Penydarren was a plateway on
stone blocks to a gauge of 4ft 2in inside the wheel flanges of the
wagons; the ruling gradient was 1 in 36. Its opening in 1802 effectively short-circuited the upper, heavily-locked section of the canal
on which congestion and delays were alleged to occur, but its place
in history derives principally, perhaps, from its having been the location of the famous but short-lived trials of Richard Trevithick's locomotive in 1804. Trevithick at this time was working on stationary
engines and an experimental locomotive at Penydarren Ironworks,
the manager of which, Samuel Homfray, bet Anthony Hill that the
locomotive would haul ten tons of iron from Penydarren to
Abercynon. The wager was won on 21 February 1804, when the
locomotive took down to the canal five wagons loaded with pig-iron
and seventy men who had clambered aboard. (The first steam-
hauled 'standee' passengers in history?) Trevithick's locomotive
broke too many tramplates and its use on the line was discontinued,
although locomotives were later successfully employed on the tramroad before its life began to draw to a close about the middle of the
century.

   Despite the coming of railways proper, however, the rate of industrial growth so exceeded that of transport capacity that the principal
canals enjoyed a long period of prosperity; in 1851 the
Glamorganshire Canal carried nearly 600,000 tons. Thereafter, with
the continuing improvement in railway facilities, its trade and that
of the Monmouthshire Canal began to decline, although it was not
until early in this century that the final revenue loads passed over
those sections still open for navigation.

   An odd echo of the Glamorganshire Canal's long and chequered
history was heard as late as 23 February 1963 when Cardiff
Corporation, which in 1944 had acquired that part of the undertaking within the city boundaries, closed down the last active unit of
the former Navigation Company, being about 265yd of railway
authorised by the Glamorganshire Canal Act 1882 to link a GWR
siding leaving the South Wales Railway east of the bridge over the
Taff with sidings around the sea lock and canal basin. Of this industrial railway, then of some three track miles, it is pleasant to recall

Page 33 (Top) Tramroad viaduct at Risca, Mon, *circa* 1825, showing Kingson's passenger coach and a descending 'mineral' train; *(bottom)* Opening ceremony at Swansea Station, South Wales Railway, 18 June 1850. *(Courtesy British Library; Author's collection)*

Page 34 (Top) Movable bridge across the Monmouthshire Canal at Mill Street, Newport, in GWR days; (bottom) Freight train crossing Crumlin Viaduct, viewed from the Monmouthshire Canal towpath. (British Rail)

that at least one of its few locomotives was emblazoned with the city's coat-of-arms as evidence of municipal ownership.

COMING OF THE RAILWAYS

With industry and population expanding very quickly – some one hundred blast furnaces were blown-in around Dowlais and Merthyr alone, while the population of Glamorgan County was to increase from 70,000 to over 850,000 during the nineteenth century – the canal-and-tramroad system became under increasing strain, not merely from the growth of the basic coal and iron industries, but also from their closely related activities such as sawmills, refractories, limekilns, tinplate works, and small forges, all springing up as mushrooms of the Industrial Revolution. Already, too, local resources of iron-ore were proving inadequate, and import from fresh sources began in the 1830s through Cardiff and the Glamorganshire Canal. In 1864 the Ebbw Vale Company was to take-over the working of the West Somerset Mineral Railway to secure iron-ore from the Brendon Hills. Exports, too, were moving out of South Wales by tram, canal, and sea – iron rails, cannon, bar- and pig-iron and, increasingly, coal. The time was ripe for real railways. In the outside world the Stockton & Darlington was opened in 1825, the Liverpool & Manchester (the first real inter-city railway) five years later. South Wales was not far behind, with the Taff Vale Company incorporated in 1836 and opened, along the now classic Cardiff-Merthyr battleground, in 1840–41. And already sheeps (or more correctly, perhaps, wolves) eyes were being cast towards this nascent Eldorado by major railway interests in England. The prospectus for the South Wales Railway Company was issued within three years of the opening of the Taff Vale line; the London & North Western and the Midland, and much later (by devious means and route) the Manchester, Sheffield & Lincolnshire followed, and by 1850 the Border was physically crossed.

Before this theme is developed further, mainly on a geographical basis, it may be as well to anticipate the time-scale by depicting the strategic picture of the South Wales railway system as it was completed by the end of the century; first, the trunk routes with England:

1. The original South Wales Railway (GWR) via Gloucester (and later through the Severn Tunnel) running directly

along the seaboard through Newport, Cardiff and Swansea into the South West corner.

2. The GWR/LNWR route from the Midlands and North via Shrewsbury and Hereford to Newport, throwing-off at Pontypool Road a line to Aberdare and Swansea.

3. Two London & North Western Railway routes, one from Abergavenny across the Heads of the Valleys to Merthyr, and a later one from Craven Arms (the Central Wales Line) down to Llanelli and Swansea.

4. A back-door Midland Railway entrance, mostly over other people's lines, from Hereford through Brecon to its outposts in and around Swansea.

5. Edward Watkins' extraordinary back-door access, by arrangement with the Cambrian (Mid-Wales), from the isolated section of MSL/GC lines in the Wirral Peninsula and North Wales down to Talyllyn and Brecon; a meandering route which although much split-up among different railway companies, was even an officially-recognised route for freight traffic to and from the North Eastern Railway.

These then were the railway 'gateways' into South Wales: Severn Tunnel Junction, Pontypool Road, Abergavenny, Hereford, Craven Arms and Talyllyn. The entry routes neatly cut across the area at various latitudinal levels.

The second main group of railways, beginning with the pioneer Taff Vale, comprised the numerous internal and basically local lines running down the valleys to the ports. Thirdly, these railways in their turn promoted smaller 'laterals' like the Pontypridd, Caerphilly & Newport, the Rhondda & Swansea Bay, and the Vale of Glamorgan, each of which ran across part of the region with the object of diverting coal traffic from the normally nearest ports to more distant docks (eg from the Rhondda to Newport or Swansea instead of Cardiff). Mainly because of rate problems and more expensive working, such lines usually proved not to be as profitable as their promoters had hoped, but they certainly fluttered a few dovecotes.

Thus the railway map of South Wales was in criss-cross form, with the valley lines predominating. The distribution of the railways in relation to the various ports as it appeared immediately prior to the grouping under the Railways Act, 1921, is quite striking as illustrative of both the complex nature of the system, and its highly competitive nature; the most strenuous port versus port rivalry was that in the east, between Newport, Cardiff, Penarth, and Barry:

Newport:	GWR, LNWR, Alexandra (Newport & South Wales), Brecon & Merthyr.
Cardiff:	GWR, LNWR, Taff Vale, Rhymney Railway, Barry Railway, Cardiff Railway.
Penarth:	Taff Vale, and Penarth Harbour Dock & Railway (worked by TVR).
Barry:	Barry, and Vale of Glamorgan (worked by Barry).
Port Talbot:	GWR, Port Talbot Railway & Docks, South Wales Mineral Railway, Rhondda & Swansea Bay.
Briton Ferry:	GWR, R & SB.
Neath:	GWR, Neath & Brecon, R & SB.
Swansea:	GWR, LNWR, Midland, R & SB, Swansea & Mumbles, Swansea Harbour Trust (the two latter purely local).
Llanelly:	GWR, LNWR, Llanelly & Mynydd Mawr, Burry Port & Gwendraeth Valley, Nevill's Dock & Railway Company (local)
Burry Port:	GWR, Burry Port & Gwendraeth Valley.
Kidwelly:	GWR, Gwendraeth Valleys.
Milford Haven:	GWR, Milford Haven Dock & Railway (internal).
Fishguard:	Fishguard & Rosslare Railways & Harbours Company (at Fishguard, worked by GWR).

It is of interest that two of the major Welsh railway companies, the Alexandra (N & SW) and the Barry were incorporated primarily as dock companies, changing their titles later to emphasise their railway aspect and thus, incidentally, to obtain trustee status for their stocks.

THE SOUTH WALES RAILWAY

The orientation of so much of the regional system on the direct linkages between the industrial valleys and the nearest ports makes it easy to develop on this basis the more detailed studies which follow, covering the respective sections of the lateral railways as one progresses east to west. Since the main lateral, the South Wales Railway, constituted in a railway sense the physical base of the system, and was also the only trunk railway to intersect the whole of the region, an introductory review of its origin may be helpful at this stage. Nor should we overlook the fact that by 1923 this company's not always loving parent, the GWR, controlled all but some 200 miles or so of the regional rail network, and all the major ports.

Discussions and consultations for the promotion of a trunk railway between London and South Wales had begun as early as 1836, in which year a committee was formed numbering no fewer than seventy-eight persons and including some of 'the best people' to represent South Wales. The eyes of the Paddington board and management, however, were not directed only towards the Principality but beyond it to Ireland, which was becoming the objective of rival schemes for communication with England. The prospectus for the South Wales Railway Company was issued in 1844, the same year in which, at the other end of Wales, the rival Chester & Holyhead Railway was incorporated; the SWR was in fact *ab initio* a creature of the Great Western. The SWR Company obtained its incorporation Act without difficulty (Royal Assent. 4 August 1845), the £2,500,000 capital being fully subscribed, one-fifth of it by the GWR. The railway was a grand concept in the London & Bristol tradition: a main line of some 143 miles from Chepstow, along the Severn's north bank to Newport, thence via Cardiff, Bridgend, Port Talbot, Neath, Swansea and Llanelly to Carmarthen, and through the Pembrokeshire hills to Fishguard on the west coast, with a branch to Pembroke Dock. (The company's Act of 1846 authorised extension from Chepstow to Awre, whence the Gloucester & Dean Forest Railway, by concurrent Act, completed through to Gloucester.)

Although all the auguries for a successful alliance were present at the outset – the GWR to nominate six directors, to have powers to make agreements, and (from 1846) a lease to the Great Western at a guaranteed rent of five per cent – the whole relationship very quickly went sour, for a variety of reasons. Firstly, in making Fishguard the objective of the South Wales promotion, the GWR had in mind Government encouragement to open-up routes to Ireland, and the opportunity to compete with the proposed route via Holyhead. The guarantee to the South Wales was therefore subject to the completion of the latter through to Fishguard. When by 1849 it became apparent that the state of things in Ireland and general economic conditions rendered the Fishguard project temporarily untenable, Paddington got very tough, and refused to modify the agreement. Secondly, the conditions under which the

GWR supplied equipment and staff were too onerous. Thirdly (and to many readers this will be rank heresy!) the gauge was wrong, inhibiting proper development of the important and growing South Wales mineral traffic.

This statement needs to be examined in the context of the opening itself. This took place in sections, on 18 June 1850 from Chepstow to Swansea, though the Wye Bridge at the former place was not finished for through traffic until two years and one month later; and from Landore (Swansea) to Carmarthen on 11 October 1852. Extensions to Haverfordwest and to Neyland ('New Milford') on the northern shore of Milford Haven opened on 2 January 1854 and 15 April 1856 respectively, the branch from Johnston (Pem) to Milford Haven, built by the Milford Railway Company but worked by the GWR, following on 7 September 1863. Meanwhile the GWR had reluctantly consented to a new agreement with the SWR, whereby the Fishguard extension would be temporarily postponed; half-a-century was to elapse before some of Brunel's unfinished engineering works on this line were to be completed.

The third adverse factor in the early fortunes of the South Wales Railway, the gauge of the railway itself, deserves perhaps greater consideration in a book of this kind than the other factors already mentioned, which are described at length in previous histories. In the context that the South Wales Railway was basically an extension of the Paddington empire, initially with GWR men as chairman and as chief officers, and with Isambard Kingdom Brunel as the supervising engineer, it was virtually axiomatic that it was to be laid out to the broad gauge of 7ft 0¼ in. Except that at its western end beyond Pembrey, where it comprised only a single line of the inadequate Barlow (inverted v-shaped) rails, which soon had to be replaced at the expense of the SWR (!), it was splendidly engineered. Following as it largely did the coastal strip, it was more nearly level than any other railway in South Wales. These favourable stretches comprised twenty-four miles from what is now Severn Tunnel Junction through Newport and Cardiff, three miles through Bridgend, nineteen miles between Margam Moors and Neath, and some twenty-six miles along the shores of the estuary from Gowerton to Carmarthen, a total of seventy-two level or almost level miles out of ninety-two. On the other hand, there are three challengingly steep 'gables' over Llanharan, between Llantrisant and Pencoed, over Stormy Down between Bridgend and Margam, with a ruling gradient of 1 in 79 eastbound, and over Skewen Bank between Neath and Swansea, with 1 in 88 westbound and 1 in 91 eastbound. The worst summit of the lot on the old route is that up to the 789yd Cockett Tunnel west of Swansea, with ascents at 1 in 52 going west from Landore, and 1 in 53/50 coming east from Gowerton. All these banks are now less formidable with the advent of diesel traction. Brunel made two deviations from the line originally authorised, one over Stormy Down to avoid the notorious shifting sand dunes of Kenfig, and one between Kidwelly and Carmarthen to avoid the heavier terrain inland. There were, however, other engineering problems: several swing or opening bridges had to be provided over navigable rivers, while several ancient tramroads which happened to be there first had to be crossed on the level.

THE GAUGE DIFFICULTY

Apart from its rows with Paddington, the main disadvantage under which the South Wales Railway laboured during its relatively short life as a separate company was the choice of the broad gauge. Of other railways in South Wales only the Vale of Neath and four other small local lines subservient to the South Wales adopted it at their inception – and again, the engineer of the Vale of Neath was I. K. Brunel. The decision to adopt the broad gauge for the SWR and its satellites was in accordance with Paddington philosophy at the time, but only a decade previously Brunel had advised the promoters of the TVR to use the standard gauge of 4ft 8½ in, partly because of the curvature of the TVR main line along the banks of the River Taff above Radyr, and partly because he foresaw that this local railway would extend its system into the narrow valleys; the extent to which the TVR would develop through freight traffic with other railways was evidently not foreseen at the time Brunel's advice was sought. Moreover, he was tendering this advice at a time when the London & Bristol Railway Company had not yet been incorporated: the Taff Vale in this respect was only one year its junior, having obtained its own Act in 1836.

The South Wales' chickens came home to roost when the South Wales Railway found that even with the growth in the coal trade, it could attract little freight traffic into England. Although forced to provide a series of tranship stations with the standard gauge local railways along its main line, the SWR found that freighters still preferred their business to move in standard gauge wagons (and many of them were beginning to possess their own) direct from valley to port and thence by sea, rather than have it transhipped at Newport, Cardiff, Stormy Down or Llanelly; this objection was particularly strong in the case of coal traffic because of the risk of additional intermediate breakage. Ironically, the GWR itself had begun by the early 1850s to obtain large supplies of coking coal from the Lower Rhondda for use in its locomotive coke ovens at Bristol; probably this traffic passed from the Great Western Colliery via the Dinas Branch of the TVR, opened in 1841, and Pontypridd to Cardiff for shipment, but see also page 123. Meanwhile, standard gauge routes were being opened into and out of South Wales, from 1854 by Hereford-Pontypool Road and the Newport, Abergavenny & Hereford, and by the LNWR into the northern part of the industrial belt via the Merthyr, Tredegar & Abergavenny route from 1862 onwards. The laying of a third rail into Paddington in 1861 underlined the writing on the wall by affording through communication of a sort between South Wales and London via Pontypool Road, the West Midland Railway, Oxford and Reading. Even earlier, the TVR had 'seen off' the SWR by firmly refusing to make a broad gauge connection with the latter at Cardiff(the Bute Street Junction Branch, opened 1854 for the purpose of exchanging traffic in Cardiff), and the SWR had to provide it at its own expense, the first piece of mixed gauge in South Wales. In 1866, over 250 South Wales freighters petitioned against the continuance of the broad gauge; by 1872 it was gone from South Wales, but in the meanwhile the family squabbles between the GWR and the SWR had ended in an inevitable amalgamation on I August 1863.

With the absorption of the SWR into the Paddington fold, the Vale of Neath, the Monmouthshire, and a number of other local railways, some twenty in all, which will be encountered as this story develops, the stage was set for the long high summer of the GWR to run its rule across the base of the Principality and into some of the most valuable parts of the coalfield. As with the lines acquired by the GWR, totalling over 500 route miles, parts of the systems built up by the LNWR and by the companies which remained independent until the 1920s also included mileage which was originally tramroad; some of it, in modern guise, is still in use today. As the years passed, other of the early tramroads were superseded either wholly or in part, or became redundant, or survived as elements of colliery or other local industrial systems which do not form part of this book. A few lingered into the late twentieth century as works lines under the respective banners of the National Coal Board or the

British Steel Corporation. Elsewhere, many a crumbling bridge pier or broken abutment, a few stone sleeper blocks in a grass-grown embankment, or the way the sheep go along a narrow shelf on a hillside, mark the way the old rails ran and the heritage they gave to railway history.

CHAPTER III

Eastern Monmouthshire (Gwent)

Of the various gateways into South Wales listed in the preceding chapter, three – Newport, Pontypool Road and Abergavenny Junction – are located within twenty miles of one another along the north-to-south courses of the parallel rivers Usk and Afon Llwyd (or Afan Llwid, take your choice), which join at Caerleon, three miles above Newport. Much the most important of these is the former county town of Newport, the commercial capital of Gwent (as Monmouthshire is now known), and a centre of canal, tramroad and railway activity for nearly 200 years. Hemmed in to landward by, and now largely built upon five hills each some 350ft high, Newport's strategic situation between the outfall of the rivers Usk and Ebbw into the mouth of the Severn assured it a turbulent history in which there figured successively and bloodily the early warring tribesmen, Romans, Normans, Welsh princes and English kings, Cavaliers, Roundheads, and even the Chartist rioters of 1839. Equally this situation secured its place as a focal point of transport development as the mineral wealth of the valleys began to pour down towards the Bristol Channel during the Industrial Revolution, and as rail traffic grew between England and South Wales. Similarly, the physical restraints of the encompassing hills dictated the courses of the early canal and tramroads, respectively around the east side of the town and through the Usk River gap into the Eastern Valleys, and around the West or Cardiff side by way of the Ebbw River gap into the Western Valleys. Only the main line of the South Wales Railway struck through the centre of Newport, by virtue of Brunel's bold and costly bridge-and-tunnel engineering, neatly dividing the commercial part of the town on the seaward side from what developed as the residential pattern on the rising ground to landward.

This geographical division between the two groups of valley railways which meet at Newport conveniently aids the study of railway evolution as between Eastern and Western Monmouthshire/Gwent respectively, rather than approach it in strict chronological sequence.

For many a home-coming native as for the railway enthusiast, there is an emotional aspect, almost a magic, in the approach to Gwent from eastward. The original route of the South Wales Railway via Chepstow is shut in by higher ground along the north bank of the Severn, but coming from London or Bristol by way of the Severn Tunnel the descent through Pilning can be dramatic, as the train bursts out of Patchway Tunnel and affords on a clear day the first sighting across the water of the hills of Wales, misty-blue to the north-west. Through the Tunnel itself (in which in times past, with any luck, one might by cautious peering through a half-dropped corridor window encounter the splendid noise and spectacle of a double-headed freight train blasting up towards the English side), Severn Tunnel Junction disclosed itself as a complex of marshalling yards and locomotive depot leading on across the Caldicot Level. Prior to the 1960s this was a flat, rather uninteresting stretch, in olden times reclaimed from and retained against the risk of long-remembered Severn floods, but in 1962 there was officially opened the first section of the Richard Thomas & Baldwin Group's (now British Steel Corporation's) integrated Spencer Steelworks, today better known as the Llanwern plant. This great undertaking stretches for some 3½ miles between the main line and Severn's edge, connected to the former by a flying junction at the eastern end (Bishton), and by a flat junction – the main line is four-tracked – at Steelworks West at the Newport end, near the site of the former Llanwern station, closed in 1960.

The Llanwern plant covers some 1,700 acres and is served by nearly forty miles of internal railways. As an interim expedient until the deep-water iron ore terminal at Port Talbot should be ready, iron ore was imported through Newport Docks and taken to the works by a shuttle service of trains composed of conventional tippler wagons. With the completion of the Port Talbot ore terminal and with the introduction in February 1976 of the first of the new-type high-output blast furnaces at Llanwern, there began the much-publicised operation of the heaviest freight trains in Great Britain: three Class 37 diesel-electric locomotives each of 1,750 hp hauling twenty-seven 100-ton wagons with a gross payload of 2,079 tons of ore making a gross trainload of 2,740 tons. Operations began with five Port Talbot–Llanwern trains daily, with a projected service of seven, automatic loading and discharge enabling empty return journeys to be restarted in under four hours, with maximum permitted speeds of 60mph.

From 6 August 1979 regular operation of these trains was taken over by Class 56 diesels of 3,250hp each (two per train), releasing Class 37s for use in pairs on the fifteen daily trains, each of thirty-five merry-go-round wagons, to Aberthaw power station. By introducing the more powerful Class 56s on the Llanwern ore trains, from 29 September 1980 the loading went from twenty-seven wagons to thirty, payload increasing to 2,316 tonnes and trailing weight to 3,048, laden.

Iron ore apart, the volume of actual and potential traffic to and from the Llanwern plant in 1980 afforded a formidable example of what railways could do with the right sort of business, including around 25,000 tons of coking coal received weekly, 8,000 tons of steel strip forwarded to Ebbw Vale, and about 5,000 tons of steel slab weekly to Margam for the BSC Port Talbot plant; other finished output went away on Freightliner or Speedlink services.

NEWPORT

Approaching Newport from Severn Tunnel Junction at the zenith of the railway network in the early 1920s, the traveller would observe in succession two branches on the left hand side towards the River Usk; first (from East Usk Branch Junction) the East Usk Branch, of which more anon; and second, from Nettlefold's Branch Junction, the private industrial branch of that name. The latter was officially taken out of use on 10 March 1974. Following almost immediately on the right are the triangular Maindee Junctions with the route to Pontypool and beyond, now the only access from Newport to the Eastern Valleys. The railway now crosses over the muddy Usk (in bygone days with a glimpse of a Bristol Channel paddle-steamer moored at the pontoon below). At the period of which we write, the main line would next pass over both the remains of the Monmouthshire Canal and the Eastern Valleys line of the former Monmouthshire Railway & Canal Company. This latter railway, now obliterated at the Newport end by highway development, had no connection here with the main line, but passed under it and round the south side of the town to the docks area. Until 1874, this circular loop formed the only means of connection between the Eastern

Valleys and the South Wales main line of the GWR.

Although strategically situated for passenger business, Newport Station (High Street for many years, to distinguish it from Dock Street and Mill Street) was initially isolated from the local railways, while as both freight and passenger traffics expanded its operating capacity became severely limited by the bridge over the River Usk to the east, and by the tunnel under Stow Hill to the west.

The early histories of both bridge and tunnel were not without adventure, the opening of the railway being delayed by the accidental burning-down of the original timber bridge during its construction in 1848, while the tunnelling operations 200ft below Stow Hill were alleged to have drained the wells from which part of the town then derived its water supply. Both these operating defiles were in due course opened-out; a second Hillfield Tunnel was completed in 1911, being slightly longer than the adjacent original (742yd), while the widening of the Usk Bridge was carried out in stages between 1911 and 1925.

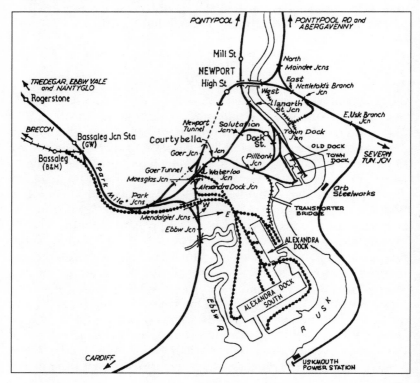

Until the 1960s the layout of Newport station was traditional, with a Down main platform incorporating the offices and amenities (the station was largely rebuilt between 1923 and 1930 in imposing style with modern offices, including the Monmouthshire Club as tenants). There were Up and Down middle tracks, an island Up platform, with outer face used either as a relief through line or for local trains, and a Down main platform with a bay at either end. In connection with the growth of traffic expected to accrue from the opening of the Llanwern steelworks, the layout was altered in the 1960s to its present form, with six tracks through the station (four through the tunnels), with a high degree of reversible working. The Up and Down middle tracks have now basically become the Up and Down freight lines, enabling this traffic to be kept normally to the south side of the main line right through from Cardiff to Bishton. Both faces of the old Up island platform are now normally used for passenger trains, while the former Down platform is used normally by parcels and freight trains, although occasionally by passenger trains.

In 1906 the station was being used by 110 originating or arriving passenger trains a day, with 85 passenger and 150 freight trains passing through. Fifty years on, when all local passenger services were in being, some three-quarters of a million tickets were issued annually, excluding 300,000 platform tickets: the Welsh are splendid at welcoming and 'seeing-off'. Saturday was the great day for local travel, with a big influx from the valleys for shopping and football. Newport was also something of a Mecca for railway enthusiasts, because it was the first place at which you could see a purely Welsh railway, in the shape of the Brecon & Merthyr passenger train. The fact that the locomotive bore a remarkable resemblance to a GWR 2–4–0T was perhaps not surprising inasmuch as Swindon had courteously lent the drawings, but the coaches were likely to be distinctly 'vintage', to use a currently much overworked word. Every vintage has its bouquet, however, and the B & M vintage carriage had a bouquet all its own, compounded of faded upholstery, shag, beer and coal dust, but with an additional aroma acquired on each trip past the Bargoed coke ovens. Apart from the B & M, there was another stranger in the camp at Newport, in the shape of an LNWR local train to the Sirhowy line, probably with a Webb 0–6–2T heading a rake of four-wheelers. With the main Newport goods depot adjoining the passenger yard on the Down side, a corresponding space on the Up side was occupied by a locomotive depot until 1915, when because of traffic growth and lack of space it was transferred to Ebbw Junction (Maesglas) on the other side of the tunnels.

THE EASTERN VALLEYS

The South Wales Railway already described was thus a strictly east-west axis line through Newport, having originally no direct branches of its own into the valleys on either side of the town. The branches, in origin, derived mainly from the early canal-and-tram-road pattern. Even before the canal and tramroads, however, Newport had begun a maritime trade with Bristol and other coast-wise ports, mainly by means of small craft loading at pills or creeks on the banks of the Usk, and if necessary drying out on the mud at low tide; development became very rapid with the opening of the Monmouthshire Canal in 1799, and of the tramroads from the Western Valleys about six years later. The coming of the canal now to be described, and of the tramroads from the Western Valleys, was to bring a number of private wharves along the west bank of the Usk, belonging mostly to the various freighters, with short tram-roads connecting with the canal basin and with the first dock proper, the Newport Town Dock; the last-named however was not authorised until 1835, its original section being opened in 1842.

The Monmouthshire Canal Navigation Company is important to South Wales railway history because, unlike its neighbour the Glamorganshire Canal Company based on Cardiff, it was the possessor of a number of tramroads which it later converted into railways, and so enabled it in the coming Railway Age to play an important part in the politics and strategy of the region. *Per contra,* the Glamorganshire left its bid to become a railway company far too late to have any chance of success.

By its Act of 1792 the Monmouthshire Canal Navigation Company was incorporated mainly for the purpose of carrying traffic between the collieries, ironworks, limestone quarries and other industries and the riverside at Newport; the Act incorporating the Newport Dock Company already mentioned authorised the canal company to subscribe to the former. The canal originally began near Newport Bridge but was later extended about a mile westwards and south of the town to Pillgwenlly, mis-spelt 'Pingwelly' in the company's Act. Going up into the valleys, the canal divided into two arms at Crindau on the eastern outskirts of Newport. The western arm terminated at Crumlin, while the eastern arm ran to Pontnewynydd, about a mile above Pontypool, which was the nexus of an industrial area including ironworks – iron had been made there since the sixteenth century – collieries, tinplate (including the once famous 'Pontypool japanned ware'), wireworks, and other activities with which the names of the Hanburys, the Harfords and others are historically associated.

Each arm of the canal was about eleven miles long and involved heavy engineering, for which Thomas Dadford junior was responsible. The Newport section and the eastern arm had forty-two locks and the western thirty-two, with total rises of 447ft and 370ft respectively. Practically the whole of this canal was open for traffic by 1799, and in 1812 the waterway line of communication in Eastern Monmouthshire was completed by the 35-mile Brecknock & Abergavenny canal. This branched off the Monmouthshire at Pontymoile, below Pontypool, continuing via Abergavenny and thence up the easily-graded Vale of Crickhowell to Brecon – a route which subsequently figured in more than one abortive railway promotion, there being no mineral resources north of the canal to provide worthwhile traffic expectation.

As stated earlier, both these canal companies had powers to build feeder tramroads within specified distances of the waterway, or for them to be built by or on behalf of freighters. Thus from 1795 onwards the Monmouthshire Company and other promoters built up around Pontypool a network of tramroads of which the earliest and principal, the Blaenavon Tramroad of 1795, ran for five miles northward from the canal-head at Pontnewynydd to the Blaenavon Ironworks. This tramroad threw off branches from its western side to ironworks and collieries at Abersychan, Varteg and Cwm Ffrwd, while other tramroads were built lower down the canal, from Pontymoile to Blaendare and Trosnant. Like most of the Monmouthshire's tramroads these lines were nearly all originally built with cast-iron edge-rails to the 3ft 4in gauge, but it soon became evident that this combination afforded very poor haulage capacity, a horse often being able to haul only one wagon, while broken rails were frequent. Following a report by Benjamin Outram in 1800, the majority of the Monmouthshire's tramroads were converted to plateways of 4ft 2in gauge, but this system in its turn ran into difficulties with the introduction (mainly in the Western Valleys) of steam locomotives, which broke-up the tramplates. The Monmouthshire had other troubles, however; freighters became dissatisfied with unreliable service and with rate discriminations, while some of the principal personalities were having to face both ways (and goodness knows how one or two of them must have enjoyed it!) as directors or shareholders of the canal company on one hand, and as freighters on the other.

PERSONALITIES

This situation was exemplified in the person of Crawshay Bailey (1789-1872), for a long period MP for Newport and the Monmouthshire Boroughs, who with his elder brother (Sir) Joseph was related to the Crawshays of Cyfarthfa, and who came as youngsters from their native Yorkshire to seek their fortunes in the South Wales valleys. In this they succeeded admirably by a combination of family patronage, native wit and immense industry, the elder at Nantyglo and Blaina (where Crawshay later joined him) and the younger initially at the Aberaman Ironworks and collieries in the Aberdare Valley. Both were prominent and energetic in the affairs of the B & A and Monmouthshire Canals respectively, and in the promotion of rail connection with their respective works. Crawshay became immortalised in South Wales folk-lore as having introduced one of the early steam locomotives in South Wales. Although technical evidence of its existence seems slender, there was nothing slender about the words of the song, which like *Sospan Fach* was sung (and maybe it still is) for generations on pay nights, or after a notable victory by the Newport rugger team, or most often in the past on the arrival of the last train at valley stations on Saturday nights. The original ditty does not often find its way into the milk-and-water versions of some folklorists; the first two lines went:

Crossher Bailey had an engine, and the engine wouldn't go,
So they pushed the bloody engine all the way to Nantyglo...

Having betrayed at the early age of six a promising interest in railway history by enquiring at the family breakfast table next morning, the meaning of certain words of this song as heard through the bedroom window the previous night, purposeful glances ensued across the table, followed by a rapid change of subject. But the next time the family went in state by train, perhaps to Tenby or Weston-super-Mare, I pointed to the magnificent Great Western 4–4–0 bringing in our train, and inquired in a loud and

Page 51 Armorial devices of South Wales railway companies: Taff Vale, Rhondda & Swansea Bay, Cardiff, Barry. *(British Rail* and *Curator of Historical Relics, BRB)*

Page 52 (Top)   An ex-Taff Vale Railway 0-6-0T pushes a load of empties up the 1 in 13 cable-assisted Pwllyrhebog Incline, out of the Rhondda Valley; *(bottom)* Loaded coal trains from the Rhondda Valley *(left)* and the Rhymney Valley *(right)*, both hauled by GWR 0-6-2Ts, below Walnut Tree Viaduct, which carried the former Barry Railway over the Taff Vale main line. *(R. J. Doran; British Rail)*

penetrating voice, 'Dadda, is *this* Crossher Bailey's bloody engine?'

The Bailey Brothers, Crawshay especially, were devil's advocates in the affairs of the canal companies, prodding the Monmouthshire in particular to get into the world of railways proper, to which immense stimulus had been imparted by the opening of trunk lines in England. Ambitious proposals for railways to connect South Wales and England had foundered, but the Taff Vale Railway was open by 1841, and the South Wales, the Vale of Neath, and the Newport, Abergavenny & Hereford companies were all in the early stages of promotion, and were to be incorporated by 1845-46. The Monmouthshire Canal Company on the other hand, although highly prosperous financially, was in serious difficulty, both with its freighters, and with the more progressive of its shareholders. It was a 'toll road' and not a carrier, so did not really control the traffic which passed over it. Its system was physically inadequate to the boom that was rip-roaring through the valleys – the population of Newport had soared from less than 800 in the 1790s to 1,100 in 1801, and was to reach 14,000 half-a-century later (in 1989 over 128,000). The Monmouthshire Canal was carrying over 130,000 tons of coal and iron traffic a year, while with the aid of the traffic brought down by tramroads from the Western Valleys and its freedom from shipping dues, Newport in the 1830s had been exporting five times as much coal as Cardiff, before the exploitation of the steam coal seams in the Rhondda and Aberdare Valleys and the development of Cardiff Docks.

In this situation the canal company came under pressure not only from a 'ginger group' of its own shareholders, but also from local interests seeking to promote railways from Newport to Nantyglo either via the Western Valleys or via Pontypool, Blaenavon and 'over the tops' at the heads of the valleys. Nor is it perhaps surprising that these promotions had the active support of members of the 'ginger group', not least Crawshay Bailey.

While the canal company was still dithering whether or not to convert itself into a railway undertaking, and was having a route surveyed between Pontypool and Newport (which was the bigger bottleneck, because in the Western Valleys there had been through tramroad communication of a sort with Newport since 1805) a 'Monmouthshire Railway Company' incorporated in 1846 reached agreement to buy out the canal company, but this early example of an agreed take-over collapsed because not enough canal shareholders were agreeable to conversion of their shares.

In 1845 the canal company screwed up its courage, or was pushed over the brink as the case may be, and obtained an Act to make railways between Newport and Pontnewynydd with an extension into Newport Town Dock (in substitution of the tramroad already connecting the docks with the canal), to become carriers, and to raise more capital. Three years later the company had to come back for another Act raising more money, extending the time for completion of the railways, abolishing the right of freighters to run their own locomotives on its lines whether railways or tramroads (with some minor exceptions where locomotives could not yet effectively work because of curves or gradients), and changing the name of the company to The Monmouthshire Railway & Canal Company. In a play on these initials, the company became known to railwaymen as 'The Mouse, Rat & Cat Company', though whether this had allusion to the local fauna or to the MR & CC's cat-and-mouse games with other companies is a matter of speculation.

NEWPORT TO PONTYPOOL

Without ploughing through the dismal undergrowth of lawsuits and other frustrations which delayed this programme, it can be recorded that with the exception of the few sections mentioned in the preceding paragraph, the whole of the MR & CC tramroads had been converted to standard gauge railways by 1855; this was partly financed out of revenue, but also involved a charge to capital account of nearly £21,000.

By this time the company had already brought into use its railway communication between Newport and the Eastern Valleys, the first of its properties to be built as a 'modern' railway and not initially as a tramroad. The new railway to Pontypool was 8¼ miles long, and was opened as a single line for passenger traffic on 1 July 1852 and as a double line for mineral traffic in 1854. Its original and temporary terminus in Newport was at Marshes Turnpike Gate, near the present Shaftesbury Street roundabout, but on 9 March 1853 the passenger service was extended a quarter of a mile into Newport (Mill Street) Station, which could just be glimpsed from the South Wales main line on the higher level, and which was not far from an interchange with the canal at Moderator Wharf. Two years later (May 1855) the Eastern Valleys line, passing under the South Wales Railway immediately eastward of the latter's High Street Station, became connected, for freight traffic only with the Dock Street terminus of the Western Valleys lines, the passenger services of which had used it since 4 August 1852. This extension also provided rail access from the Eastern Valleys to Newport Town Dock. Thus from 1852 until 11 March 1880, a few months before the MR & CC became amalgamated with the GWR, there were three separate passenger stations in Newport: Dock Street for the Western Valleys, Mill Street for the Eastern Valleys, and High Street for the South Wales main line.

Northward from Newport the Eastern Valleys line ran generally parallel with the canal but to the east of it, the continuously rising gradients being relatively easy by South Wales standards, until between Panteg and Pontypool they stiffened to 1 in 56 and then 1 in 54; Panteg was the location of a major ironworks for about twenty years prior to 1895, when it was converted to steel-making. Several collieries, notably Henllys Slope on the mountainside of Mynydd Henllys, had quite lengthy tramroads of their own to connect them with the railway. The principal engineering work on the line was a short tunnel close to the original Llantarnam Station, which in the mode of so many early rural stations, was halfway between the villages of Malpas and Llantarnam, but served neither effectively.

PONTYPOOL AND ITS BRANCHES

The initial terminus of the line was at Pontypool 'Town' Station or 'Newport Road', which to distinguish it from Clarence Street on the Taff Vale Extension Railway, was later renamed Pontypool (Crane Street); although industrial cranes were already familiar objects, it is more probable that this name derived from a nearby hostelry, The Three Cranes. Beyond Pontypool, and following closely the course of the Afon Llwyd, the company extended its railway to Blaenavon, 5¾ miles. on 1 June 1854 (for passenger traffic, 2 October). This branch was built mainly on the course of the Blaenavon Tramroad of 1795 and partly absorbing the formation of the canal above Pontymoile, but once it forsook the latter near Pontnewynydd it rose continuously at between 1 in 42 and 1 in 48½, terminating beyond Blaenavon passenger station in an end-on junction with the private lines belonging to the Blaenavon iron and steel works and collieries; some collieries on the west side of the valley were connected by rope-worked inclines.

Three other branches of the MR & CC diverged westward from the Blaenavon Branch north of Pontypool. At Pontnewynydd

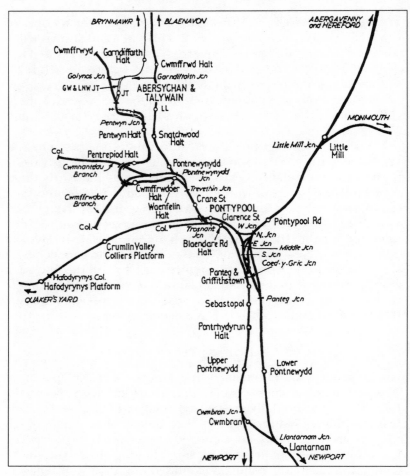

Junction, immediately south of the station of that name, a 33-chain double line led to Branches Fork Junction, whence the Cwmffrwdoer Branch of 1¼ miles followed a narrow valley to collieries rejoicing in the names of Plas-y-coed, Gellydeg, and Tirpentwys, with a private line extending beyond the last-named to Tygwyn Colliery. Part way along this branch was the Graigddu claymine opened later by my grandfather and situated on the ruling gradient of 1 in 18, which made shunting very tricky. Both the Cwmffrwdoer and the adjacent Cwmnantddu Branch, two miles in length which diverged from it at Branches Fork Junction, and which enjoyed a ruling gradient of 1 in 19, were single track, both opened in 1870, and surviving until the 1960s. In order to minimise the risk of breakaways, these branches were worked with the locomotive at the Pontypool end of the train. These and similarly-situated branch lines in South Wales were exposed to the recurrent risk of mining subsidence and earth movement which in my own time brought about the closure of the Graigddu clay workings.

A third and later branch line, opened 18 September 1879, turned westward off the original Blaenavon Branch, a quarter of a mile north of Pontypool, at Trevethin Junction, from which little place a Lord Chief Justice of England, locally born, was to take the title of his barony. This was the Talywain Branch, one of the last railways to be built by the MR & CC during its independent life. From Trevethin Junction it climbed at 1 in 48 in a tight half-circle to pass over the top of both the Cwmffrwdoer and Cwmnantddu Branches and to take up a course parallel with and to the west of the Blaenavon line. At Abersychan & Talywain, nearly four miles above Pontypool, it connected with the complex of private lines serving the ironworks and collieries, and finished up at the Varteg Collieries. In part it replaced, on a more suitable alignment, one of the earliest Monmouthshire Canal tramroads, the 'Cwmffrwd Railroad'. The top end of this last-named, about three-quarters of a mile, diverged slightly westward of and below Abersychan & Talywain to serve several collieries and the old British Ironworks, and was separately identified as the Cwmffrwd Branch. The Talywain was the only one of the branches just mentioned to have a passenger service, and if there was ever any confusion between them in correspondence or telephone conversations this must have been enhanced from 1912 onwards, when in connection with the introduction of railmotor cars, the GWR opened new halts at Cwmffrwd and Cwmffrwdoer. Now, Cwmffrwd Halt was not as might be assumed on the Cwmffrwd Branch, but between Abersychan and Cwmavon on the original Blaenavon Branch, on the east side of the valley, while Cwmffrwdoer Halt was not as might be supposed on the mineral branch of that name, but between Pontypool and Abersychan & Talywain on the Talywain Branch! I would remind any reader who is now saying to himself 'it could only happen in Wales', that at the relevant times and indeed until the nineteen-seventies, all these places, in defiance of any historical reason, were technically in England...

At Abersychan & Talywain the MR & CC line from Pontypool met the LNWR coming down from the mountains at Brynmawr, a story which belongs to the next chapter.

EARLY RULES ON SMOKING

With its railway hat on, the Monmouthshire was not always happy, and (to mix metaphors) became a bit of a byword; its maintenance and other conditions on occasion evoked sharp comment from Board of Trade inspecting officers. Its rule book of 1869 appeared to evince little confidence in locomotive reliability, as witness Rule 55:

> When the Way is obscured by steam or smoke (*owing to a burst tube or other cause*), no approaching Engine is allowed to pass through the steam, until the Engine-driver shall have ascertained that the way is clear...
> [The italics are the author's]

Rule 78 which dealt with passengers smoking (not allowed in stations, only on trains) was a masterpiece of complexity in regard to the permissible permutations according to train formation: smokers were required to fill up one complete compartment before a second could be used for smoking, while in the first-class it was not allowed in any case unless there were more than three first-class compartments on the train. Since 'prisoners in charge of the police and persons afflicted with insanity' were required if practicable to have not merely a compartment but a whole carriage to themselves, while drunks had also to be confined 'in a separate place' by the guard until arrival at the next station... there must have been some fun on the valley trains on Saturday nights, if all these rules were observed.

INVASION FROM THE NORTH

By the time that these railways completed the MR & CC network in Eastern Monmouthshire, the company was reaping the whirlwind of its earlier hesitancy and internal dissidence, and was becoming hemmed in by bigger brethren, not all brotherly in their attitudes. Both the Midland and the London & North Western Railways were keenly interested in getting into South Wales, not merely to Newport and Cardiff but also to Neath, Swansea and even Brecon, in order both to carve off for themselves some of the icing from the industrial cake, and to forestall if they could the further penetration northwards by the GWR.

The immediate link with the Monmouthshire Railway from the north was forged by the Newport, Abergavenny & Hereford

Company, incorporated 3 August 1846, for a line from Hereford through Abergavenny and the eastern outskirts of Pontypool to the MR & CC's proposed Newport & Pontypool line at Coedygric Farm, a mile below Pontypool; between Abergavenny & Hereford the NA & HR acquired three old tramroads known as the Llanvihangel, Grosmont and Hereford 'Railways' respectively; their acquisition was strategic, in order to clear the ground, and very little physical use was made of them by the NA & HR.

Despite the support and encouragement of the LNWR, bestowed not in kindness but by attempts (ultimately unsuccessful) to acquire it, progress of the NA & HR was delayed by the aftermath of the first Railway Mania and by the marching and counter-marching along the English-Welsh border and in and out of Parliamentary committee rooms of the LNWR, the GWR, the Oxford, Worcester & Wolverhampton, and the Midland companies. Eventually, after the Shrewsbury & Hereford Railway had opened throughout to passengers on 6 December 1853, the NA & HR followed on 2 January 1854, from Hereford (Barton) to the Monmouthshire at Coedygric. The Worcester & Hereford opened throughout between 1859-61. Until 31 December 1854 the NA & HR was worked by its fairy godfather, the LNWR, a feature later to prove significant being that the newcomer had obtained (by agreement, not statute) running powers over the Monmouthshire into Mill Street. The NA & HR took over the working from 1 January 1855.

Meanwhile, the NA & HR was at last getting a move on with its second route for which it had obtained powers in 1847: the Taff Vale Extension from the main line at Pontypool Road (Coedygric North Junction) up the Cwm-y-Glyn and on through the Glyn and Bryn Tunnels, 280 and 398yds, to join the Taff Vale Railway at Quakers' Yard, 15½ miles from Pontypool Road. This was a strategic lateral route of the highest significance, not only opening up a growing colliery district, but crossing almost every valley between the Afon Llwyd and eventually the Cynon, and connecting with all the railways that served them. (The River Cynon flows through what is generally known as the Aberdare Valley). Passing initially under the Monmouthshire's Newport-Pontypool line just south of Crane Street, the Taff Vale Extension ascended the Cwm-y-Glyn to Hafodyrynys and the first tunnel on a ruling gradient of 1 in 45, before soaring over the valley of the Ebbw and the Monmouthshire's railway and canal by means of the mighty Crumlin Viaduct.

CRUMLIN VIADUCT

This viaduct was one of the great structures of the Railway Age in South Wales, embodying something of the graceful tracery of Brunel's timber bridges with the robustness of iron construction, yet avoiding the almost contemptuous arrogance with which the Barry Railway was to fling its steel-and-masonry viaducts across the Taff and Rhymney Valleys as it marched into Monmouthshire half a century later. Crumlin was designed and built by T. W. Kennard to the requirements of Charles Liddell, the NA & HR Engineer. At the time of its construction it was the third highest structure of its kind in the world, including canal aqueducts, the maximum height above the river bed being 208ft. It comprised in all ten spans of 150ft each from pier to pier, but towards the western end an upthrust of rock enabled an intermediate masonry pier to be inserted, with seven spans and six piers to the east of it, and three spans with two piers to the west. The total length was 1,658ft, of which 1,500ft was in metal, requiring 1,300 tons of cast-iron and 1,250 tons of wrought-iron, most of it made at a foundry set up on the site. The total cost was £62,000. In 1928 the viaduct was re-decked by the GWR, the iron plates being replaced by 1,140 steel ones requiring 110,000 rivets; during this work, which took about two years, single-line working was instituted and was then made permanent by gauntletting the two tracks, so as to avoid trains crossing on the viaduct. Crumlin Viaduct had been in continuous use for 107 years when the railway closed in 1964, and its demolition began the following year; it had outlasted by nearly two decades Brunel's timber viaducts in the Dare Valley.

The first 5½ miles of the Taff Vale Extension from Pontypool Road to the east side of the viaduct were opened on 20 August 1855, while the branch of 1¼ miles descending at 1 in 42 to join the Monmouthshire's Ebbw Vale line at Llanhilleth Junction was opened shortly afterwards in two stages; first to the NA & HR's own goods depot at Llanhilleth on 3 September, and then to the junction with the Monmouthshire on 20 October. The second section (3¼ miles) of the Taff Vale Extension main line was opened with due ceremony on 1 June 1857 from Crumlin to Tredegar Junction (Pontllanfraith), where it passed under the Sirhowy Tramroad; the latter had yet to be converted into a standard gauge railway, but when so completed in 1865, the Tredegar Junctions became very important for exchange of traffic. Including Bryn Tunnel, the last section of the TVE to be opened during the independent life of the

NA & HR, on 11 January 1858, was the final seven miles to the Quakers' Yard (Low Level) junction with the TVR, sixteen miles from Pontypool Road, but after the NA & HR became amalgamated with the West Midland Railway (1860) and the latter with the GWR (1863), the line was pushed on from Quakers' Yard through the Duffryn or Quakers' Yard Tunnel, a single-line bore of 703yd, to join the Vale of Neath Railway at Middle Duffryn Junction, 20¼ miles from Pontypool Road. This final section was opened on 18 April 1864 for goods traffic, and for passengers on 5 October. The continuation of the Pontypool-Swansea route through Aberdare, Hirwaun and Neath is covered in subsequent chapters.

Thus the NA & HR and its successors became possessed of a trunk route into the heart of the South Wales coalfield, over which millions of tons of black gold were to flow for the greater part of a century, not only to the Midlands, London and the South Coast (the GWR alone drew some seventy per cent of its locomotive coal from South Wales in the days of steam traction) but, in World War I, far away over Shap and Beattock summits to the coaling basis of the Grand Fleet. Although the little Brecon & Merthyr Railway traversed twenty-one junctions in forty-seven miles, twelve of them with other railways, there was probably nothing to rival the significance in traffic volume of the twelve junctions in twenty miles with which the Taff Vale Extension tapped the mineral resources of other railways, principally, in their sequence from Pontypool Road:

Llanhilleth Junction with the Nantyglo and Ebbw Vale lines of the MR & CC (later GWR);
Penar Junction with 'Hall's Tramroad' line (later GWR);
Tredegar Junction (Pontllanfraith) with the Sirhowy line (later LNWR);
Maesycwmmer Junction with the Brecon & Merthyr, by means of a branch 58ch long, opened by the GWR on 28 December 1863;
Hengoed and Penalltau Junctions with the Rhymney Railway;
Llancaiach Junction with TVR Llancaiach Branch;
Taff Bargoed Junction with the Taff Bargoed Joint Line of the Great Western and Rhymney Railways to Dowlais;
Quakers' Yard (Low Level) Junction with the main line of the TVR, and at the High Level Junction with the Quakers' Yard & Merthyr Joint Line of the Great Western and Rhymney Railways;

Middle Duffryn Junction with the Vale of Neath Railway, and in the same area with the Aberdare line of the TVR, and with important private lines notably those of the Powell Duffryn group.

Concurrent with and following this penetration by the Taff Vale Extension of the NA & HR across Monmouthshire into Glamorganshire, the further development of railways in East Monmouthshire fell into three main phases: the consolidation of its acquisitions by the GWR after a bitter and not wholly successful fight to keep out the LNWR, the infiltration of the latter through the north-east corner of the county, and the building of some further railways to complete the map as it eventually became.

THE WEST MIDLAND

The carve-up of the railways leading into Monmouthshire from the north led in 1860 to the formation of the West Midland Railway Company by amalgamation of the Oxford, Worcester & Wolverhampton, the Newport, Abergavenny & Hereford, and the Worcester & Hereford companies the ink was scarcely dry on this deal when the West Midland promoted a Bill to lease the MR & CC, thus renewing an unsuccessful Bill by the former constituent to obtain access to Newport some fifteen years earlier, but almost at the eleventh hour the Monmouthshire shareholders rejected the lease after their directors had agreed to it.

THE MONMOUTH BRANCH

The pace of events had now indeed become very rapid. In 1861, the West Midland acquired on lease the Coleford, Monmouth, Usk & Pontypool Railway, which like quite a few railways in Wales and Ireland, was long in title but short in mileage – little over twenty-one miles. This company had its origin in 1853 in the quest of the South Wales ironmasters for additional ore resources. Both the Crawshays and Bailey brothers had interest in sources in the Forest of Dean, and Crawshay Bailey became chairman of the CMU & P company. This little railway with the long title diverged eastward from the Hereford-Pontypool Road line at Little Mill, two miles north of Pontypool Road; it was opened to Usk on 2 June 1856, and onward to Monmouth (Troy) on 12 October of the following year, with a branch to Coleford sixteen years later. It might even have formed part of a through route from the ironstone fields of Northamptonshire had anything come of the grandiose Worcester, Dean Forest & Monmouth Railway, authorised in 1863 but never built: several of Crawshay Bailey's colleagues were directors of this latter company. The Coleford, Monmouth, Usk & Pontypool thus never developed into more than a pleasant rural backwater; it was worked from its inception by the NA & HR, which treated it very much as a poor relation.

The early 1860s saw three important developments. On the Great Western the arrival of the mixed gauge into Paddington from 1 October 1861 enabled coal trains from South Wales, principally from Eastern Monmouthshire and the Taff Vale Extension line, to be worked right through to London, albeit by a circuitous route which included not only the seven-mile climb, partly at 1 in 82, from Penpergwm through Abergavenny up to Llanvihangel, but also the steep gradients on the Ledbury–Colwall section of the Worcester & Hereford line. In 1862, thwarted of its bid to lease the Monmouthshire, the West Midland at last obtained statutory running powers from Coedygric Junction, below Pontypool over the MR & CC Eastern Valleys line into Newport, while also that year the critical steps were taken which were to culminate in the absorption (theoretically an amalgamation) of the West Midland Company by the GWR (West Midland Amalgamation) Act of 13 July 1863.

Two more railways in East Monmouthshire which became part of the GWR remain to be described before turning to the affairs of the LNWR. By coincidence, both were delayed and truncated versions of schemes emerging from the debris of the second Railway Mania of 1865, which scattered wasteful railway projects over South Wales like confetti on a churchyard path, including for instance two competing projects over the same ground between Newport, Caerleon and Usk, and an eastward extension of the Vale of Crickhowell Railway through Penpergwm to Raglan on the Coleford, Monmouth, Usk & Pontypool. The first of the two projects with which we are immediately concerned was the East Usk Railway & Docks, which was intended to make a connecting line from the Western Valleys railways at Bassaleg, round the back of Newport to Crindau, and to tap every other railway serving Newport on the east side and so finish up with a line down the east bank of the River Usk, including a major dock on the left bank of the river. This would be in competition not only with Newport Town Dock

and with the wharves which had been established on the west or
right bank of the river during the canal-and-tramroad era, but also
with the proposed deep-water docks on the west side of the town,
where the Ebbw joins the Usk as both flow into Severn Mouth. The
East Usk foundered on standing orders in the 1865 session, but
twenty years later was revived as a purely local venture, the East Usk
Railway Company, incorporated 6 August 1885, to make a feeder
branch some four miles long from East Usk Junction on the GWR
main line 1½ miles east of Newport station, to industrial plants
which had grown up on the east bank; the latter had hitherto been
served only by a private tramroad leading to a coal stage and wharf,
later to become Nettlefold's Branch. The powers of the East Usk
Company were taken over by the GWR under its Act of 28 June
1892, but the first section of 1½ miles to Lysaght's works was not
opened until 4 April 1898, with extension to the Channel Dry Dock
in August 1901 and to Uskmouth on 26 September 1938. The
branch was doubled in autumn 1952; in 1980 it served steelworks
and Uskmouth power station.

Of infinitely greater strategic importance in the 1865 session was
the Pontypool, Caerleon & Newport Railway, an individual local
company, incorporated by Act of 5 July, to make a separate route,
parallel with and to the east of the Monmouthshire's line of 1852,
from immediately south of Pontypool Road station (and with a separate connection from Coedygric Junction also) down the valley of
the Afon Llwyd through Llantarnam and Caerleon to join the South
Wales main line by twin junctions facing east and west at Maindee
on the east bank of the River Usk, some twelve miles in all. The
significance of this line to the GWR was immense. Not only was the
Monmouthshire's route through Cwmbran to Newport becoming
increasingly congested (especially since the MR & CC had admitted
NA & HR and LNWR trains into Newport) but goods and mineral
traffic to and from Cardiff or elsewhere via the South Wales main
line had to be worked round the south side of Newport, and transferred through a laborious and costly tranship station established in
1852 at Waterloo Junction, on the west side of the town.

Not only to avoid these limitations, but also to open up a new
direct route from the Eastern Valley towards the main GWR system
eastward, the GWR subscribed £50,000 to the PC & N Company,
helped it to keep its powers alive, and came to an 'arrangement'
which was virtually a take-over; by 1871 Sir Daniel Gooch was
chairman of a board composed wholly of Paddington nominees.

The bigger company was in no great hurry to see the line completed pending the gauge conversion of nearly all the GWR lines in South Wales in 1872, but two years after the latter event the main section from Pontypool South Junction to Maindee Junctions with the South Wales main line opened for goods traffic on 17 September 1874. The direct link, Pontypool North Junction – Panteg Junction (avoiding Coedygric Sidings), followed on 21 December, enabling the GWR to switch most of its passenger trains into its own High Street station at Newport instead of Mill Street; from 1 January 1875 a LNWR through Shrewsbury – Mill Street passenger service operated. April 1878 saw a 67-chain connection opened between Llantarnam Junction on the new line and Cwmbran Junction on the old, and in 1878-9 Eastern Valleys and remaining GWR passenger services were similarly diverted; from March 1879 the LNWR passenger trains (but not their freights) ceased to run. The original Monmouthshire route between Cwmbran and Mill Street then became a purely freight line for the rest of its life, principally for Newport Docks traffic, although on one or two occasions when there was flooding of the Afon Llwyd, passenger trains were diverted over it.

The opening of the Maindee East Loop shortened the journey for coal traffic from Coedygric not only to Swindon, Reading and London, but also via Reading to the South Coast ports and naval bases, where a large bunkering demand quickly arose for what was now acknowledged as the world's finest steam coal. Then in 1886 the seal of success was imparted by the opening of the Severn Tunnel, which not only further shortened some of the hauls for coal traffic, notably to Portland and Southampton by the gauge conversion in 1874 between Westbury and Salisbury, but also enabled the Pontypool-Hereford-Shrewsbury-Crewe route to be developed for the 'North and West' express passenger services between Plymouth, Bristol, Liverpool and even Glasgow. In summer 1914 some fifty main line and local passenger trains served Pontypool Road, plus a few North and West expresses which passed without stopping; those which avoided Newport via Maindee Loop either had Cardiff portions attached or detached at Pontypool Road, or were served by connecting trains. There was even a Birmingham–Cardiff express dignified by the suffix 'Irish Mail via Fishguard'. To accommodate this growth in business, from 1 March 1909 a new Pontypool Road station opened on a site north of the roadbridge as a 1,200ft island platform with bays for local trains. An erstwhile small boy remembers it mainly for steaming tea urns and enormous buns in glass cases, presided over by formidable ladies in black bombazine, striving to serve all comers before the doors swung open to admit a frock-coated dignitary in pill-box cap, intoning 'All now for Hereford, Shrewsbury and the North Western Line!'

This was also a great centre for marshalling freight traffic from the Eastern Valleys to Newport or Severn Tunnel Junction, for attaching and detaching traffic between the valleys, and through freight trains to and from the Midlands and north-west. The intensive line occupation over Llanvihangel summit towards Hereford was enhanced by LNWR/LMS freights joining or leaving the main route at Abergavenny Junction, and serving a generally competitive pattern of destinations as far afield as Garston Docks on the Mersey. As late as 1954, long after the peak of the coal traffic, ninety steam locomotives were shedded at the former GWR Pontypool Road shed.

THE RUNDOWN

In the rundown of passenger services in Eastern Monmouthshire, the first casualty was a wartime one. The service between Newport, Pontypool and Brynmawr via the Talywain Branch was withdrawn on 5 May 1941; the GWR had always worked this service, although from Abersychan & Talywain northwards the line was LNWR/LMS. Next, the public passenger service between Pontypool Road and Monmouth ceased on and from 30 May 1955, although workers' trains continued to serve Glascoed Royal Ordnance Factory until 24 April 1961. With the increasing impetus of the Marples/Beeching policy, the Eastern Valley service between Newport, Pontypool and Blaenavon (the last-named having acquired the suffix 'Low Level' from 19 July 1950, distinguishing it from the nearby freight depot) was taken off from 30 April 1962; its carryings had been eroded by parallel bus services since the 1930s. Then on 15 June 1964 the cross-valley passenger service between Pontypool Road and Neath closed, depriving travellers of a remarkable panorama of Welsh valley railways and junctions: twenty-six stations and halts in forty-two miles. In passenger terms, this was very much an 'in-and-out' service, short journeys at cheap fares.

Meanwhile, the old MR & CC Eastern Valleys route from Newport to Pontypool began to fade away by stages. With the reduction in coal traffic, the line between Mill Street and Cwmbran ceased to be used from 27 October 1963, traffic being diverted via the Maindee and Llantarnam Junctions. Three years later, on 28 November 1966,

Mill Street goods depot was closed, and the line southward from there (part of which had been diverted for a third of a mile in 1934 to make way for the new Kingsway road, a foretaste of the future) was closed down to Dock Street. On the original MR & CC's Blaenavon (L.L.) Branch the goods depot there closed on 7 March 1960 and the rest of the branch from May 1962, shortly after passenger service withdrawal (see above). From May 1965 Pontypool Road engine shed was closed, though not demolished until 1967, by which time the extensive array of marshalling sidings there and at Coedygric were almost wholly gone.

On 31 March 1979 the rail service ceased from Panteg & Coedygric Junction to Hafodyrynys Colliery, severing the eastern end of the old Taff Vale Extension line. The closure of the line formed part of a project, paid for by the Welsh Office, to release land for highway improvements on the south side of Pontypool, involving also the removal of other tracks and sidings at Pontypool South and Coedygric, and the provision of new loops off the main line to serve the British Steel Corporation stainless steel works at Panteg, and another industrial plant. As part of this scheme Pontypool station signalbox was abolished and colour-light signalling introduced under control of the Newport panel, with a fringe box at Little Mill, north of Pontypool.' The surviving branch to Furnace Sidings, Blaenavon (High Level) – historically the Talywain Branch – thus remained accessible from the main line via Llantarnam Junction until its official closure on 3 May 1980 following cessation of coal production at 'Big Pit', Blaenavon.

In 1980 the only passenger service using Pontypool (the suffix 'Road' was dropped from 1 May 1972, nearly eight years after closure of Clarence Street) was a basic one between Cardiff, Newport, Hereford, Shrewsbury and Crewe, although there was an overnight mail train, and one or two seasonal holiday expresses. All the intermediate stations between Pontypool Road and Hereford, except Abergavenny (suffixed 'Monmouth Road' between 19 July 1950 and 6 May 1968), were closed to passengers from 9 June 1958; this drastic change had been followed by the diversion from May 1970 of all other 'North and West' long-distance services via the Bristol or South Wales–Gloucester–Birmingham axis, continuing to Manchester, Liverpool or Glasgow over the electrified West Coast main line.

For freight, however, the 'North and West Route' remained an essential link. Mostly Class 47-hauled, nearly 150 freights a week passed through Pontypool conveying domestic and industrial coal into the Cardiff Division and taking out to the north chemicals, coking coal, fertilizers, oil, pulverised fuel, salt, steel and other products. In 1978 there were two Freightliners and two Speedlink trains each way daily. On the lighter side, from the late 1970s the route was a pioneer among those selected for the occasional special passenger trains hauled by restored, preserved steam locomotives following the lifting of the 1968 ban on steam traction on BR lines.

Nevertheless, with all but the last of the Eastern Valleys lines closed, the old hub of the system is much changed. At Pontypool the visitor now can contemplate only the shortened island platform devoid of all bays and buildings save a tiny shelter, but perchance they may still recall the locomotive shed, the vast array of sidings – and the buns in their glass cases, and those simmering tea-urns of long ago.

CHAPTER IV

Eastern Monmouthshire
Enter the LNWR

In describing in the previous chapter those railways in Eastern Monmouthshire which eventually became part of the GWR, of necessity only incidental reference has been made to the role of the London & North Western Railway. In its efforts to exploit the growing traffic potential of the region, the Euston management had already launched a frontal assault following the opening of the Shrewsbury & Hereford in 1852-53 by seeking to lease or purchase the Newport, Abergavenny & Hereford Railway – in the words of MacDermot, Euston's intention was 'to extend it' [the NA & HR] 'to Swansea and Brecon respectively'. This proposal seems to have foundered in the contemporary feeling against LNWR aggrandisement and against monopolies in general, and although the LNWR initially worked the NA & HR from its opening, the two companies later fell out because the larger, domineering partner overplayed its hand in connection with the routing of South Wales traffic.

Euston's counter-stroke was a move to lease the Shrewsbury & Hereford, which would give it complete control of the northern end of the North and West route, and would also secure access right through to Aberdare, because the Shrewsbury & Hereford had effected in 1860 an exchange of running powers which gave it this facility over the NAHR's Taff Vale Extension. The GWR and as yet still independent West Midland moved swiftly to lease the Shrewsbury & Hereford jointly with the LNWR, and so the S & H became a tripartite joint line from 1 July 1862; both GWR and LNWR thus inherited S & H running powers over the NA & HR and its Taff Vale Extension line. LNWR trains began running south of Hereford from 1 September 1862.

The next move for the LNWR was to use these running powers as

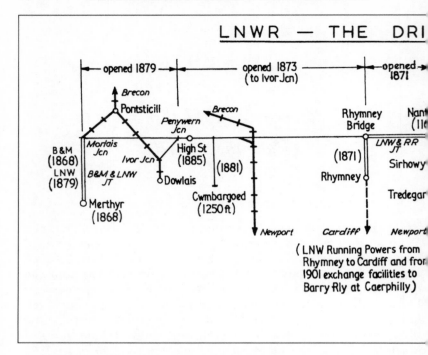

a springboard to push up through the north-eastern corner of Monmouthshire into the industrial area lying along the mountainous limestone ridge which forms the northern outcrop of the coalfield, traversing in succession from east to west the head of every intervening valley. The situation was ripe for such railway development, because although by mid-century the ironworks, collieries and limestone quarries along the Heads of the Valleys between Abergavenny and Merthyr were linked with the seaboard by a mixture of canals, tramroads and existing or nascent 'real railways', transport to and from the north west and Midlands was still restricted to the devious pattern of coastwise shipping, and the yet incomplete Taff Vale Extension. The position was particularly burdensome to the entrepreneurs in the area around Brynmawr, Nantyglo and Blaina some ten miles west of Abergavenny, who not only thought the Midlands trade offered great opportunities, but were increasingly anxious to obtain external supplies of ironstone to offset the growing shortage and declining quality of the local ores.

At the period at which this chapter opens, such ironmasters as

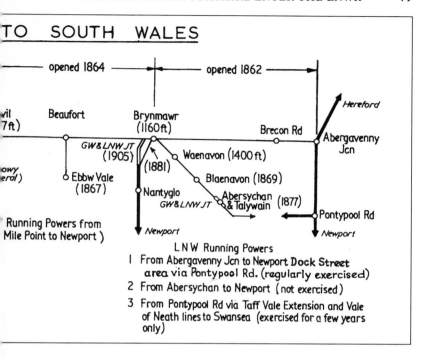

TO   SOUTH   WALES

——— opened 1864 ——— ——— opened 1862 ———

Beaufort   Brynmawr   Brecon Rd
                (1160ft)   Hereford

vil
7ft)   Abergavenny
                GW&LNWJT   Jcn
owy   (1905)
eral)   Ebbw Vale   (1881)   Waenavon (1400ft)
           (1867)
                           Nantyglo   Blaenavon (1869)
                           GW&LNWJT   Abersychan
                                      & Talywain (1877)
Running Powers from   Pontypool Rd
Mile Point to Newport)   Newport   Newport

            L N W Running Powers
I From Abergavenny Jcn to Newport Dock Street
   area via Pontypool Rd. (regularly exercised)
2 From Abersychan to Newport (not exercised)
3 From Pontypool Rd via Taff Vale Extension and Vale
   of Neath lines to Swansea (exercised for a few years
   only)

the brothers Joseph and Crawshay Bailey of Nantyglo, Thomas Hill
of Blaenavon, the Powells of Clydach Ironworks, and the Kennards
of Garn Dyris (of whom T.W. Kennard was building the Crumlin
Viaduct) were all deeply concerned with this problem, their transport facilities eastward being limited to tramroad connections with
the Brecknock & Abergavenny Canal (opened throughout by
1800), descending steeply through the Clydach Gorge to wharves at
Llanelly and Govilon, or by inclined plane down the north slope of
Blorenge Mountain to Llanfoist. From 1829 onwards a tramroad
connection by tunnel under the canal led onwards to the
Llanvihangel Railway or Tramroad, affording a somewhat dilatory
and precarious route to Hereford. By 1854 the NA & HR, which had
bought-out the Llanvihangel, Grosmont and Hereford tramroads
was open from Hereford to Pontypool (Road), but the lower end of
the Llanvihangel Railway to Govilon was not kept in use by the NA &
HR, and the need for a true railway link became all the more essential. Ideas in this direction were by no means lacking; indeed the
conversion of the B & A Canal into a railway had been canvassed, in
various forms, for about ten years prior to the critical year 1859, and

at one stage the NA & HR Company had been actively interested. Conversion of the canal was favoured by strong interests at Brecon, partly with the object of conserving the canal as an investment, and partly with a view to linking up with other railways being projected to Brecon, although there was practically no industry in the Vale of Crickhowell en route. Proposals for converting the canal to Brecon into a railway also featured, almost as an incidental, the conversion of the canal company's tramroad up to Brynmawr. A Parliamentary Bill on these lines, under the title of The Breconshire Railway & Canal Company, was lodged for the 1859 session, but had to be withdrawn because sufficient financial support was not forthcoming.

THE MERTHYR, TREDEGAR & ABERGAVENNY

A horse of a very different colour was also entered, but in this instance successfully, for the 1859 Parliamentary race, in the shape of the Merthyr, Tredegar & Abergavenny Railway Company. Promoted for the specific object 'to supply railway communication to the district between Merthyr and Abergavenny', this contestant (to continue the horse-racing metaphor) was brought to the starting-gate principally by a consortium of ironmasters, led by Crawshay Bailey (Nantyglo), James Hill (Blaenavon), and Thomas Brown (Ebbw Vale). Bailey became chairman, and James Hill deputy chairman of the company, which was incorporated I August 1859, with an initial authorised capital of £150,000 and proportionate statutory borrowing powers. The first sod was turned on 18 June 1860.

At first, all did not go smoothly with the MT & A project, due partly to the high cost of building into mountainous country, and partly to the reluctance of some shareholders to meet their calls. By mid-year 1861 the company was overdrawn and had to take measures to enforce payment or forfeit in respect of these large arrears. The West Midland Company, whose constituent the NA & HR had failed adequately to support the rival Breconshire scheme, evidently thought the moment opportune to introduce a Bill to lease the MT & A, to extend it to join the Brecon & Merthyr, and so to exclude the LNWR. However, the last named – not for the last time in South Wales – nipped in quickly with a tempting draft agreement to lease the local company for 1,000 years at a guarantee of five per cent plus interest on the debenture debt. This agreement was completed on 8 November 1861, was confirmed by Act of 7

August 1862, and the MT & A Company became finally absorbed by the LNWR in 1866, again on very generous terms. It is sad to think that the 1,000-year lease, had it not been overridden by this absorption, would still have had over 900 years to run when the railway finally closed in 1958... .

So Euston now was 'in', and by judicious tactics of cajolery, cunning, diplomacy, subvention, blandishment, and sometimes by downright bullying, succeeded within a period of less than eighteen years in driving across some twenty-five miles of hostile mountains into Dowlais and Merthyr Tydfil – creating in the process one of the most spectacular sections of railway in the British Isles. On its way the LNWR found it expedient to share part of its progress with three other companies, with two of which it made joint lines, and it traversed ten physical junctions, apart from those with private industrial lines. At the finish the LNWR had not only obtained access to every one of the intervening valleys, but had also snatched from under the noses of its rivals the Sirhowy route to Newport, had established through coaches between Cardiff and the northern part of its own system, had opened its own goods station on the doorstep of Cardiff Docks, and as early as 5 October 1865 had penetrated to Swansea by running powers over the Taff Vale Extension Railway to Middle Duffryn Junction, and thence over the Vale of Neath, with which it made a traffic agreement on 30 July 1865. The LNWR, however, made little use of these running powers after the opening of its Central Wales route to Swansea in 1868, consigning as much traffic as possible via the latter route from Shrewsbury; eventually the running powers over the Vale of Neath ceased to be exercised.

Thus, the creation of the Heads of the Valleys route completed the third great railway lateral across the South Wales coalfield, albeit of a different topographical character to the GWR (South Wales Railway) seaboard route, or that of the TVE-Vale of Neath through the centre of the coalfield between Pontypool and Aberdare.

Such was the strategic concept of the LNWR's major entry into South Wales; in order to complete the historical survey of railways in Eastern Monmouthshire, we can now turn to the detail of the initial penetration over the MT & A.

ABERGAVENNY

The LNWR took possession of the MT & A on 1 October 1862, having already supplied rolling stock for the opening on 29

September. Bradshaw for October 1862 showed LNWR trains starting from Abergavenny (Brecon Road) station for Brynmawr. The MT & A joined the West Midland's Hereford–Pontypool line by south-trailing junction ½-mile north of the latter's Abergavenny station. In 1863 the WMR constructed passenger platforms on its own line 175yd north of the junction and from March 1864 some branch trains connected at this (now GWR) station with main line trains, reversing south of the junction. In 1862 Euston had complained that the traffic required a northerly junction; by 1866, with extension planned to Dowlais and consequent heavy flows of minerals expected through Birkenhead, the need was urgent. The ¼-mile north curve (LNWR Act 1867) was reported as opening on 22 June 1870. With it came a station north of the new junction, the 1863 station closing, replaced by sidings. The south curve remained (see below). After the extension to join the Rhymney Railway (1871) the second junction station – built, with GWR agreement, by the LNWR – acquired formidable nameboards as the junction for numerous places including Cardiff, which must have presented problems for passengers with through tickets to that city via the GWR route!

NIGHTS OF SONG

Abergavenny Junction had its great moments, notably on Friday nights before the biennial Rugby Union clash of Scotland versus Wales at Murrayfield, when to the procession of trainloads of Welsh supporters from GWR stations, there was added a quota of LMS specials from the Heads of the Valleys, the singing from the coaches momentarily overborne by the eldritch shrieks exchanged between the train engines and the North Western 0-8-0s or little Webb 0–6–2Ts closing-up behind to bank a heavy load up to Llanvihangel. But in the cold grey of a winter's Sunday morning, the return was likely to be much quieter.

About 1884 a private siding was laid in from the south curve to serve the Abergavenny Lunatic Asylum (local pronunciation, *Loonattic Assilum*) to which the LNWR had running powers; GWR men averred that these were needed because anybody who had to work on, let alone build, such a railway as the MT & A could only finish up in one place... the real object was to deliver coal and stores.

From the junction, the MT & A line made a wide half-circle of half a mile to its 'town' station in Abergavenny (Brecon Road), close to which was the LNWR engine shed, opened in 1867. According to Hawkins and Reeve, by 1880 there were two buildings, covering twelve roads. Enlarged in 1896, the shed had an allocation of some forty locomotives, including an old 2–2–2, with burnished brass plate, *Engineer South Wales*, coupled to the LNWR engineer's saloon. Just a stabling point from November 1954, the shed closed on 4 January 1958.

From Brecon Road the MT & A line descended, partly at 1 in 60, to cross the River Usk by a spidery, seven-span girder bridge, and the crunch was on. In the next eight miles, almost under the shadow of Blorenge Mountain (1,832ft) on the left, and with the Sugar Loaf (1,954ft) and the Black Mountains away to the north, the line rose about 1,000ft, with a ruling grade of 1 in 34 near Govilon (where it began to turn away from the Brecon & Abergavenny Canal), but mostly at 1 in 38–40 with a few slightly easier pitches where there were stations. Perhaps the most spectacular piece was at Gelli Felen, where on reverse curves it clung to a shelf on the hillside, with a steep drop on the right-hand side, having turned at Gilwern into the formidable gorge of the River Clydach. For much of its course the railway followed that of Baileys' Tramroad, built in 1822 to a gauge of 4ft 4in, leading from Nantyglo Ironworks through Brynmawr to the canal at Govilon; to enable the railway to be built, the 'Messieurs J.&C. Bailey' conveyed the line to the MT & A Company, no doubt on terms not unfavourable to themselves. Even in the 1950s there were places where the original course of the tramroad, too sharply curved for the railway to follow, was separately identifiable.

Between Clydach and Gelli Felen were two pairs of tunnels, the pair named after the former place being respectively 302yd and 330yd long, and the Gelli Felen pair, 386 and 352yd. The second bore was in each case added when the line was doubled between Abergavenny and Brynmawr. This doubling was mandatory under one of the MT & A's Acts, but both the original company and the LNWR had to obtain extensions of time, and the work was not finally completed until 1877. One of the difficulties was that much of the additional formation had to be cut out of the mountainside.

REDOUBTABLE ENGINEERING

All this redoubtable engineering was the work of John Gardner, a civil engineer who does not seem to have built many railways, though he acted as consultant to quite a number. It is delightful to recall that while Gardner was thus building a railway by which the LNWR was to drive on into what the GWR was to regard as its sphere of influence, he was also acting as engineer to the Nantwich & Market Drayton Railway, by which the GWR was to obtain running powers into the North Western's stronghold at Crewe!

Nearing Brynmawr, there was in early days a 'Brecon Boat Siding,' an odd name to be met over 1,000ft up, but derived from its being established to connect with a tramroad by which the Brecon Boat Company, a by-trader on the canal, conveyed traffic to and from its wharf far below.

Brynmawr was 1,160ft above sea level, claimed to be the highest town in Wales. Locomotives were thankfully watered here, wisely too, because the ensuing climb westward up to the short Beaufort Tunnel involved a mile rising at 1 in 88. Brynmawr station was situated on the boundary between Monmouthshire and Brecknock, but just within the latter county, the line being located within a southerly enclave of Brecknock from east of Gilwern, with the Blaenavon Branch, about to be described, re-entering Monmouthshire at Waenavon, the first station on the branch. With the reorganisation of county boundaries in 1974 things became much tidier, the whole course of the old railway in this area (though now largely obliterated by the Heads of the Valleys trunk road) being south of Gwent's boundary with Powys to the north (Ordnance Survey 1:50,000 Sheet 161, 1974). Brynmawr was also the junction for Baileys' private railway to Nantyglo, and with its comparatively modern successor, but the rather complex story of these connections belongs to Western Monmouthshire.

Upon the opening to Brynmawr, a mail coach connection was provided thence to Merthyr, and a horse-bus to and from Blaina. The former must have been quite an adventure for passengers, especially in bad weather.

BRYNMAWR TO BLAENAVON

Leaving the MT & A main line for the moment to continue its switchback progress westward (as tabulated in the chart on pp 70/1, the Blaenavon Branch was built to serve the great ironworks, iron-stone mines and collieries in the upper part of the Afon Llwyd above Pontypool. Blaenavon had been reached by tramroad from the south in 1796, and by MR & CC railway in 1854; with the opening of the MT & A from Abergavenny to Brynmawr in 1862 it was logical to move across the intervening ridge south-east of the latter and down into the industrial area between Pontypool and Blaenavon. A 'Brynmaur, Blaenafon & Pontypool Railway' Bill for a line between these places was promoted in the 1865 session, but failed on standing orders. In addition to its main line between the places described in its title, it included two eastward branches from Waenavon to serve Pwll Du Ironworks and other potential sources of traffic below the western face of Blorenge Mountain. More successful in the following session was the Brynmawr & Blaenavon Railway Company, which under the auspices of the LNWR obtained its Act of incorporation on 16 July 1866, becoming vested in the LNWR (which appointed two directors) in 1869. Another director was a local coalowner, John Jayne, whose name was for many years commemorated by Jayne's Branch Junction with the private railway to Milfraen Colliery, from a point on the Blaenavon Branch immediately south of Waenavon station.

Turning away first eastward and then south-east from Brynmawr, the single-track 'Bed & Breakfast Line' climbed steadily at 1 in 40 or so for two miles to Waenavon; even with a banking engine, fully-loaded freight trains often had quite a job to maintain the standard timing of ten minutes (12mph). Apart from its lonely situation in wild and remote country, Waenavon had several distinctions: until 1974, by reason of its location on the county boundary it was a 'frontier post' between England and Wales, and at 1,400ft above sea level was the highest public station on the LNWR and indeed in England and Wales; after the closure of Leadhills in Scotland in 1939, it became the highest on the LMS system. To those who did not know it in all its moods it must have seemed a quiet place, but even as late as 1939 there was a score of booked trains on the two shifts for which the signal box was open, enhanced by the movements of banking engines, and complicated by the fact that two passenger trains could not cross there. Waenavon owed its existence as a block post, telegraph and train staff station from 20 March 1871 (passenger traffic from 1 September in the same year) to the fact that when the branch was opened the full 4¾ miles from Brynmawr to Blaenavon on 1 November 1869 (passengers 1 January 1870), it soon became necessary to break the long section and to provide such facilities at the summit.

From Waenavon the branch descended on similar gradients, past Furnace and Tyre Mill Sidings adjoining the iron (and later steel) works to Blaenavon station ('High Level' from 1950 to distinguish it

from the former GWR establishment lying below and to eastward).
The LNWR was by no means satisfied to stop short at Blaenavon,
however, wanting to push on down the valley to serve the collieries
and works around Abersychan and Talywain. A branch 1½ miles in
length was made from Blaenavon to Varteg Hill Colliery and other
neighbouring pits, the former having hitherto been served by an
inclined plane across the valley to Cwmavon on the MR & CC line.
In 1877, therefore (passengers 1 May 1878) the LNWR pushed on
another 3¾ miles from Blaenavon to Abersychan & Talywain; a
head-on collision with the GWR thrusting up from Trevethin
Junction, as described in the preceding chapter, was avoided by an
agreement to vest in the two companies as a joint line the half-mile
of double track through Abersychan & Talywain station, although
this was an LNWR-type structure. Because of its 1 in 45 inclination
up the western hillside the Varteg Hill Branch could not be used for
the Blaenavon-Abersychan extension, which ran parallel to the original MR & CC line to Blaenavon but at a higher level along the west
side of the valley. At Garndiffaith Junction above Abersychan, the
LNWR threw off a short spur to Golynos Junction with the
Cwmffrwd Branch, over which the LNWR was allowed running
powers. Neither these powers, nor others granted to the LNWR
from Abersychan & Talywain through Pontypool to Coedygric
Junction, seem to have been exercised, although the LNWR and its
successor the LMS continued to work between Abergavenny
Junction and Newport.

   The withdrawal of passenger service between Pontypool and
Brynmawr in 1941 has already been mentioned in Chapter III;
freight traffic had remained fairly heavy despite the closure of
Blaenavon iron and steel works during the depression of the 1930s,
but thereafter fell away, the GWR working reduced numbers of coal
trains through to Newport. Blaenavon LMS locomotive shed,
erected 1881, closed on 5 September 1942. By 1953 through freight
ceased above Furnace Siding, Waenavon and Abersychan &
Talywain stations being closed for general public freight traffic in
1954 and 1965 respectively. North of Blaenavon the former
LNW/LMS tracks remained in situ up to Waenavon for possible
opencast mining working. North from Furnace Sidings was lifted in
1961.

   Although the story of the Merthyr, Tredegar & Abergavenny line
west of Brynmawr belongs to subsequent chapters, enough should
have been said by now to convey the impression that both scenically

and operationally, this was one of Great Britain's most remarkable railways. (It was, incidentally, also one of the most expensive to work, the average coal consumption alone being of the order of 90lb/mile). As it switchbacked along the tops before the final steep and curving descent into Merthyr, one might be lucky to travel on a fine day with curlew and plover hovering and wheeling against a back-cloth of great clouds sailing, and far below as the head of a valley was crossed, even the grey industrial haze touched with the magic of sunshine. You would not be so lucky to travel the hills on a day when the cloud base was down below 1,000ft and the train would be immersed in damp, clinging cotton wool – but then you might be fortunate enough to be party to an impromptu choral rehearsal in the incongruous auditorium of an LMS open saloon superannuated from the Manchester-Blackpool Club Train; in the 1930s the Abergavenny District could muster a complete train of these vehicles.

BATTERED BY BLIZZARDS

The worst conditions to which the railway was prey was snow, which thanks indeed to goodness I never encountered personally, but my friend and sometime colleague, the late J.M. Dunn, who laboured manfully in the Motive Power Department of the district, recalled hair-raising (or freezing!) experiences around Christmas 1927, when no fewer than fourteen locomotive engines were snowed-up at various places along the line, and a train with forty passengers on board was stuck for twelve hours at Nantybwch, 1,165ft up. Apart from the enginemen, one can well imagine the stress of stationmen battling through the blizzard to check signal lamps shown as 'light out' on cabin indicators, trackmen struggling to free frozen points, or clambering into the tool van before setting off to rescue a belea-guered train. It was, too, a railway of characters as well as character; there was a signalman who on occasion could be seen gesturing and declaiming to his unresponsive levers, and might be suspected to be slightly 'round the bend', but this was only Old Huw (or Trevor, or Bleddyn, or Ivor, or whoever) rehearsing his sermon for the devout of Bethel the following Sunday. Of drivers, Dunn recalled a certain 'Mad Dai', whose appearance half-out of the cab would cause waiting passengers to blanch, step back, and decide the next train would be better – a long wait, too. As one of this ilk told a colleague of mine, 'Well, sir, you see, I came on to the railway to *drive* the trains, like'. But despite all the hazards, the LNWR and LMS had a fine record of safety on this line; one can find few reports of serious accidents beyond the classic pile-up of a runaway Webb tank and its coal train in 1910 on the Ebbw Vale Branch, after an alert signalman (not writing a sermon at the time) had diverted it into a dead-end. In 1925, the driver and fireman of an 0–6–2 side tank were killed on the GWR at Tir Phil, when their goods train went over the bank into the River Rhymney, due to a wash-out.

These were railways on which to learn the business – the hard way. The Abergavenny District, suitably remote from Euston and in LNWR days largely entrusted to 'the man on the spot', was a severe testing-ground for men and machines. The first District Traffic Manager, Joseph Bishop (a family well known on the LNWR) ruled gubernatorially at Abergavenny for some 35 years; the district afterwards produced three general managers of the LNWR or other railways, while during my own service Mr C.H. Tait presided at Abergavenny and his brother was LMS District Traffic Superintendent at Swansea. (Unless one was very senior indeed, one did not raise reference to 'Harry Tate's Railway', Harry Tate being a famous music-hall comedian of the period).

Operating rules were necessarily stringent, the maximum speed allowed anywhere being 30mph for passenger trains and 20mph for freight, with numerous more severe restrictions; passenger trains were not allowed to exceed 25mph in descending from Brynmawr to Abergavenny. (This steeply downhill stretch was incongruously the 'Up' line, to conform with the Newport-Shrewsbury direction). In 1939 the 3.25am passenger from Shrewsbury to Merthyr, which had run semi-fast behind a GWR locomotive from Hereford to Abergavenny Junction, then pounded up the 8¼ miles from Brecon Road to Brynmawr at an average speed of 21 mph, but a summer-Saturdays through train from Blackpool to Merthyr, probably worked by two LNWR Super D 0–8–0s, was allowed thirty-one minutes for the ascent. A splendid sight on this incline would be a two-engined freight train of which the front portion would be for Merthyr, followed by the wagons for the Blaenavon Branch, the engine which was to work the latter forward from Brynmawr acting as banker in rear, with the front and rear portions moving-off in opposite directions at Brynmawr. At one time the Le Chatelier counter-pressure brake was fitted to a number of engines to aid control in descending, but was attended by maintenance problems through cylinder wear.

The ultimate in motive power for the Abergavenny District lines was the mighty 0–8–4 tank designed by H.P.M. Beames for the LNWR in 1921, when traffic was still relatively heavy, but these locomotives did not come into service until the first year of the LMS in 1923. There were thirty of them in all, of which about twenty worked in South Wales, being divided between Abergavenny, Blaenavon and Tredegar sheds; they weighed 88 tons in working order, and the coupled wheelbase of the 4ft 5in driving wheels (the third pair being flangeless) was 17ft 3in. Despite various troubles, some of which were put right by modifications, and a tendency to come off the road in sidings especially, they were immensely powerful – the tractive effort was nearly 30,0001b – and on occasions worked without difficulty passenger trains of from ten to thirteen coaches. The maximum load of freight which they were allowed to take without a banker from Abergavenny to Brynmawr was only sixteen vehicles, and they were allowed an extra five minutes in which to do it. This was far below the achievement of the type on its initial tests, but was more likely governed by allowance for wind and weather, and for the ability of the train to be stopped by the brake-van in the event of a break-loose. The 0-8-4Ts were banned by the GWR from its former Rhymney Railway section, and it is perhaps of interest that of other South Wales railways only the former Barry and the Port Talbot used locomotives with eight-coupled wheels without a pony truck in front. Be that as it may, the Beames 0–8–4T's represented a notable climax in the story of the LNWR lines in South Wales, although with the further decline in freight traffic, they were eventually transferred elsewhere. Two only survived to carry British Railways numbers and with the withdrawal of 47931 at the end of 1951, the 0–8–4T wheel arrangement became extinct on former LMS lines.

A final note about Abergavenny. Was there anywhere else in Wales other than Brecon Road, where banking-in-rear took place regularly in both directions? Apart from the assistance given up to Brynmawr, it was also customary when required to bank up towards the Junction, with its half-mile at 1 in 40/52/40. Add to this the more distant overtones of LNWR/LMS locomotives assisting both LMS and GWR trains from the Junction up to Llanvihangel, and there must have been some noisy moments at Abergavenny. Whether it is noisier now I know not, but if so it is from lorries and cars, for with the rundown of industry along the line between Abergavenny and Merthyr, and the facility to use alternative routes under nationalisation, the railway lost its through freight services from 22 November 1954, and its passenger trains from 6 January 1958 – an unusual instance of the withdrawal of freight facilities preceding that of the passenger services. Brecon Road goods station, however, remained open until 5 April 1971 for local traffic worked from Abergavenny Junction.

ABORTIVE SCHEMES

During the 'Second Railway Mania' of the mid-1860s, a pink rash (the last word being in most cases the operative one) of railway promotions broke out along the existing axis of the Coleford, Monmouth, Usk & Pontypool Railway, mentioned in the preceding chapter as running eastward from the NA & HR at Little Mill Junction, and opened in 1856-57. These were intended to lead eastward to Worcester (the Worcester, Dean Forest & Monmouth), to Stonehouse on the Bristol & Birmingham (the Severn Junction, and the Monmouth, Forest of Dean & Standish Junction Railways) and the Eastern Extension of the Vale of Crickhowell. The last-named, pursuing in part the lost cause of the Breconshire Railway & Canal Company, had obtained an Act (14 July 1864) to build just over five miles of line from a junction with the MT & A near Llanfoist up to Crickhowell, with an envisaged western extension towards Brecon; the 'Eastern Extension' was to have left the Coleford, Monmouth, etc line at Raglan, to cross and make junctions with the Hereford–Pontypool main line at Penpergwm, and to join the Vale of Crickhowell near Llanfoist. Least palpably impracticable of all these schemes – which if they had a common thread, was to open up an alternative route to the Midlands and in particular to afford access to alternative supplies of ironstone in that area and in the Forest of Dean – was the only other one apart from the Worcester, Dean Forest & Monmouth (p63) to obtain an Act of incorporation, namely the Abergavenny & Monmouth Railway Company (5 July 1865). This was yet another brainchild of Crawshay Bailey, supported by Abraham Darby of Ebbw Vale and others, with John Gardner as engineer. The railway was to extend for 12¾ miles east from the MT & A's intended south-trailing Abergavenny junction with the Hereford-Pontypool line to the Coleford-Monmouth route just east of Dingestow, thus smartly short-circuiting the Vale of Crickhowell's Eastern Extension via Penpergwm. The last named was rejected by Parliament, and with the eventual collapse of all the other schemes as potential trunk outlets, the Abergavenny & Monmouth itself disappeared into limbo, there being no point in its ending-up at Dingestow.

Although his name crops up again more than once in writing about other railways in succeeding chapters, now, in closing the chapter which deals with Abergavenny, is the moment to record that Crawshay Bailey came in his closing years to live nearby at Llanfoist House, where he died in 1872. As a promoter and sometimes turbulent director of canal, dock and railway companies he fought indefatigably for the development of the South Wales railways. When he died, the Second Railway Mania was over, and there were already over 900 miles of railway in South Wales – the basic network established, Crawshay Bailey lies in Llanfoist churchyard, hard by one of the most triumphant of his promotions, the Merthyr, Tredegar & Abergavenny Railway. Though he and his railway are long gone, both have yet an assured place in the history of the South Wales railways.

CHAPTER V

Western Monmouthshire
(Gwent)

With one notable exception dating from as late as the 1880s, all the railways leading from the industrial valleys of Western Monmouthshire down to the west side of Newport were of tramroad origin, converted to railways during the middle of the nineteenth century. From east to west, these valleys followed the courses of the rivers Ebbw Fach ('Little Ebbw'), the Ebbw Fawr ('Big' or main Ebbw) – these two joining at Aberbeeg, fifteen miles from Newport – and the Sirhowy, which runs into the Ebbw above Risca. All three rivers have their sources in the mountains, now in the County of Powys, which rise beyond the northern outcrop of the coalfield; the valleys down through which they lead are narrow, hemming-in both industry and transport arteries, until at Risca the base of the valley broadens out, leading through Tredegar Park to final confluence with the River Usk at the point where, south-west of Newport town, both rivers spill into Severn Mouth. The land here being flat and on the eastern edge of the Wentlloog Level towards Cardiff, was largely clear of buildings when the tramroads arrived. In fact, much of it was made up by ballast dumped from ships, and afforded an ideal site for the development of larger docks following the advent of rail transport.

All the early tramroads (using the term in its generic sense, since some were plateways, and others 'railroads' using edge rails) followed the common pattern of being built initially to serve the ironworks near the valley-heads, the latter also having early rail communication with the limestone quarries and local coal workings. As coal mines multiplied and tended to become deeper, there was no more room for them in the increasingly crowded valley bottoms, and fresh sinkings were driven up onto the slopes, whence came the suffix 'Slope' to many colliery names; always these pits needed transport outlets, often on steep inclined planes, and sometimes overhead ropeways. Before the major development of coal output for landsale or bunkering the main commodity carried by the tramroads was iron, from the Blaina and Nantyglo Ironworks in the Ebbw Fach, from the Ebbw Vale and Beaufort works in the main Ebbw valley, and from the Sirhowy and Tredegar works at the head of the Sirhowy Valley. The social consequences and complications of establishing new industrial communities in these bleak and inhospitable valleys may be imagined, starting as they did with makeshift housing and inadequate, slow-expanding services of roads, water, sewage and medical care, all in the context of intensive immigration from many parts of the British Isles, notably Staffordshire, Northumberland and Durham, and parts of Scotland and Ireland.

The Western Arm of the Monmouthshire Canal had reached Crumlin in the Ebbw Valley, 11½ miles rail distance from Newport, by 1799; in the same year a connecting tramroad built by the canal company was opened from the canal-head to Beaufort Ironworks at the head of the main valley, while connection to the ironworks in the Blaina-Nantyglo area at the top of the Ebbw Fach was achieved in the 1820s. MacDermot's official *History of the GWR* records that eventually the Monmouthshire Company owned thirty miles of tramroads in the Western Valleys, besides which 'there were no less than 72½ miles of tramroads in the Western Valleys alone connected with the Monmouthshire lines but belonging to independent companies or private individuals'.

Typical of the latter, and destined to survive not merely into the Railway Age but (in part at least) to the present day, was 'Hall's Road', which was owned and built by one Benjamin Hall, son-in-law and protégé of Richard Crawshay the Cyfarthfa ironmaster, Hall was the father of (Sir) Benjamin Hall, later Lord Llanover, who as Chief Commissioner of Works was responsible for the clock tower of the Houses of Parliament and hence of the national timepiece, Big Ben. Thus while diesel locomotives trundle today over part at least of the tramroad course laid out by the father, millions daily gaze at and listen to the clock installed by the son: from tramroads to television, a fascinating journey in time... Hall's Road was built in 1805, leading from the Monmouthshire Company's Ebbw Vale tramroad a mile or so above Risca, and running parallel with the main tramroad which it shared with the river and canal for nearly three miles nearly to Newbridge, whence it turned away westward into the Sirhowy Valley to terminate above Argoed at Hall's Manmoel Colliery, about nine miles.

THE SIRHOWY TRAMROAD

A few miles further west, at the head of the Sirhowy Valley, the Sirhowy Ironworks had been opened before the turn of the century, being connected with the Beaufort Ironworks north of Ebbw Vale by the Rassa (or Rassau) railroad of 1794; the Rassa formed part of a network of inter-connecting tramroads built mainly to obtain limestone from the Quarries at Trevil and elsewhere along the high ground to the north.

In 1800 a consortium was formed between Richard Fothergill, Matthew Monkhouse (both lessees of the land on which stood the Sirhowy Ironworks), Samuel Homfray, the highly successful ironmaster of Penydarren near Merthyr, and others, to acquire from Sir Charles Morgan a lease of highly favourable mineral land about a mile south of Sirhowy. Sir Charles, grandfather of the first Baron Tredegar, was probably well disposed to the syndicate as his daughter was married to Homfray, while the ironworks and the town which grew up round them were named Tredegar in his honour; the township from its inception was highly feudal in pattern, houses, shop and school all being provided by the company, as was typical of so many such industrial communities in South Wales.

Naturally one of the first objectives of the new consortium, even before its ironworks went into blast in 1802, was to ensure a transport outlet to Newport for its products: rails for new railways, cannon for the wars, pig and bar iron for the London market, and so on. Equally, the canal company was alert to the need to extend its communications into the Sirhowy Valley, although an extension of the canal from its Western Arm at Risca would raise problems of levels, lockage, and water supply. The Tredegar partners however had powers under their lease, so far as Sir Charles Morgan was concerned – and he by ownership of lands through Tredegar park and around the mouth of the Ebbw virtually controlled the available egress to the sea – to build a tramroad down to the canal at Risca or to tidewater. The canal company therefore sought to come to an arrangement with the Tredegar faction, and the outcome was a joint but potentially precarious arrangement, embraced within the Monmouthshire Canal Act of 26 June 1802, whereby the canal company was empowered to build a nine-mile tramroad from the Monmouthshire Canal Dock at Newport, via Bassaleg and Risca to join the intended Sirhowy Tramroad at Nine Mile Point, with a six-mile branch tramroad to its existing tramroad at Crumlin Bridge.

THE GOLDEN MILE

One mile of this tramroad through Sir Charles Morgan's Tredegar Park on the outskirts of Newport was however required to be built and maintained by him, this being the famous Park Mile, extending in railway days from Park Junction to Bassaleg (originally Pye Corner). The Tredegar ironmasters were authorised to form The Sirhowy Tramroad Company, from Nine Mile Point to the Sirhowy Furnaces, also (in this instance as a partnership and not as a company) to make a connecting tramroad from Tredegar Ironworks to Trevil Quarries, and from Nantybwch to the Union Ironworks, Rhymney.

The Act provided that the Sirhowy Tramroad Company and Sir Charles Morgan were authorised to charge the same tolls and rates on their respective portions of the throughout system as the Monmouthshire Canal Company, so that Sir Charles and his successors accordingly became entitled to levy toll on one of the biggest railborne flows of coal in South Wales, eventually worked by four different railway companies over six parallel tracks through Tredegar Park – no wonder the Park Mile became known as the 'Golden Mile'. This continued until the GWR bought out the tolls in 1923. (See also pp93, 104-7).

These tramroad links with Newport were brought into use in 1805, with the exception of the short piece linking Risca with the Ebbw Vale network north of the canal head at Crumlin, this being opened in 1829.

THE OLD RUMNEY

Only one of the Western Monmouthshire tramroads leading towards Newport and destined to become part of the railway network remains to be mentioned, and was the longest yet built as a complete line of route. This was the Rumney Railway, known as the 'Old Rumney' to avoid confusion with the later Rhymney Railway. It was incorporated as a company in 1825 but was actually a tramroad of 4ft 2in gauge, engineered by George Overton, and opened in 1826. It extended for nearly twenty-two miles from the ironworks at Rhymney down the east bank of the Rhymney River (thus contriving to remain wholly in Monmouthshire), until near Machen, the river having rounded the shoulder of the mountains and having turned sharply southward to enter the Bristol Channel just east of Cardiff; the tramroad continued its own easterly course to make junction with the Monmouthshire tramroad from Newport at the top end of the Park Mile. The masonry viaduct by which the Old Rumney crossed over the River Ebbw to join the line to Newport bears the date 1826, and the company's name, now over 165 years old. This is one of the few substantial engineering relics of the tramroad age still in railway use. The most impressive structure of tramroad origin in Western Monmouthshire, however, was for long the 'Risca Long Bridge' of thirty-two arches which carried the Monmouthshire's link line to the Sirhowy Tramroad across the valley floor at Risca; the transition at either end of this bridge was too sharp for normal rail practice, while at the north end, the tramroad ran through a private works. The Long Bridge was therefore by-passed by a deviation on embankment authorised by the MRCC Act of 1853, passed out of railway use in 1855, and such parts of it as had not already disappeared to build houses were demolished, some fifty years later, its memory surviving in the 'Bridge End Inn' – no longer at the end of a bridge.

TRAMROADS INTO RAILWAYS

Most of the tramroads had a long innings of half-a-century or more before their conversion into railways. Such conversion became inevitable as traffic progressively outstripped both capacity and the possibility of effective control on the basis of toll roads open to all and sundry. With the introduction of steam locomotives operated both by the tramroad companies (in the case of the Sirhowy from 1829) and by the more progressive freighters, steam-hauled trains tangled with horse-drawn trams and with passenger traffic. The last-named had begun between Newport and Tredegar in 1822 with a horse-drawn carriage on rail wheels, toll being paid at every gate. As elsewhere the steam locomotives broke-up the rails or tramplates, while the variety of designs and condition of maintenance of the freighters' wagons added to the general disarray; at Pye Corner (Bassaleg) where the Old Rumney joined the Monmouthshire, the local pub waxed prosperous on teamsters 'waiting for the road', or just deciding to stop for a pint.

As stated in Chapter III, the MR & CC was forced to take powers in 1848 to get rid of the freighters' horse traction and private locomotives and to convert its tramroads into standard gauge railways, worked by the company's own locomotives. The Sirhowy proprietors similarly obtained an Act (25 May 1860) changing the name of the undertaking to the Sirhowy Railway Company, and authorising conversion of the tramroad into a standard-gauge railway within three years, plus an extension to Nantybwch, while the (Old) Rumney Railway was also re-incorporated as a railway company by its Act of 1 August 1861, with powers to alter the tramroad line and levels, and for a branch from Machen to the Rhymney Railway near Caerphilly. Only partly-built (p121), it opened for freight, without ceremony, during 1864. The chairman was Lord Tredegar, grandson of the Sir Charles Morgan from whom the Tredegar Ironworks consortium obtained its lease. Lord Tredegar (first baron of that title in 1859) was supported on the Rumney Railway board by Crawshay Bailey.

STATIONS AT NEWPORT

The first Western Valleys station at the Newport end was at or near the Courtybella Zero Distance Post, between what is now the main line and the Usk (opposite Belle Vue Park). The gauge when this station first came into use for passenger services on 21 December 1850 was the tramroad one of 4ft 4 in, and passenger traffic had to be suspended during the MR & CC gauge conversion Beyond and around Courtybella lay a muddle of tramroads leading to the canal basin, the Town Dock, and various wharves (Sirhowy Tramroad traffic for instance using its own quay, the Tredegar Wharf). So far as a body corporate can have feeling, the South Wales Railway bursting forth from Newport Tunnel on its way to Cardiff and Swansea in 1850, must have felt like Captain Cook landing among the aborigines.

The Courtybella station was short-lived, the MR & CC pushing on eastward for a mile or so to Dock Street Station on 4 August 1852. Dock Street was linked up to the Eastern Valleys station, Mill Street, in May 1855 and was used by all the Western Valleys passenger services until opening on 1 January 1879 of the direct connection from Park Junction to Gaer Junction, west of Newport

Tunnel on the GWR main line, enabled them to be concentrated at High Street from 11 March 1880. Dock Street continued in use as a goods station for many years afterwards, including through workings of LNWR/LMS trains from Abergavenny.

The troublous and somewhat tardily executed conversion of the Monmouthshire's Western Valley lines was practically complete by 1855, for passenger traffic to begin from Dock Street to Nantyglo – the original station, an extension of a quarter of a mile northward being added three years later – and from the junction at Aberbeeg to Ebbw Vale. Three short Newport branches, Courtybella Junction to Town Dock, Pillbank Junction to Dock Street, and a ¼-mile loop avoiding Dock Street, from 'Salutation Junction' (named after a local pub) to Llanarth Street Junction on the extension from Mill Street, were opened at the same time; the last-named ran through the streets and was abandoned in 1907, although remnants lingered until swept away for road improvements. The link between Risca and Nine Mile Point (where the GWR had a connection of its own, independent of the Sirhowy, to the Penllwyn colliery tramroad), was completed by the MR & CC in November 1855. The conversion of the Sirhowy Tramroad into a railway was completed in 1863 or soon afterwards, passenger traffic beginning on 19 June 1865 with three trains a day (as required by a later Act of 5 July 1865) between Sirhowy and Dock Street, the journey of twenty-three miles with four intermediate stops at Tredegar, Blackwood, 'Tredegar Junction' (Pontllanfraith) and Risca taking 1½ hours. Several alterations had been made to the alignment of the original tramroad, which in places passed through the village street during conversion to a railway.

ENTER THE BRECON & MERTHYR

In recording the conversion into a railway of the last-comer of the tramroads into Newport, the 'Old Rumney', it is necessary to say something about its acquisitor and to honour its full but rarely used title, the Brecon & Merthyr Tydfil Junction Railway Company. If ever a railway had 'character', it was the little B & M. Starting its career in an unassuming way in 1858-60 with powers to make a railway over the hills between Brecon and Dowlais, it embroiled itself in a series of fierce contests and real or abortive alliances with much bigger neighbours, thinking naught to fighting the Taff Vale, the Rhymney, and the London & North Western Railways more or

less simultaneously, scattering prodigally in its wake draft agreements, running powers, writs, shareholders' petitions, and takeover
bids. For two years it was in receivership, and even had its authorised amalgamation with another company (the Hereford, Hay &
Brecon) pronounced void by the Court of Chancery after agreement had been reached (p204). Through the mists of virtual insol-
vency it promoted extensions to Cardiff, and nearly had running
powers to Swansea thrust, unsought, upon it by a Parliamentary
Committee.

But it did get to Newport. We left the Old Rumney with powers
(1861) for adaptation into a passenger railway and for sale or lease
to the Monmouthshire or West Midland. Little improvement had
been made, and the bigger neighbours seemed uninterested, when
by Act of 28 July 1863 the B & M was authorised to extend to and
acquire the Rumney, with rights over the Rhymney, to which, by
further powers in 1864, it could form a junction. This gave it a
route not only for the valuable coal and iron traffic from the east
side of the Rhymney Valley, but also through running from
Bassaleg into Newport. It was not until after he had carried out two
unsatisfactory inspections, however, that the Board of Trade
inspector passed the line for passenger traffic, which began to
Newport (Dock Street) on 14 June 1865. Owing to prolonged
dispute with the Rhymney Railway over their respective proposals
to build through the valley between Bargoed and Dowlais Top (at
one time the surveyors' pegs for the rival schemes overlapped), it
was not until 1 September 1868 that the Brecon & Merthyr's two
separate sections were joined together and its trains could work
through between Brecon and Newport; this ancient feud was for
years afterwards unconsciously commemorated by the division
between 'Northern Section' and 'Southern Section' in the B & M
working timetables.

BATTLE OF GIANTS

By the 1870s the stage was set for something much bigger than
local   rivalries.   Here   were   these   native   companies   –
Monmouthshire, Sirhowy, Brecon & Merthyr – only recently emer-
gent from the tramroad trammels and with overlapping interests
along the Park Mile, diligently engaged in a fast-growing business
of moving down to Newport large quantities of coal, iron, and
incipiently steel, with a huge consequential boom in shipbuilding

and ship repair, and in industries relevant to these basic products. By 1865, the limited shipping facilities of Newport had already attained an annual throughput of more than 750,000 tons of coal alone, and a major scheme for new docks was with Parliament. Sirhowy–Nantybwch opened on 2 November 1868. By 1870 the Sirhowy's directors were proudly describing the dividend as 'the usual ten per cent', although the Monmouthshire's return had fallen from twelve to around five per cent. In this atmosphere of potential mergers and takeovers the LNWR had already reached Nantybwch from Brynmawr (p121), was probing down into the Ebbw Valleys, and looking down into the Sirhowy. Thanks to its gauge conversion, the GWR was able in 1872 to connect with the Monmouthshire at Waterloo Junction, obviating the wretched tranship station, and was looking up into the valleys, not least at the downward thrusts or its Euston rival. To tidy up this area, the PC & NR (p104) was carried over the South Wales Railway in order to avoid main line/docks traffic conflict, and on 2 April 1885 (not 1886 as in MacDermot) the Board of Trade wrote to Paddington with permission for mineral traffic to use the new ¾-mile Park Junction–Ebbw Junction 'Western Loop', made for through running between the Western Valleys and the South Wales main line in the Cardiff direction. Ebbw Junction was the scene of a nasty accident on 28 September 1907, when a freight train over-ran the junction and collided with a passenger express, one person being killed. In World War I, to help out the motive power position Barry Railway locomotives began working freight trains over this curve, between Rogerstone Yard (between Bassaleg and Risca) and Barry Docks, and continued to do so until the grouping.

THE MIDLAND'S INTERVENTION

There was yet a third protagonist in the takeover stakes, the Midland Railway, which as early as 1846 had supported the grandiose but abortive scheme for a Welsh Midland Railway from Worcester to Brecon and Swansea (p205). By subscription to the Worcester & Hereford Railway, the Midland in the tortuous way of these matters had the right of running powers over the West Midland (NA & HR and Taff Vale Extension) right through Middle Duffryn down to Swansea. (I have found no evidence that they were ever exercised, but the key to the door was there). In 1870 a delegation of Midland directors and officers visited Newport

Docks, reconnoitred the local railways, and was all ready to join the fray a few years later. Space does not permit a blow-by-blow account of the wheeling and dealing, double-talking and double-crossing which ensued among the various pillars of Victorian rectitude who controlled the destinies of these railways. But (if you have got to mix metaphors, do it wholesale) the dogs of war seem to have been unleashed by the Sirhowy directors, in making it known they were prepared to opt out of being a public railway, being apparently anxious to concentrate on their iron-mastering, and to get rid of their railway while the going was good. Anyhow, the Sirhowy was offered either severally or jointly to the Monmouthshire, the Great Western, and (unknown to Paddington!) the Midland. Thinking the rabbit was practically in the bag so far as Paddington was concerned, the GWR in 1875 obtained powers to build a cut-off line from Nine Mile Point to run behind Newport to its Pontypool, Caerleon & Newport Railway near Caerleon, very much in the pattern of the abortive East Usk scheme of 1865. This would not only have diverted from the Monmouthshire much valuable traffic – including Aberdare coal which, since the Sirhowy's conversion in 1865, had been passing south on to that railway by means of the connection established by opening of the Taff Vale Extension in June 1857 between Tredegar Junction (Pontllanfraith) and Gelligroes Junction – but would also have obviated the payment of tolls for Lord Tredegar's Park Mile. Under this duress, and with the Midland defecting from the proposal to acquire the Sirhowy jointly with the MRCC, the last-named caved-in, granting the GWR full running powers from 1 August 1875, amalgamation following, by Act, from 1 August 1880.

Nobody at Paddington seems to have remembered how Euston had snatched the Merthyr, Tredegar & Abergavenny Railway from under the West Midland's nose. A month before this agreement between the MR & CC and GWR was signed LNWR locomotives and officials had mysteriously appeared on the Sirhowy Railway, and it then became known that – repeating the MT & A take-over technique of some thirteen years previously – Euston had smoothly and slickly agreed retrospectively with the Sirhowy on 21 August 1875 on working the line and for application to Parliament to purchase the Sirhowy undertaking, achieved by the LNWR (Sirhowy Railway Vesting) Act of 13 July 1876. If there was champagne at Paddington to celebrate the takeover of the Monmouthshire, it was probably non-vintage, and powers for the

Nine Mile Point-Caerleon diversion were quietly forgotten.

Meanwhile the Midland, having given up so far as the Monmouthshire was concerned, was in process of capturing the Hereford, Hay & Brecon Railway further north, but in 1874 had promoted a Bill with the MR & CC to lease the Brecon & Merthyr, which the B & M board and its ordinary shareholders found acceptable; this would have given the Midland running powers through to Newport over the Old Rumney, and would have afforded access into Merthyr and Dowlais. (What the LNWR thought of this, having paid a lot of money to reach Merthyr jointly with the B & M, scarcely bears contemplation). But the debenture holders of the B & M petitioned against the Bill, and that was the end of it; bereft of any access to South Wales except via the HH & B and the Neath & Brecon Railways to Swansea, the Midland concluded a face-saving agreement with the LNWR 'to avoid unreasonable competition in South Wales' (which really meant only the non-use of Euston's running powers to Swansea via Middle Duffryn) and backed out with what grace it could muster. In view of Derby's capital commitments in connection with the Settle & Carlisle project, it was probably a wise decision at the time; conceivably also, the Midland's experience of 'diplomacy' in South Wales was helpful in its doing down of the Great Western over the acquisition of the Somerset & Dorset Railway, behind Paddington's back, in 1875.

MODERN BRANCHES

Under the aegis of the new owning companies after the absorptions of the 1870s, the West Monmouthshire branches were set for a long period of traffic growth, which the GWR and LNWR were much better geared to meet than their local predecessors would have been. In the high peak of the coal industry immediately prior to World War I, there were some twenty collieries on the Blaina and Nantyglo Branch and in the Sirhowy Valley, and seventeen on the branch through Ebbw Vale to Beaufort. All these branches were double track except at their northern extremities, but at the Newport end the Park Mile eventually had six tracks: two were added on the west side for use by the GWR and the Pontypridd, Caerphilly & Newport Railway (pp104-7) in 1885-86, and the second GWR pair of the four tracks on the east side were in use by March 1898. Quadrupling was completed northwards to Risca by June 1910, and as a child I 'played trains' with the green flag with which my grandmother waved the ceremonial train through the remodelled Risca station. Beyond Risca, gradients became progressively more severe, reaching 1 in 52 at Ebbw Vale, and from Aberbeeg through Blaina to Nantyglo nothing easier than 1 in 68, until at Nantyglo the ruling grade was 1 in 47. The Sirhowy line was somewhat easier until from Sirhowy northward the rise was 1 in 42; no wonder you could hear the trains go up the hills!

The worst gradient of all in this district was 1 in 24 on the Cwmtillery Branch, opened by the Monmouthshire Railway in 1858 and about one mile in length, which diverged from the Ebbw Fach (Blaina) Branch at Abertillery into the little side valley of the Tillery stream, and which at one time served five collieries. Greatest of these was Cwmtillery Colliery, which when it celebrated its centenary in 1950, was claimed by the National Coal Board to have won no less than 32 *million* tons of coal. This valley was the scene of an enterprising venture by the GWR in 1911–12 when, the branch being considered too steep for motor trains, a Milnes-Daimler bus was put on a service, Cwmtillery–Abertillery (then second-largest town in Monmouthshire)–Aberbeeg–Llanhilleth.

THE BRYNMAWR & WESTERN VALLEYS

Penetration by the LNWR into the top end of the Ebbw Fach Valley had a curious history. The Monmouthshire Railway in its advance up the valley had stopped short a quarter of a mile beyond Nantyglo station, but had the option to take lease of a part of the railway which the brothers J. & C. Bailey had built in substitution for their earlier tramroad between Nantyglo and Brynmawr; indeed, Airey's map of 1876 shows (un-corroborated) an MR & CC goods station on this railway at Brynmawr. But in 1871, the year before Crawshay Bailey died, the brothers had sold their business to the Nantyglo & Blaina Iron Company, which in 1881 leased the Brynmawr-Nantyglo section of their line to the LNWR. The latter continued to use it for access to various works, and down the valley by running powers to Rose Heyworth Colliery Siding (4½ miles from Brynmawr) until early in the twentieth century, when the LNWR and GWR joined forces in a Bill for acquiring the separate, already authorised, Brynmawr & Western Valleys Railways connecting the LNWR with the GWR, a quarter of a mile north of the latter's Nantyglo station. It was alleged that the promotion of this separate railway was necessary because of the exorbitant terms sought by the Iron Company for the acquisition of its own line, which as it stood would be expensive to adapt for passenger purposes, especially in view of its connection with the Merthyr, Tredegar & Abergavenny line, being east of the latter's Brynmawr station. The Iron Company opposed the Bill in terms which elicited from *The South Wales Gazette* the comment that 'the... company have been the prime obstacle in the way of this public convenience', which if correct would appear to be the first instance of a railway being promoted solely for such a limited purpose as the provision of toilet facilities! The B & WVR Bill, promoted locally, received Royal Assent on 13 July 1899. Two years later, when nothing had been done, and following an approach from the Duke of Beaufort to both companies, the GWR and LNWR took over its responsibilities jointly, confirmed by the Brynmawr & Western Valleys Railways (Vesting) Act of 31 July 1902, the line being built and equipped to LNWR standards.

Running parallel with the Iron Company's line on sharply falling gradients from Brynmawr, the 1¼-mile single-track joint railway – the last offshoot from the LNWR's Abergavenny–Merthyr line – opened formally on 12 July and to freight on 1 August 1905. From their inception on 28 May 1906 the passenger trains worked to and from Newport as a projection of the GWR Nantyglo–Newport service, although the LNWR ran a few passenger trains between Nantyglo and the MT & A line until World War I. The LNWR continued to operate local freight traffic over the Iron Company's line for some years after the B & WV opened, the lease finally expiring in 1918. By 1939 there was only one daily mineral working booked between Brynmawr, Blaina and return over the joint line. From Brynmawr southward the passenger service was withdrawn on 30 April 1962 and the line closed completely in November 1963 down to Coalbrookvale; thence down to Aberbeeg was singled in 1971, while coal traffic from Beynon Pit at Coalbrookvale ended in September 1975.

THE BEAUFORT BRANCH

More fortunate latterly has been the adjoining ex-GWR branch – traditionally known as the Beaufort Branch – up through Ebbw Vale immediately to the westward. Iron and steel have always made a major contribution to its traffic, and despite current uncertainties steel is still the mainstay of the Ebbw Fawr. Beaufort Ironworks at the head of the valley had been opened as early as 1780, nine years before what later became the Ebbw Vale Company's works lower down, while in 1837 the new Victoria Ironworks and the Ebbw Vale Company's Victoria Colliery nearby led to the adjacent passenger station being also named Victoria. Steel-making by the Bessemer process was adopted at the Ebbw Vale Company's plant about 1868 but in the depression following World War I the works closed down, with disastrous effect on the valley's economy. In 1935 the plant was acquired by Richard Thomas & Co and modernised to become three years later the first continuous wide-strip mill in Great Britain for the production of tinplate. Until after the formation of the British Steel Corporation, Ebbw Vale continued to make its own iron with a consequent heavy movement of imported ore through Newport Docks and up by rail, but under the BSC iron-making ceased at Ebbw Vale and steel slab was railed to the works from Llanwern.

The Ebbw Vale Company took over part of the historic Trevil Railroad connecting its works with the limestone quarries on the slopes of Mynydd Llangynidr north of the MT & A, converting it into a standard gauge line which attained an altitude of about 1,600ft above sea level. In 1940 some thirty-three locomotives worked fifty-seven miles of steelworks domestic network and leading to the quarries, the Trevil line to the latter being closed.

British Rail's ex-GWR Ebbw Vale Branch ended (in 1980) at the steelworks, passenger trains having ceased at the same time as on the neighbouring Aberbeeg–Brynmawr line. The single-track ex-LNWR/LMS branch from Ebbw Vale Junction west of Beaufort down to Ebbw Vale (High Level), 1½ miles long and opened on 1 September 1867, lost its passenger trains on 5 February 1951 – two months earlier than had been fixed, due to a coal economy measure – and was closed completely on 2 November 1959. The neighbouring LNWR/LMS passenger service from Nantybwch down through the Sirhowy Valley to Newport was withdrawn on 13 June 1960, though private siding traffic kept the line open until 30 April 1969.

'HALL'S ROAD'

This early tramroad has already been mentioned as leading off the Monmouthshire's Western Valley line at Hall's Road Junction and extending in a north-westerly direction towards and into the

Sirhowy Valley. Following the working of the Sirhowy Railway by the LNWR from 1875 and its acquisition by Euston the following year, there was a temporary interruption of the Great Western running powers for the Aberdare coal trains over the Sirhowy line, and as an insurance the GWR acquired a lease of Hall's Tramroad in 1877. Restoration of the running powers delayed the intended conversion of the tramroad into a railway, but with impending colliery developments in the northern part of the Sirhowy Valley, the four miles between Penar Junction, 1¾ miles west of Crumlin on the Taff Vale Extension line, and Manmoel Colliery were opened as a standard gauge railway on 10 March 1886. It was not until September 1912 that the 4¾ miles southward from Penar Junction to Hall's Road (or Tramroad) Junction were similarly opened. In April 1911 there was opened the Cwmcarn Branch, about a mile in length, leaving Hall's Road between Cross Keys and Abercarn; following closure of Cwmcarn Colliery, the branch railway also closed in November 1968. The only double-line section of Hall's Road was that of half-a-mile between Rhiw-Syr-Dafydd signalbox and Colliers Arms on the part of the line north of Penar Junction. It was also only on this part of the line that a passenger service (and a rather odd one) was provided, beginning on 14 March 1927 with auto-trains working between Pontypool Road (sometimes Clarence Street) and Penmaen and Oakdale Halts via Crumlin, which last-named was occasionally a trip termination/reversal point. Oakdale Halt closed from 12 September 1932, and the Friday afternoons-only passenger workings to and from Penmaen Halt ceased from 25 September 1939.

In more recent times, the lower part of Hall's Road was taken out of use on 21 December 1967, but three years later was rehabilitated in order to permit the final closure of the Sirhowy line, traffic from Markham Colliery being diverted over Hall's Road instead of through the Tredegar Junctions and down the Sirhowy line, on which all other freight traffic had already ceased. The 2½-mile Oakdale–Markham Colliery line saw its last train on 21 December 1979, and was closed ten days later.

BATTLE FOR NINE MILE POINT

Thus the Sirhowy Tramroad and Railway passed into history, but before it passes also out of this story, it is worth recalling how as part of the LNWR it figured in one of the most bitter and protracted railway battles in South Wales history. Just as the Great Western and the LNWR had fought and bought their way into the Monmouthshire coalfield, so also did the Glamorgan-based local railways in their turn cast envious eyes upon the industrial wealth of Monmouthshire, and sought to become invaders in their turn. Curiously, it was not one of the bigger brethren, but the pugnacious and persistent little Brecon & Merthyr, which was first off the mark in 1865, proposing an 'Ebbw Valley and Cardiff Junction Railway' to begin at a triangular junction at Machen on the B & M's recently-acquired Old Rumney line; thence it would cut through Machen Mountain by a mile-long tunnel, emerging at Nine Mile Point. A short branch was intended to the MRCC south of the latter's junction with the Sirhowy Railway, thus neatly avoiding payment of tolls, while the main stem bore up into the Ebbw Valley to connect with the Monmouthshire's Western Valleys line between Cross Keys and Abercarn. The Bill for this line was withdrawn, and over twenty years elapsed until first the Rhymney Railway Company and then the Bute Docks Company (predecessor of the Cardiff Railway Company) obtained powers for a roughly similar line between Caerphilly and Nine Mile Point; both these powers became time-expired.

By the early 1900s things began to move again. Apart from the continuing progress of the collieries served by the GWR in its Western Valleys, new sinkings were being made on the east bank of the Sirhowy River across from Nine Mile Point, in particular the new colliery of that name opened by Burnyeat Brown & Co. This was on the line of the ancient Penllwyn Tramroad of which some two miles had been acquired by the LNWR along with the Sirhowy Railway Company. The junction with this tramroad had been south of Nine Mile Point, however, so hitherto the LNWR had been required to pay tolls to the GWR as successor to the MRCC for any traffic passing over it; accordingly the LNWR made two new junctions with the Penllwyn and modernised it as far as Ynysddu (Lower). Whoever could get through the mountains to Nine Mile Point was therefore likely to attract valuable traffic to Cardiff, Penarth, or Barry Docks.

By 1905 the thrusting Barry Railway had not only penetrated the valleys of the Taff, Rhondda and Rhymney, but had also established connection with the B & M (Old Rumney) at Barry Junction (Duffryn Isaf from 1929) above Bedwas, thus penetrating what was then technically English soil. Even before the connection to the

B & M was opened the Barry had come forward with a scheme to tunnel through the mountain to Ynysddu on the Sirhowy, and thence up to Penar Junction on the Taff Vale Extension. Two years later the battleground shifted back to the Caerphilly-Machen-Nine Mile Point axis, and either separately or jointly the Barry, Rhymney, LNWR and GWR were involved in competing schemes. Even the little B & M was also involved, because it was prepared to grant running powers to the Barry to Bassaleg (and so to Newport!). To show the lengths to which protagonists were prepared to go in order to buy an alliance, the Barry at one stage was willing to adjust a proposed junction so that one of its intended lines would pass for *two chains* over B & M metals, thus presenting the latter with mileage revenue! The Barry also went to great lengths to placate the Cardiff and the Taff Vale companies, the latter of which was making threatening noises for a line of its own from Cardiff to Machen. So the battle was transferred to Westminster, where after costly and protracted hearings in committee, the Barry's scheme was approved (Royal Assent 28 August 1907) and the others' failed. But for the principal protagonist, it was an empty victory. A clause was inserted in committee whereby the Barry's rates on its authorised new railways were required to be the same irrespective of destination. Since Barry Docks were further in distance than the other competing ports, the legal requirement could only be met by excessive reductions in its existing rates from the Rhondda and other collieries nearer to Barry, whereas the economics of its Sirhowy scheme clearly depended on its being able to undercut its competitors' ton-mile rates, for example, to Cardiff. The Barry returned in 1911, but in the company's own words 'the facilities granted by Parliament proved unworkable', and with the outbreak of World War I in 1914, the grand design quietly lapsed. The Barry's promotional expenses alone were reputed to be of the order of £100,000.

Today one can look in vain on the latest Ordnance Survey map for the name of Nine Mile Point, the focal point in the battle for the Sirhowy. Mynydd Machen looks peacefully down on the valley, undisturbed by tunnelling or trains: the unconquered mountain.

ALEXANDRA DOCKS & RAILWAY

The last arrival of the railways serving Newport, the Alexandra (Newport & South Wales) Docks & Railway Company had one of

Page 101 (Top)   Serried ranks of privately-owned coal wagons, awaiting shipment orders at Roath Dock sidings, Cardiff, in the heyday of the export trade; (bottom) Two British Rail Class 56 diesel-electric locomotives bring some 2,300 tonnes of iron-ore from Port Talbot into Llanwern Steelworks, in 1979. (British Rail)

Page 102 Changing scene in the coalfield: Senghenydd, terminus of the Aber Valley Branch. *(Top)* A busy scene in Rhymney Railway days; *(bottom)* The same area, photographed by the author in 1949. *(Author's collection; L&GRP)*

the longest titles and, at nine, the shortest (owned) route mileage of any of the constituent companies amalgamated with the GWR under the Railways Act, 1921, although additionally it owned over 100 miles of dock railways and connections.

The company had its origin in the serious concern which by the middle of the nineteenth century became evident among freighting and shipping interests at the manifestly growing inadequacy of the Newport Town Dock and riverside wharves to cope with the expanding trade of the port and with the progressive increase in the size of ships. Notwithstanding its expansion from its original five acres to 11½ acres in 1858, the Town Dock was not only too small, but its relationship to the river involved a shallow depth over the sill, which limited the draught of ships that could get in. Early in the 1860s therefore, a subscription list was opened to promote a new and larger dock, with a better entry through open land nearer to the mouth of the Usk, in the ownership of Lord Tredegar. This nobleman headed a list of subscribers including Crawshay Bailey and other representatives of the iron trade at Cwmbran, Nantyglo, Tredegar and Rhymney.

The Alexandra (Newport) Dock Company was duly incorporated in 1865, the name of the proposed dock being presumably adopted as a compliment to Princess Alexandra of Denmark, who had married the Prince of Wales (later King Edward VII) in 1863. The Act of Incorporation also authorised connections between the dock railways and the Western Valleys line of the Monmouthshire, with the South Wales Railway both at Maesglas and 'where it passes under the Western Valleys line', and – most interestingly – with the Monmouthshire's Eastern Valleys line near Crindau, to the north east of Newport. This last-named scheme would have curved round the north side of the town, partly in tunnel; into modern times, an engineer's yard on the Eastern Valleys line was known as 'Tunnel Yard', possibly because of this or after the adjacent canal tunnel under Barrack Hill. The abortive East Usk Railway & Docks scheme of the same session, for a railway from Bassaleg round the north side of Newport and for a dock on the east bank of the Usk which would have been in competition with the Alexandra project, also intended a connection with the latter's Crindau Branch, but none of it came to pass, and while there are now plenty of junctions and a tunnel in that vicinity, they are all highway works.

For some years after its incorporation the Alexandra Company was in financial difficulty due to trading troubles arising from the

Franco-Prussian War of 1870 and its aftermath, and bank failures of the Second Railway Mania of the 1860s. Due not only to these factors, but also to the decision to build the Pontypool, Caerleon & Newport Railway, the Alexandra's Tunnel Branch was allowed to lapse after three extensions of time, although it was shown as 'authorised' on Airey's map as late as 1876. Running powers to the proposed docks were made available to the Monmouthshire, Great Western, B & M, and LNWR with powers to the first-named three to subscribe to the undertaking. As regards the connections with the GWR the Alexandra, in view of the impending change of gauge, neatly backed both horses each way by obtaining powers to make these connections mixed gauge (which in the event proved unnecessary) or 'on the same gauge as the GWR between Newport and Cardiff'!

THE PC & N RAILWAY

The original Alexandra North Dock was at length opened in 1875, and the first section of the South Dock in 1894; two subsequent extensions of the latter eventually afforded a total deep water area of 125 acres. Water had hardly been let into the first dock when the company and its supporters, including the Corporation of Newport, the shipping interests, and influential freighters, started to campaign vigorously for direct rail access between Newport and the Glamorganshire coalfield based on the Rhondda and Aberdare valleys. There were several good reasons for this. The steam coal measures in these valleys were now being exploited at astonishing speed, and whereas in 1846 Newport had shipped 130,000 tons more coal than Cardiff, by 1875 Cardiff in the space of nine months had exported over a million tons more than Newport. Both Cardiff Docks and its principal artery, the Taff Vale Railway, were already grossly overloaded, with a fleet of ships constantly moored in the roadstead waiting for berths, and coal trains standing block-and-block on their way to the port. A new pattern was evolving, too, in the coal trade itself. The days of one-man colliery ownership, or partnerships, were drawing to a close as limited liability companies took their place from 1856 onwards, leading to the next step whereby groups of collieries were formed under the control of big firms like Powell Duffryn, Ocean Coal, and Cory's. Those iron companies which found that they could not effectively compete in steel-making turned to the coal seams under their feet, while ship-

ping agents and foreign buyers were demanding the planned shipment of mixed natures of coal, in particular the mixing by
controlled dockside tipping of the soft bituminous coal generally
found in Monmouthshire with the drier steam coals of Glamorgan.

The principal protagonists of a railway link between Newport
and Glamorgan were J.C. Parkinson, who (not inconveniently) was
both managing director of the Alexandra Dock Company and pres-
ident of the Newport Chamber of Commerce, and Sir George
Elliot, MP, both of whom were also associated with Powell Duffryn
Collieries, which Sir George by then virtually controlled. Although
the mere threat of their intention to promote a railway between
Newport and the Glamorgan coalfield was sufficient to cause the
TVR and GWR to reduce by about 2p a ton, their joint rate for
traffic from this coalfield to Newport, the promoters were unsuc-
cessful in their attempt to penetrate beyond Pontypridd into the
Aberdare Valley to link up with Nixon's private railway, or to bypass
Lord Tredegar's Park Mile with its invidious tolls. The Act of 8
August 1878 incorporating the Pontypridd, Caerphilly & Newport
Railway authorised a railway of 5¼ miles from a junction with the
TVR at the south end of Pontypridd Station to another junction
with the Rhymney Railway near Caerphilly (see map, p. 136),
together with running powers over the Caerphilly Branch of the
B & M through Machen to Bassaleg Junction. By a further Act of 2
August 1883, the PC & N was authorised to build some two miles of
railway (should the owners of the Tredegar Park Mile Railway not
themselves build it) between Bassaleg Junction and the Alexandra
Dock Company's line. The price paid for this access to the
Glamorgan coalfield included tolls to the Rhymney, B & M Railways
and the Tredegar Estate, and a special payment to the B & M for
banking engines between Caerphilly and Machen, together with an
agreement (1884) with the TVR for working PC & N freight trains
through to the Alexandra Company's exchange sidings; the agreement with the Taff Vale was in consideration of the PC & N withdrawing its proposed line to the Aberdare Valley.

The PC & NR left the TVR immediately south of Pontypridd
Station, (the junction being controlled by a TVR signalbox emblazoned 'Pontypridd, Caerphilly and Newport Junction' in full)
crossed over the River Taff on a masonry viaduct, and after passing
the interchange sidings between the two companies, traversed the
rocky Glyntaff Cutting, the only engineering feature of note on the
railway. Thence it followed the east side of the valley of the River

Taff down to Nantgarw, the double track gradually climbing away along a shelf on the hillside on gradients ranging from 1 in 159–212, until making a junction with the Rhymney Railway at Penrhos Upper Junction, whence 1½ miles of RR tracks were used through Caerphilly Station to an end-on junction with the B & M Caerphilly Branch near the site later used for the RR locomotive works. The engineer for this line, which was one of the few in South Wales where the gradients were continuously against the loaded coal trains, was (Sir) James W. Szlumper.

CONFRONTATION AT BASSALEG

An attempt to open the new route was made on 7 July 1884, when a train of twenty-seven wagons of Powell Duffryn coal was worked through by the TVR from their Aberdare Branch to Caerphilly, accompanied by what was for this occasion a fraternal band of TVR, Rhymney, PC & N and B & M representatives. At Caerphilly, a B & M locomotive was added for the steep switchback on to Machen, possibly also to lend some appearance of legality to the proceedings. This was soon to be invoked, because at Bassaleg Junction the GWR signals were held against the train, and the party was met by officials of the GWR, increasing to five the number of railways represented in what now became a confrontation of bowler hats on the ballast. Alfred Henshaw, the B & M traffic manager, (who was later to become the Alexandra's general manager) produced a 'permit' the validity of which was claimed under the B & M's running powers over the Park Mile to Newport. This document was rejected on the grounds that it could not cover a movement arranged by the PC & N and engined by the Taff Vale! So the train had to be stabled while the GWR party went off to wire Paddington for instructions; it sat there, while no PC & N traffic moved beyond Bassaleg, until eighteen days later, when Paddington gave way. The GWR must have realised its objection was both open to question and dog-in-the-manger, because the Park Mile legally belonged to the Tredegar Estate, while in 1883 Parliament had authorised a separate double track for use of the PC & N along the Park Mile, although this did not become available through to West Mendalgief Junction until April 1886. Meanwhile, PC & N traffic passed over parts of six different railways in the nineteen miles between Pontypridd and Newport Docks.

The making of these additional tracks for the accommodation of the PC & N traffic along the Park Mile posed problems, because if they had been made to the east of the existing tracks, it would have been necessary for PC & N trains to make two fouling movements right across the Western Valley lines and back again at Bassaleg and Park junctions respectively. An arrangement was therefore reached whereby the use of the original tramroad alignment and successor tracks thereon were transferred to the newcomer, and additional tracks were cut out of the shallow hillside for the use of the GWR and its running-power 'tenants' (p94). On 14 September 1891 a separate line for Up trains (i.e. 'down' the valley towards Newport) some two miles long was brought into use between Gwaun y Bara Junction and Machen on the Caerphilly–Machen section in order to ease the gradient for loaded coal trains, hitherto faced with a 1 in 39 climb on the single line between those stations. First authorised by the PC & N Act of 1882 but superseded by a different route under that company's Act of 8 August 1887, and known then as the 'Machen Loop Line', it was transferred to the B & M after completion in consideration of the receipts being shared 50–50 between the two companies.

THE ALEXANDRA TAKES OVER

Although the PC & N was from its inception an associate of the Alexandra Dock Company, having been promoted in conjunction with the latter, the dock company's financial troubles had pushed aside any question of integration. As early as 1882 however, the Alexandra Company had obtained powers to change its title to The Alexandra (Newport & South Wales) Docks & Railway Company, a change which *inter alia* had relevance to the qualification of shares for trustee status. Similarly, at other South Wales ports, the Barry Dock & Railways Company became the Barry Railway Company in 1891, and the Bute Docks Company became the Cardiff Railway Company in 1897. (The ADR in 1906 proposed a further and somewhat audacious change of name to 'The Newport & South Wales Railway Company', but this clause was struck out of the company's Bill by the House of Lords Committee).

In the year following its change of title, the Alexandra by virtue of the Newport Dock (Transfer) Act of 1883, took over the Newport Town Dock (the 'old dock') with effect from I January 1884, the purchase price being £149,000 against the Newport Dock Company's share and loan capital of nearly £483,000. Largely because of its own limited capacity and the competition of the new docks, the old company was by that time unable to meet in full the preference dividends, on which there were large arrears of interest. But it was to be some years after the railway grouping of the 1920s before all shipments at the old dock ceased and it was finally closed and filled in. In 1897 therefore, the ADR saw its way clear to bring forward a Bill to purchase or lease the PC & N, with which it had already been authorised, in 1890, to exchange mutual running powers. This brought about an instant and powerful riposte from the Taff Vale, which sought to secure its own direct access to Newport by acquisition of the PC & N, together with running powers over the Park Mile and portions of the GWR. The ADR prevailed in obtaining by Act of 6 August 1897 its acquisition of the PC & N. In the following session the TVR made a last, unsuccessful, effort to obtain running powers over the PC & N and the Park Mile, together with power to acquire property at Herbert Street, Newport, for a goods or locomotive depot, but these powers were not granted, nor any more heard of this TVR invasion of Newport.

The TVR nevertheless continued to work the ADR mineral traffic between Pontypridd and Alexandra Dock until 30 April 1906, when the ADR, having accumulated by now a heterogeneous collection of locomotives, including ten tank engines from the Mersey Railway when the latter was electrified, took over the working itself, using also some locomotives hired or borrowed from the Rhymney Railway when necessary.

PASSENGER SERVICES

Although the PC & N had been refused running powers to Newport (High Street) in 1883, the Alexandra began a passenger service between Newport and Pontypridd over the PC & N on 28 December 1887. The GWR took over this service on 1 January 1899, and after an interruption during World War I, extended it to Merthyr. On 1 September 1904, the ADR began a local service between Pontypridd (Tram Road) Halt, east of the TVR station, and Caerphilly, later extended to Machen, utilising two steam rail-motors built by the Glasgow Railway & Engineering Company of Govan, and calling at seven intermediate ground-level halts, of which Upper Boat derived its name from a canalside hamlet lower down. Some of these services, as for instance on market or football days or first thing in the morning, added a trailer which might well turn out to be one of the American-type coaches acquired early in the century from Barnum & Bailey's circus train. It is odd that although the ADR was a Newport-based company and had its head offices there, it operated no passenger services into or out of the town after 1898.

The ADR continued full of enterprise in port development and railway aspiration until the outbreak of World War I. In 1906 for instance, it obtained retrospective Parliamentary powers to operate buses for passengers, mails, goods, etc, between any places within the County Borough of Newport, except in competition with Newport Tramways. With two ex-London & South Western Railway Milnes-Daimler 14-seaters it put on a service from 1 January 1906 between the Docks Office and the Corporation tram terminus at Pwllgwenlly in Dock Street and, if required, continuing on to High Street station. Two further vehicles were acquired and the service, confined to the docks area from December 1917 when the trams reached the dock gates, ceased in 1933.

Somewhat belatedly, in 1911 the ADR flung itself into the competition to obtain access to the Sirhowy Valley, obtaining powers in that year to make a railway from near Bassaleg Junction up the west side of the Ebbw Vale to join the LNWR at Nine Mile Point, with a short branch to the Black Vein and Penllwyn collieries. The Act also contained a clause requiring that where the railway would pass by Danygraig House, Risca (my grandparents' home) it was to be in tunnel or by the operation known as cut-and-cover. Some minor changes in the scheme were the subject of a further Act in 1914, but with the outbreak of war in that year, no more was heard of it.

In the current era, time has dealt hardly with these railways. Local passenger services were withdrawn between Pontypridd, Caerphilly and Machen on 17 September 1956, while the last section of the PC & N to remain open for freight, between Pontypridd and Glyntaff goods depot (the only one of its kind on the ADR outside Newport) was officially closed on 29 July 1967; the PC & N alignment is now but a scar on the hillside. Between Caerphilly and Newport, a workmen's service continued until I July 1963, when it also ended with the closure of the former Rhymney Railway workshops at Caerphilly. The B & M Newport passenger service had also closed down on 31 December 1962, since when the 'Old Rumney' remained open only east of Bedwas to serve the colliery at the former place and a stone quarry at Machen. The

Down section of the Caerphilly–Machen branch remained open as a single line for freight traffic from the Rhymney Valley to Newport until 20 November 1967, when such traffic was diverted via Penrhos and Walnut Tree, Radyr and Cardiff. Through the Park Mile one single line serves the rump of the B & M, and two the Western Valley direction, but with no physical connection between the two at Bassaleg; where once a constant procession of trains moved over six parallel tracks, they now appear few and far between. At the bottom end, only the abutments remain of the ADR bridge that carried the valleys traffic over and above the South Wales main line on its way to the docks. Here too there was later contraction, with Maesglas Junction–East Mendalgief Junction, including Monmouthshire Bank Sidings, taken out of use on 3 September 1979, and the Dock Street Depot–Town Dock Sidings similarly on 29 October 1979. (See Chapter XII).

CHAPTER VI

Cardiff: The Protagonists

Cardiff, capital city of Wales, for long Britain's third largest port, and still an outstandingly important centre of commercial and maritime trade, has a turbulent history to which Romans, Vikings, Normans, the rival factions of Welsh and English and of the Civil War, and within living memory raiders from the sky have all contributed. Less blood-thirsty, but in its way equally fascinating to the student of railway history, is the in-fighting between railway, canal and dock interests, which went on almost unremittingly from early in the nineteenth century until the first quarter of the twentieth.

Topography is the common dominating factor. Cardiff lies 11¾ miles west of Newport across the Wentlooge Level, flat land reclaimed long ago from the Bristol Channel, along which the modern high-speed *Inter- City 125* purrs at a restrained 90mph on a dead level course which for eight miles between Ebbw Junction and the crossing of the River Rhymney on the outskirts of Cardiff is almost dead straight. Cardiff has another similarity with Newport, inasmuch as it is bounded on either side by rivers: from east to west the Rhymney, the Taff, and the Ely, with the Glamorganshire Canal formerly reaching tide-water close to the latter pair. Within the four miles crow's flight between crossing the Rhymney at Rumney (sic) River Bridge Junction and the Ely's outfall into the channel below Penarth Head there was crammed the great acreage of docks and railways (of the latter, five different companies in 1921, six with Barry running powers) by which the commercial greatness of Cardiff was established.

Equally important was the layout of the hinterland. The Rhymney River as it neared Cardiff had no railway following its course, while the Ely coming in from the west afforded an exit towards Swansea for the South Wales main line. The way up into the valleys, though, was primarily through Taff Vale; by means of the Walnut Tree Gap, a giant fault in the limestone outcrop at Taff's Well seven miles north of Cardiff, the river, four railways, the canal, and the main Cardiff-Merthyr road were all able to jostle their way through to the sea. Coincidentally, this topographical feature whereby access to the hinterland was through a defile also occurred in the case of Newport at Risca (Gwent), about the same distance from Newport as Taff's Well is from Cardiff. It would be tidier but less interesting to be able to record that the growth of Cardiff, its docks and railway system, was carefully planned, to match the

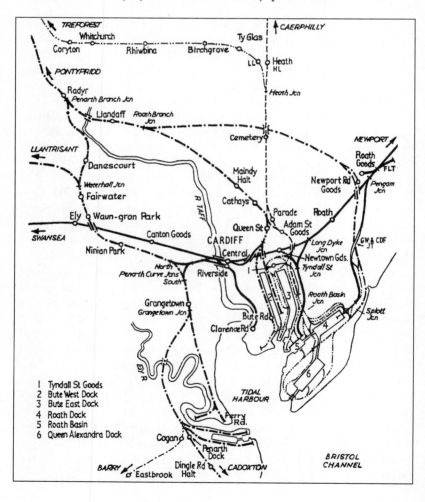

growth of industry in the hinterland. But nobody planned, or was allowed to plan, our railway system – George Hudson had the entrepreneurial vision, William Ewart Gladstone the political foresight, but the latter's efforts were frustrated by vested interests and fears of monopoly.

Much of the history of the railways serving Cardiff, more particularly the local lines, is thus concerned with their relationship, problems and frequent conflict with the dock interests as much as with each other as rival railways. This situation had such a profound effect on railway strategies and fortunes that some preliminary identification of this problem and of the protagonists which it involved seems essentially preferable to a mere catalogue of the railways serving Cardiff and its adjacent competitive ports of Penarth and Barry.

THE CANAL BASIN

The first shipping terminal relevant to this story was the Glamorganshire Canal Company's basin adjacent to the mouth of the River Taff on its east bank side, and entered from tidal waters by a sea lock; the basin and the channel leading inland from it were opened in 1798, and extended for about a mile to where the South Wales Railway was to pass over the canal just east of Cardiff General Station. As mentioned on p32 the canal basin and the numerous wharves adjoining it were served by the Canal Company's own tramroad, but this did not become connected to the GWR until the opening of the latter's Riverside Branch in 1882.

In 1839, the year in which the Bute West Dock was opened and the year immediately previous to the inauguration of the Taff Vale Railway's first section, over 200,000 tons of coal alone, as well as large quantities of iron, were brought down by the canal. Various improvements were made over the years, even after traffic had begun to decline with the development of Cardiff Docks and connecting railways, but eventually the basin was useful only to coasters. The Glamorganshire Canal was acquired by the Marquis of Bute in 1885 and figured in an unsuccessful proposal in 1898 to convert it into a railway. In 1943 Cardiff Corporation obtained Parliamentary powers to acquire and abandon the canal, but the basin lingered on until the gates of the sea lock were accidentally burst open in 1951 and all the water, like the money before it, ran away.

THE BUTE DOCKS

When the sea lock and basin were opened in 1798, the population of Cardiff was only about one thousand. The creation of the central dock system now to be briefly described, with all its associated industrial and commercial activities, helped bring about an explosion of population to nearly 60,000 by 1871, when at last Cardiff's population eclipsed that of Merthyr Tydfil, hitherto the largest town in Wales. Mostly this was due to the enterprise and personal investment of the second Marquis of Bute (1793-1848), rightly described as the founder of modern Cardiff, by whom and by his successors the docks were financed, built, owned and managed until 1922. Although this represented an enormous personal and family undertaking, it was by no means a disinterested public benefaction – not only did the land on which the docks were built belong to the Bute estate, but also the marquis was the owner of large mineral rights in the hinterland, leading to considerable embarrassment when conflict arose between the coalowners and ironmasters and their ground landlord the dock owner, while from the earliest days there were clashes between the dock interest and those of the railway companies over questions of access, charges and shunting arrangements. Moreover, as the trade of the port grew, the Bute interests faced financial problems arising from the basic fact that the dock revenue did not earn a margin of profit sufficient adequately to write down the investment on the older docks as they became obsolescent through the increased size of ships. Cardiff soon outstripped Newport as the largest South Wales coal shipping port until overtaken by Barry, but this distinction had a reverse side: colliers were not much beloved of shippers for more general cargoes as they usually came home in ballast, so that apart from iron-ore and timber, the port was long under-utilised for imports.

Recognising the inadequacy of the canal sea lock for the growth of traffic, the second marquis constructed the Bute West Dock, opened in 1839; the Bute East Dock followed in 1855-59, being opened under the auspices of the Bute Trustees, whom the marquis had appointed prior to his death in 1848, the heir to the title being a minor. In 1874 the trustees opened the Roath Basin, connected with the East Dock but having also its own entrance lock seaward. By this time the trade of the Bute Docks (imports and exports together) amounted to some three million tons annually, and the enormous expansion of the smokeless steam-coal trade from the Rhondda and Aberdare Valleys was soon threatening to overwhelm the dock facilities. A Parliamentary committee was to be told that people could walk from one side of a dock to the other on the decks of the ships moored in it, and that there was great congestion and delay on the railways from the valleys. Coal and coke traffic on the TVR had grown from a modest 41,000 tons in 1841 to 4½ million tons in 1873, although the latter figure included shipments from Penarth Dock, opened in 1865.

The last dock to be undertaken by the trustees was the Roath Dock, authorised by Parliament in 1883 but not opened until 1887. By this time the marquis and his trustees had decided that the status of personal responsibility in relation to the docks could not be sustained, especially as the Bute estate could no longer from its income finance further needed expansion, and from 31 December 1886 the docks undertaking vested in the Bute Docks Company, incorporated by Act of 25 June of that year; the enormous investment (estimated at £2.4 millions) by the marquisate remained in the form of share and loan capital of the company. In later years the marquis made generous concessions to help the undertaking in its difficulties. By this time the Bute dock monopoly had been whittled down through the opening of the Ely Tidal Harbour on the east bank of the River Ely, near its mouth, in 1859; of Penarth Dock on the opposite bank in 1865; and most importantly of the Barry Dock & Railways in 1889. Nevertheless, the coal trade was still expanding, and in 1913 the coal exports of Cardiff were 10½ million tons compared with eleven million tons at Barry.

The formation of the Bute Docks Company was by no means the last major change in the organisation of the dock system, but at this stage it is necessary to introduce the other principals concerned with the movement of traffic to and from the docks, apart from the Bute interest itself. From early on, the marquis provided the docks with an internal railway system, worked from the 1860s by a fleet of steam locomotives bearing on their tank sides as sole insignia the marquis' coronet; eventually this system amounted to more than 120 miles of dock lines and sidings, and involving some ten junctions with the four railway companies feeding and clearing the port.

THE TAFF VALE RAILWAY

The Taff Vale was the original and long the paramount of the independent South Wales railways, opening-up and largely dominating the rail access to Cardiff's hinterland, and for nearly half a century enjoying a monopoly position in respect of a huge slice of the region's industrial traffic. It was born partly as a local consequence of the congestion on the Glamorganshire Canal as early as 1835, but more broadly as the natural outcome of the realisation that the region must have railways as the long-term succession to the canal-and-tramroad era. The company was incorporated by Act of 21 June 1836, the promoters being mainly ironmasters and other industrialists of whom the most notable were (Sir) John Josiah Guest, head of the great Dowlais Ironworks, and Walter Coffin of Dinas, who was the first man to open up coal mining in the Rhondda Valley, incidentally building his own tramroad which was to become an important feeder to the TVR. The latter's initial connection into the Rhondda was one of several branches authorised by the Act of Incorporation, the main line being that between Cardiff and Merthyr Tydfil, where connections were authorised with the tramroads serving the ironworks of Pen-y-darran, Dowlais and Plymouth. The Act prescribed several features which later were conveniently repealed: anyone who could obtain permission to do so could use their own engines and carriages on it, the maximum speed of trains was not to exceed 12mph, and dividends were not to exceed nine per cent (between 1870-88, until the opening of Barry; the dividend on the ordinary shares averaged 12½ per cent, making it one of the most prosperous railways in Great Britain).

Cardiff (p130) to Navigation House (p154) opened 8 October 1840, and to Merthyr 21 April 1841 (postponed from 12 April). The 24½-mile main line was single at first (but see p140), doublings being Cardiff–Taff's Well in mid 1846, to Navigation House a year later, and to Merthyr 1861-2. From these small beginnings there evolved by direct construction or by the acquisition of eight local companies a system of 124½ route miles, 411½ single-track miles including sidings, extending into the Rhondda and Aberdare valleys, westward through Penarth to the outskirts of Barry, to Cowbridge and Aberthaw in the Vale of Glamorgan, and into the area around Llantrisant.

In its relationship with the Cardiff Docks interest, the TVR by its Act of incorporation obtained powers not only to serve the Bute West Dock, but also to make a branch to Cogan Pill on the west bank of the River Ely where alternative shipping facilities were clearly envisaged. Not surprisingly, the latter proposal was not very acceptable to the Marquis of Bute, who secured its withdrawal in return for an agreement to let the Taff Vale have a long lease of part of the

Bute West Dock, the railway company to provide and maintain the coal shipping appliances. The TVR accordingly built a branch line into the dock from East Branch Junction (below Queen Street Station), and brought it into use in 1848, but the arrangements with Lord Bute became a source of serious trouble later on.

THE RHYMNEY RAILWAY

Following the arrival of the South Wales Railway in 1850, the next local protagonist to appear on the scene was the Rhymney Railway Company, incorporated 24 July 1854 to make a line of 9½ miles from the Rhymney Iron Works to a junction with the Newport, Abergavenny & Hereford at Hengoed. The promoters were encouraged to think that their Cardiff traffic would be carried over the Taff Vale branch (opened in 1841 from Stormstown Junction on the TVR main line) to Llancaiach, between Hengoed and Quakers' Yard on the NA & H. Fortunately for the Rhymney (because this roundabout route could never have coped with the increasing traffic of all three companies) the Llancaiach connection fell through, so by Act of 2 July 1855 the RR extended its main line from Hengoed, past the west side of Caerphilly to join the TVR at Walnut Tree Bridge Junction, Taff's Well, whence the TVR conferred running powers down to Crockherbtown Junction, immediately north of the present Queen Street Station in Cardiff. From Crockherbtown the RR was authorised to make its own line to the seaward end of Bute East Dock.

The Rhymney Railway enjoyed the strong support of the Bute interests, since it would afford a rail outlet for the marquis' important mining interests then being developed in the territory it was to serve. Powers were granted for the Bute Trustees to subscribe to the initial capital, and the leader of the trustees, John Boyle, became the first chairman of the company, while the trustees paid for the construction of the Bute East Dock Branch, leasing it back to the company at four per cent.

The formative years of the Rhymney Company were very difficult for a variety of causes: lack of capital (one at least of the contractors had to be paid in stock), under-estimates of the cost of construction, landslips, and delays in opening the new collieries in the Rhymney Valley. The Bute Trustees therefore continued to prop up the Rhymney in all sorts of ways, foregoing priority of their own interest in favour of that on the preference shares when the Rhymney

defaulted on its prior charges after the opening between Cardiff
and Rhymney in 1858 (25 February for freight, 31 March for passengers). The branch to East Dock had been opened in September
1857, but could be little used until connected to the main line.
Then in 1860 the trustees offered very satisfactory terms (including
five per cent guaranteed interest on the Rhymney Ordinary stock)
for a long-term lease of the railway. Although this proposal was, not
surprisingly, acceptable to the Rhymney shareholders, the Bill
promoting it was rejected by Parliament, partly through the opposition of the Taff Vale.

WAR WITH THE TAFF VALE

From a short-lived honeymoon the Taff Vale and the Rhymney were
soon at loggerheads, the most serious *casus belli* being that whereas
the former had been required both to pay a stiff price for its access
to West Dock, and to withdraw its Cogan Pill scheme into the
bargain, the newcomer was given the use of the tips on the East
Dock for nothing! Moreover, the working of the Rhymney's trains
over the TVR through Walnut Tree into Cardiff was alleged to be
inefficient and even dangerous, with overloaded, under-powered
and inadequately-braked trains thundering perilously down the 1 in
47 gradient through the Nantgarw Gap towards Walnut Tree
Junction with whistles screaming, sparks and smoke flying from the
brake blocks, and all the drama of what was commonly known in
South Wales as 'a wild run'. So the Rhymney found its traffic liable
to unexplained delays, and was beset with an additional charge of
one old penny per ton, not in the agreement, on all traffic handed
over at Cardiff; this impost the Rhymney took to arbitration with
substantial success, but blood was now up on both sides.

   In 1861 both protagonists promoted Bills for direct lines between
Cardiff and Caerphilly, neither of which succeeded, but the next
few years were to witness a better prospect for the Rhymney. That
notable Victorian strong man, Cornelius Lundie, arrived from the
Blyth & Tyne Railway to stiffen the management, virtually taking
charge for the next forty years. The TVR was too concerned with
growing congestion on railway and docks alike, and with the
Penarth project, to impede seriously the Rhymney's second attempt
for its own direct Caerphilly–Cardiff line; more importantly for the
Taff, its initial resistance obtained for it the valuable concession of
access to Bute East Dock.

Page 119 (Top) Runaway in the Eastern Valleys: an ex-GWR 0-6-0PT comes to grief in 1955 on the steep Cwmnantddu Branch; *(bottom)* The landslip in April 1930, which brought about the closure of the Brecon & Merthyr Railway's Rhymney Branch above New Tredegar. *(South Wales Argus (New-port); British Rail)*

Page 120 Scenes from the past. *(Top)* Through train for Aberystwyth, climbing away from Merthyr over the LNWR/B&M Joint Line, behind two Brecon & Merthyr locomotives, an 0-6-0ST leading an 0-6-2ST; *(bottom)* High in the hills at Nantybwch, a trio of ex-LNWR 0-6-2Ts meet on passenger trains from Tredegar *(left)* and Merthyr *(right)*. *(K. A. C. R. Nunn, W. A. Camwell)*

Two Rhymney Acts of 25 July 1864 not only authorised the Caerphilly–Cardiff line and the connection east of Caerphilly to the termination of the B & M's Machen–Caerphilly branch at the road between those places, but also confirmed heads of an agreement with a powerful new ally the LNWR, no less. The latter's physical entry into Cardiff over RR metals had to wait another seven years for completion, but meanwhile the Rhymney obtained from its new partner valuable aid in financing new rolling stock under a rent-hire arrangement. Then in 1867 the Rhymney concluded another important agreement, this time with the GWR, for the Taff-Bargoed Joint Railway by which iron-ore for the Dowlais furnaces was to be hauled up from Cardiff, so that by 1871 the RR was poised for fresh expansion, albeit incurring also heavy expenditure on new lines, new equipment, and track widening.

ENTER THE LNWR

In its westward drive along the MT & A line towards Merthyr, the LNWR had extended from Brynmawr to Nantybwch, 4¼ miles, on 1 March 1864. Both the North Western and the Rhymney were facing at this time the efforts of the puny, penurious, and pushful little Brecon & Merthyr Railway to enter this territory from the Dowlais direction, and as a tacit part of their agreement the new allies jointly resisted this intended invasion, by constructing as a joint line the Rhymney's proposed extension to meet the LNWR at Nantybwch. This very steep line in wild country descended at 1 in 35 from Nantybwch towards Rhymney Bridge, where the line joining the RR at Rhymney itself turned left down the valley at a similar inclination, while the LNWR continued towards Merthyr. An amusing feature of the joint line was that it boasted two sets of mile posts reading in opposite directions, those of RR design from Cardiff, and those in LNWR style from Abergavenny Junction.

The Rhymney-LNWR through route was completed on 1 April 1871 by the opening of the former's extension from Caerphilly through the tunnel of 1 m 173yd under Cefn On Mountain down to Cardiff, and on 5 September (for public traffic 2 October) the Rhymney-Nantybwch joint line. The ceremonial opening of the latter was conducted at a high level in more senses than one, Nantybwch being 1,165ft above sea level, the participants including civic dignitaries from London and Cardiff, John Boyle & Co and the austere and autocratic LNWR chairman Sir Richard Moon.

Through working between the two systems began at once. The LNWR diverted onto the RR all of its coal traffic for Cardiff originating in the upper part of its lines in Monmouthshire; this traffic had hitherto suffered from transhipment at Newport due to the GWR being still broad gauge, while LNWR coal traffic from its Monmouthshire pits for shipment at Penarth (and later, Barry) was handed over to the RR at Ystrad Mynach. The LNWR also provided through coaches between Cardiff and both Liverpool and Manchester, which lasted until World War I. On 1 October 1875 it opened its own freight depot and warehouse at Tyndall Street, Cardiff, for access to which a half-mile of North Western track was built from LNWR Junction on the Rhymney. In the great days of railway prosperity, Cardiff traders had a choice of through goods wagons to Manchester by at least three different railways: Great Western, Taff Vale, and LNWR. The last-named was at one time running as many as six goods trains daily each way with its own locomotives between Cardiff and Abergavenny, and as late as 1929 the author hitch-hiked a lift into Cardiff on an LMS Fowler Class 4 0–6–0 going down light to Tyndall Street Goods, the only bit of 'Midland' in the Welsh capital...

Although it eventually comprised only just over fifty route miles of track (including its share of joint lines) the Rhymney developed into a compact, powerful, efficient and prosperous undertaking. Four years after the opening of the important lines just mentioned, it again failed to pay any Ordinary dividend at all in 1875, the year of a big coal strike, but between 1880 and 1897 the dividend averaged nine per cent.

THE GWR IN CARDIFF

Considering that its predecessor, the South Wales Railway, was the first to open communication between South Wales and England, and that the Great Western Railway soon became the most important railway in the city, eventually absorbing all the local companies and Cardiff Docks, it may seem odd to introduce its local role so late in this chapter. But both the South Wales and its successor the GWR seem to have been less involved than were the local lines in the early strife between these native railways, the Bute Docks interest and each other. That this was so was probably due to the pre-occupation of the South Wales Company with completing its trunk route to Swansea and West Wales, to its initial under-estimation of the traffic potential of the hinterland (an error shared by Brunel himself, as is clear from his recorded opinion), and to the adoption of the 7ft 0¼in gauge.

The South Wales Company having entered Cardiff from Newport in 1850, crossed the River Taff immediately west of its passenger station, and headed up the Ely Valley to Llantrisant and thence to Port Talbot, Neath and Swansea, all reached at the same time. It was on 19 April 1858, barely four years before the GWR would renew the lease and work the SWR as part of its own system before amalgamation, that the latter opened its 1¼-mile Bute Docks Branch. The SWR leased two coal tips at East Dock, reached through this branch, about which there is a bit of mystery. MacDermot's official history shows that the Bute Docks Branch was broad gauge from its opening until the general gauge conversion of 1872, yet the Taff Vale Railway records show that up to 43,000 tons of coal a year were being moved by that railway 'to the SWR tips' until 1872. This was most likely the coking coal from the Lower Rhondda pits for shipment across to Bristol for the GWR locomotive coking ovens there; it could reach the docks over the standard gauge connection between TVR and GWR at Bute Street Junction, close to the break-of-gauge tranship-ment station. At this period, however, the TVR was providing loco-motive power for the Bute Docks, and it is possible that other tips were used temporarily for this traffic from the TVR: the latter had no means of working broad gauge wagons. On the other hand, the SWR tips at East Dock (to which the GWR added a third at Roath Basin after the latter's opening in 1874) also received coal from the GWR's broad-gauge associates in the Ely, Llynvi and Ogmore valleys, and some from the Monmouthshire pits, transhipped at Newport. Hence the spectacle, puzzling to a stranger, of loaded coal trains passing each other in opposite directions between Newport and Cardiff, as was also the case over the Pennines, notably on the MS & L and L & Y Railways.

OTHER BRANCHES

Apart from the Riverside Branch, already mentioned as having been opened (14 September 1882) from the west side of Cardiff passenger station to serve wharves and industrial sidings along the canal basin, the only other major connection between the GWR and the dock system was the Roath Dock Branch, 1¼ miles long (of which a quarter-mile in the middle was made jointly with the Cardiff

Railway, as the Bute Docks Company had by then become). Opened on 2 November 1903 from the main line at Pengam Junction at the eastern outskirts of the city, it served the last of the Cardiff Docks, the 52-acre Queen Alexandra, brought into use in July 1907, with the completion of which the total deep-water area of the Cardiff Docks amounted to 165 acres, with quays totalling some 38,000ft.

PENARTH

Not forming part of the Cardiff Dock system, but rivals of it, two neighbouring ports to the west of the city were of immense railway significance. By the mid 1850s dissatisfaction among traders and shippers at slow development and increasing congestion at Cardiff led to promotion of the Ely Tidal Harbour & Railway, the latter being from Penarth Junction on the Taff's main Cardiff–Merthyr line at Radyr, 5¼ miles north-west from Cardiff Bute Road. The subsequent Act of 21 July 1856 was followed by another on 27 July 1857 changing the title to Penarth Harbour Dock & Railway, with powers to build a dock as well, in the lee of Penarth Head on the opposite side of the mouth of the Ely. Crawshay Bailey MP was chairman of the company. The railways, which totalled some 8½ route miles, separated at Grangetown Junction to serve the installations on either side of the river, that to the Tidal Harbour being opened in the summer of 1859 and to the dock in 1865. Meanwhile a furious row had broken out between the TVR and the Bute Trustees, who all along had objected to the proposed dock and harbour, and when the TVR agreed terms in August 1862 (sanctioned by Act of 1863) with the PHD & R to lease and work both dock and railway for 4½ per cent and half the surplus profits, the Bute Trustees sued the company for breach of the agreement whereby in 1846 the Taff had withdrawn its authorised Cogan Branch on the Ely in return for the expensive lease of part of the Bute West Dock. The case went to the Lords, who decided that the Taff had not broken the agreement, but that in equity the rates to be charged for Penarth traffic should not undercut those at Cardiff. The TVR influenced as much traffic as it could to Penarth, as this incidentally relieved the pressure on its main line and yards south of Radyr; in its year of opening Penarth dealt with three-quarters of a million tons of all natures of cargo (mostly coal) and within twenty years this figure had risen to 2.8m tons.

BARRY DOCK & RAILWAYS

Much the same factor, but on a much bigger scale and with even greater repercussions, brought about the establishment in 1884 of the Barry Dock & Railways Company (from 1891, for reasons already explained in connection with the ADR, the Barry Railway Company). Seven miles south-west of Cardiff, with a sheltered deep-water approach, Barry from 1865 onwards had been the location of several abortive railway promotions, the first of which failed largely because it flirted with the Broad Gauge and with the GWR, already abhorrent to the coal trade. But in the 1880s, when coal shipments from Cardiff had risen to over eight million tons a year and when only the opening of Penarth Dock had afforded any interim relief to congestion, the coal traders and shippers combined under the leadership of David Davies of the Ocean Collieries to make a modern port at Barry, with rail connections to the coalfield. 'Dai Davies yr Ocean' was just the man for the coming battle with existing vested interests; in his earlier life he had built parts of the Cambrian and the B & M Railways, and he was an acute and successful business man, backed by colleagues with plenty of money behind them.

The spark that lit the fuse in the row between the Davies faction and the Bute-Taff Vale interests, was a clause in the Trustees' 1882 Bill for the Roath Dock, to increase by one (old) penny a ton the charge on coal shipped not only at the proposed dock, but at all the existing Bute Docks as well. The first Bill for the Barry scheme was rejected in the following session, so the promoters offered to buy the Bute Docks: Davies had threatened that they 'would make the grass to grow in the streets of Cardiff'. On 14 August 1884 the Barry Bill received Royal Assent (the two submissions to Parliament had cost £70,000) and on 18 July 1889 the company opened its first dock, seventy-three acres and the largest enclosed dock in the country. With a fitting sense of theatre, Davies had arranged for trains of coal from the Rhondda and Aberdare Valleys to approach in time for the opening ceremony, as part of which the coal began to flow down into the hold of the inaugural vessel as the champagne began to flow down the throats of 2,000 invited guests.

Barry was served by a relatively short and simple railway system. From Cadoxton Junction at the eastern end of the dock area the main line turned northward through rural terrain to Drope Junction, 6¾ miles from Barry, where a branch went off westward to tap the GWR main line at Peterston, and beyond it the Ely, Llynvi and Ogmore areas of the coalfield. After crossing over the GWR main line on an imposing masonry viaduct comprising nine arches each of 45ft span, with a maximum height of 84ft, a short but important steep little connection from the GWR at St Fagan's came in at Tynycaeau Junction (7¾ miles); the original Barry main line carried on through Tonteg Junction, with a connection down to the TVR main line for Aberdare, etc, traffic, and thence ran parallel with and at a higher level than the Taff Vale past Pontypridd to terminate by a junction with the TVR in the Rhondda Valley at Trehafod, nineteen miles from Barry. Cadoxton to Tynycaeau Junction opened for freight on 13 May and on to Trehafod on 18 July 1889, after Barry to Penarth (p128). Later extensions were from Tynycaeau eastwards across the Vale of Taff at Walnut Tree, first to Penrhos Upper Junction in the Nantgarw Gap south-west of Caerphilly (opened 1 August 1901) to draw off traffic from the Rhymney Valley including that of the LNWR, and then (2 January 1905) from Penrhos Lower Junction right across the Rhymney Valley to join the Brecon & Merthyr above Bedwas, and so to penetrate what was then technically England.

Because it could not follow the floors of the valleys but had either to cross them, or in the case of the Rhondda main line to use a back way along higher ground, the Barry lines involved some heavy engineering. North of Wenvoe station was the Wenvoe Tunnel (1m 108yd), and between Treforest (BR) and Pontypridd another of 1,373yd, while the later lines into and across the Rhymney Valley involved huge and lengthy steel-on-masonry viaducts at Walnut Tree, Penyrheol, and Llanbradach, the last-named structure being 2,400ft long and 125ft high. Several distinguished engineers shared responsibility for design and construction: Sir John Wolfe Barry, Henry Marc Brunel (son of I. K. Brunel, over or against whose South Wales and Taff Vale Railways of some half-century earlier, the Barry was to run), and Sir James W. Szlumper, who engineered the difficult section from Trehafod southward.

Including the Cogan and Barry Island branches yet to be described, and the nominally independent Vale of Glamorgan Railway worked as part of the Barry system, the Barry's total route mileage amounted to just under sixty-eight miles, with a track mileage of 300.

The Barry venture could not be other than successful; its promoters were able to exploit so many advantages. Its docks were further 'down ocean' than Newport and Cardiff; it sometimes paid shipowners to call in for bunkering en route to the Mersey even if they had no cargo to or from South Wales. There was no burden of old, inadequate quays or appliances as at Cardiff, and – of paramount importance – there was no confusion of authority or complication of dock traffic working; the Barry Company controlled the lot. More than three million tons of coal were shipped in over 1,700 ships in 1890, in which year the company paid ten per cent on its ordinary shares, this dividend being paid without a break from 1894 to 1897, while between 1913 and 1920 it never fell below 9½ per cent. In the peak year of 1913 before World War I Barry, now the leading port, shipped eleven million of the thirty-seven million tons exported from South Wales. No wonder David Davies had modestly assured a Commons Committee during the hearing of one of the Barry Bills, 'We have five million tons of coal, and can fill a thundering good dock the first day we open it.'

THE TAFF VALE FIGHTS BACK

The TVR, which had reacted sharply to the impending start of the Barry's operations by an anticipatory reduction in rates, suffered a severe initial setback in the years immediately following, its net revenues for 1890 and 1891 being less than the 1888 figure by £110,000 and £135,000 respectively. The Taff Vale fought back vigorously, in hard-contested battles before Parliamentary Committees and the Railway & Canal Commission, the latter once reducing an award to the TVR because of 'fallacious and inaccurate' arguments, and requiring it to pay half the Barry's costs. Another battle concerned the area between Penarth and Barry, and consequently access to Cardiff via the GWR. On 20 February 1878 the TVR opened the Penarth Extension Railway up a mile of 1 in 40 to Penarth Town, and in 1885 the company promoted Bills for acquiring the Bute Docks and for building – through a nominally independent Cardiff, Penarth & Barry Junction Railway – a direct Penarth–Barry line, with a coastal loop through Sully. The Barry riposted with a direct Barry–Penarth line. The outcome was withdrawal of the Taff's Bute Docks Bill after the Lords Committee had insisted on extensive Barry running powers over the TVR, failure of the CP & BJ direct line, but Royal Assent on 31 July 1885 for the Barry's line, to join the TVR at Cogan. Sole Taff success was the CP & BJR Act of 6 August 1885, authorising the 4¾-mile coastal loop from Penarth Town to Biglis Junction on the Barry's new line (the CP & BJR) vesting in the TVR by Act of 1889). The Barry's Act of

1888 protected its docks traffic by effectively restricting TVR use of the CP & BJ to local traffic; that done, it opened its own line to Cogan on 20 December 1888, bringing itself within three miles of Cardiff. The coastal loop opened to Lavernock on 1 December 1887; the remainder, intended for 5 December 1887, was delayed by the Barry refusing access to Biglis Junction station, some 700yd west of the loop junction with the BR. The TVR thereupon opened a temporary platform at Biglis, east of the junction, from 8 July 1889, not connected with Barry services. By various ploys, including at least two hearings of the Railway Commissioners, TVR trains were not allowed over the junction and into the station until 22 May 1890, when the platform closed; ten days later the junction station was renamed Cadoxton.

THE CARDIFF RAILWAY

It is time to return to the mixed fortunes of the Bute Docks Company, with problems of increasing trade, congestion, old docks and a heavy capital burden insufficiently remunerated. Notwithstanding the Barry impact, Cardiff's trade continued to grow, due to general expansion of the coal trade. Between 1885–1914 the output of the South Wales coalfield increased steadily from 24¾ million tons to over 50 million tons in 1913. Over the same period the TVR, which eventually had some eighty collieries connected with its system either directly or over private lines, increased its coal and coke carryings from around nine million tons to over nineteen million tons. In a single week of November 1893, following the mine-hauliers' strike in August, it moved 281,416 tons, involving 70,000 wagon movements. So great was the demand for South Wales coal that some overseas customers, such as the Italian State Railways, maintained permanent buying offices in Cardiff. In the context of the present state of the mining industry, it seems almost incredible to recall that between 1888-98 the collieries were stopped on the first Monday of each month, in order to restrict production and to give both miners and railwaymen a rest. This practice was secured through the efforts of the great miners' leader, the Rt Hon William Abraham MP ('Mabon') for better wages, hours and conditions, culminating in the six months' strike of 1898 and the granting of the minimum wage in 1903 and the legislation for an eight-hour day in 1909.

It was not therefore surprising that the Bute Docks Company felt that the main solution to its problems lay in going out to fetch the coal itself instead of merely tipping that brought down by the railways. An early attempt by the TVR to acquire the Bute Docks by amalgamation (inspired by the imminent opening of Barry) failed in 1888, although the terms for exchange of capital would have been very advantageous to the railway company. Next in 1896 came the legislation whereby the Glamorganshire and Aberdare canals were acquired by the Bute interests, but less successful were proposals for far-reaching running powers over various South Wales railways, including even the Brecon & Merthyr, while a separate abortive Bill proposed the amalgamation of the Rhymney Railway and the Bute Docks companies, the dissolution of the former, and the change of the dock company's name to the Cardiff Railway Company.

The Rhymney take-over having been dropped, the change of name was authorised by the Cardiff Railway Act of 6 August 1897; that Act, with one of 12 August 1898 (varied by Act of 1906), together authorised a railway system from Roath on the east side of Cardiff, intersecting, and making a junction with, the RR at Heath, and thence through the Walnut Tree Gap into the Taff Vale to join the TVR at Treforest. Of the twenty-plus miles authorised, only the nine miles from the junction with the RR to Treforest were ever built, and completed in 1909; the sad story of the Treforest Junction fiasco belongs to the next chapter. Even while the new railway was being built, the TVR brought forward proposals to acquire by amalgamation both the Cardiff and Rhymney Railway Companies, the offer for the Cardiff shares being £1.3 million less than the nominal capital. The first Bill in the session of 1909 was tenaciously fought by both the Barry (which would have been left in almost isolated competition with the TVR in the latter's proposed new form), and by Newport interests, but the 1909 scheme failed to pass the Commons and was dropped in the following year.

In 1913, the greatest-ever year of the South Wales coal shipping trade, the Cardiff Railway Company's annual report provided for a dividend of only two per cent on £2.9 million ordinary stock Notwithstanding a capital expenditure of more than £711,000 the working of the company's railways allowed a deficit of £2,655 (net receipts from docks working were £213,000), while the report recorded that a Bill for increased charging powers had been rejected on third reading. All this in spite of a total import and export tonnage of nearly 13 million tons having been dealt with through Cardiff Docks, an increase of 1-2 million tons over 1912.

CARDIFF STATIONS

The first passenger station was the TVR's 'Cardiff', opened 8 October 1840, situated near the later Queen Street Up platform; through freight lines continued a mile further to Cardiff Docks (Bute Road from 1924), first in *Bradshaw* in April 1845 (but footnote, 'Company's carriage' connection, December 1844). After the GWR gauge conversion, with through running via Bute Street Junction, 'Cardiff TVR' was rebuilt in 1887 as 'Queen Street'. The Rhymney's original 'Adam Street' closed when its passenger service moved on 1 April 1871 to a new 'terminus', 'Crockherbtown' ('Cardiff (Rhymney)' from 1888 and 'Parade' from 1924) across the road from Queen Street. The latter had only two through platforms and a bay until 1928 but nevertheless dealt with astonishing volumes of traffic before the motor-car era, commuting 16,000 passengers daily during the week in nearly 200 regular trains, of which some twenty-five each way ran through to or from the GWR. On high days and holidays as many as fifty extra trains used Queen Street.

Under the GWR, Parade station was closed from 15 April 1928 and its trains diverted into Queen Street, which was enlarged to a total of five platforms to accommodate the Rhymney trains and the railmotor service which the Cardiff Railway had launched in 1911 between Cardiff (using the RR station) and Rhydyfelin Halt in Taff Vale, and which on 20 July 1931 was cut back to Coryton.

In the 1970s Queen Street had again been rebuilt with a single island platform and a terminal bay; the head offices of the TVR which adjoined it on its west side have been demolished to make way for property development, while on the east side the station is now flanked by the modern office building, Brunel House. To the east and south of this building are the relics of the former RR and TVR branches to the docks, which in bygone days witnessed an almost continuous procession of freight trains. Brunel House was purpose-built as the headquarters of the abortive British Rail territorial organisation abandoned in 1974, and until 1984 housed the headquarters staff of the Western Region Cardiff Division for the whole of South and SW Wales, together with a slice of England up to Hereford.

CARDIFF CENTRAL

Cardiff's principal station, on the same site since 1850, is the Great Western's 'Cardiff General', Cardiff Central since 7 May 1973, and displaying the Welsh alternative, *Caerdydd Canalog*, in the current bilingual pattern. Occupying what the estate agents would doubtless call 'a much-favoured central position between the industrial, commercial and residential districts of the capital', the station lies immediately eastward of the main line's crossing of the River Taff. In its latest form dating from 1932 after successive rebuildings, the station comprises three long island platforms (six working faces) connected by subway, with two through roads primarily for freight trains. In 1980, with the Swansea-Cardiff-London service by HST introduced in October 1976 and then working to better-than-hourly frequency, and with the intensive Coast-Valleys diesel multiple unit service, the number of trains handled on weekdays was around 150; some 5,000 commuters daily travelled to and from the Cardiff stations

THE RIVERSIDE BRANCH

After yet another of their perennial altercations, this time over access to Cardiff via Cogan Junction and the TVR's junction with the GWR at Penarth Curve South Junction, the Barry, Taff Vale and GWR reached a compromise settlement in 1894 whereby the GWR agreed to convert its Riverside freight branch of 1882 for passenger operation, and to admit thereto the respective passenger trains of both local companies from and to Penarth and Barry. (The Taff Vale was already working over the GWR through Cardiff and beyond, using the notorious Bute Street Junction until in 1896 it was supplemented by the present flyover east of the Central Station). Barry trains began to use Riverside Station, as it was then separately known, on 14 August 1893, and were extended to Clarence Road in dockland on 2 April the following year. This helped to cater for the rapidly growing commuter, shopping and commercial traffic between the coast stations and Cardiff, and in the development of both Penarth and Barry as seaside resorts – Penarth considering itself somewhat socially superior to Barry in this respect. The Barry train service between Pontypridd and Cardiff via the St Fagan's connection with the GWR, introduced June 1897, also used Clarence Road to some extent.

Upon the 1932 Cardiff General rebuilding, Riverside station became an island platform, Nos 8/9, though it remained 'Riverside' until amalgamated with General on 28 October 1940. With integration of the Cardiff–Coast services into the Valleys services via Queen

Street, for which the first DMU workings began in January 1958, the Riverside Branch closed, for passengers, and freight (excl to Curran's Siding), on 16 March 1964, and incl Curran's Siding on 8 July 1968. The island 'Riverside' platforms have since been used for parcels traffic.

BARRY ISLAND AND PIER

Barry quickly outshone Penarth as a trippers' Mecca after the Barry Railway took powers by Act of 17 August 1894 to construct a ¾-mile extension from Barry Town, across the causeway enclosing the Old Harbour, to Barry Island, which it reached by climbing at 1 in 80 from the bottom of the causeway dip. This was a standard gauge branch, in substitution of a passenger tramway authorised in the Barry's Act of 1893 but not proceeded with. The new works included enlargement of Barry station and a single platform Barry Island station (additional platform by May 1914). The branch opened on 3 August 1896 for the Bank Holiday; four days later the company obtained an Act to extend it for a further ½-mile down at 1 in 80 through a 280yd tunnel to Barry Pier. The Pier station, opened on 27 July 1899, was never used by regular passenger services, but soon became popular with Bristol Channel steamers, notably those with the famous P&A Campbell fleet, so that a big pleasure traffic developed. The Barry was encouraged to try its hand at running steamers itself, taking powers to do so under the Barry Railway (Steam Vessels) Act of 15 August 1904.

Four steel paddle-steamers were purchased. In 1905 *Gwalia* and *Devonia*, 519 and 641 gross tons, arrived from John Brown's Yard, Clydebank. *Rhos Colwyn*, 393 tons, third-hand, built 1899, followed, being renamed *Westonia*. But so many restrictions had been imposed by the Act upon the scope of voyages, and the points between which passengers could be carried, that the steamers made a substantial loss, notwithstanding the formation of a nominally separate operating company, and powers in 1907 to subscribe to the Burnham (Somerset) Pier Company. That year the fourth steamer arrived new from Brown's, *Barry*, 471 tons. By 1909 the Barry had to admit failure and the steamers were sold, *Gwalia* to the Furness Railway and the others to a Bristol company.

Campbell steamers continued to call at Barry Pier for many years, the last occasion being in the summer of 1971. By then the branch had been singled (Pier–Barry Island, 1929; Island–Barry Town,

June 1969). The final 'seasonal' passenger train to the Pier ran on 18 October 1971, though railtours continued until April 1973, the Pier extension going out of use in July 1976. In addition to the remaining regular DMU service, many excursions ran to Barry Island (much patronised in recent years by enthusiasts visiting the 'graveyard' of British Rail steam locomotives nearby, and from which much resurrection was to come) but the glamour had departed of the days when LNWR/LMS 0–8–0 goods locomotive worked through from Abergavenny, and one could hear the sigh of a Westinghouse Pump on a visiting RR locomotive.

Indeed, little remains of the once busy and prosperous Barry Railway system except the coast line to Cogan Junction and the Vale of Glamorgan line, and it is largely upon past triumphs that the statue of Dai Davies gazes down from its position outside the impressive docks office building, which shareholders alleged had cost £50,000 and which was restored in 1985 following a severe fire. But surely there can be no regrets at the Barry Company's contribution to railway history.

CHAPTER VII

The Cardiff Valleys

After grouping the GWR established and maintained for many years a 'Cardiff Valleys Division', a traffic management unit comprising mainly the former Taff Vale and Rhymney Railways together with parts of neighbouring systems. This unit also forms a convenient geographical basis for describing this part of the network, continuing the east-to-west pattern of the narrative so as to begin with the Rhymney Valley, the railways of which also afforded links with (but on occasion barriers against) the railways of Monmouthshire to the east, those of the Taff and Aberdare Valleys to the west, and the industrial conurbation of Merthyr-Dowlais to the north.

The Rhymney Railway which threaded the valley of that name from end to end enjoyed, or suffered, a remarkable number of connections with other railway companies; the former verb is on balance more apposite since the penetrators' tolls added substantially to RR revenues, while the RR itself was able to intrude into valuable new sources of traffic. Conversely, the Rhymney which for years nursed an ambition to get to Newport, but eventually had to help the PC & N to do so (Chapter V) actually extracted £10,000 a year from Paddington's pockets for some years from 1889 onwards, as a moiety of the GWR's traffic between Monmouthshire and Cardiff, in consideration of the RR giving up its Bill of 1888 for access to the Monmouthshire Valleys.

Because its main line extension of 1871 from Caerphilly to Cardiff could follow no river valley, there was some heavy climbing, at a ruling grade of 1 in 80, from the Welsh capital up to the tunnel through the mountain south of Caerphilly. From its arrival in 1858 on its original route down to the TVR at Walnut Tree until 1865 when junction was made with the B & M branch from Machen, the RR had Caerphilly to itself, but then in succession came the PC & N to Penrhos Junction (with running powers through Caerphilly and on to the B & M), the RR's own branch north-westward to Senghenydd, completed in 1894, and the two junctions made by the Barry Railway, first of all at Penrhos Upper Junction (1901) to exchange traffic with the RR and LNWR at Aber Junction, and later in 1905 from Penrhos Lower Junction passing to the west of Caerphilly and then turning eastward across the valley to join the B & M. With the addition of various inter-connecting loops, Caerphilly became the nexus of the RR system, with lines radiating in all directions except to the north-east, a gap which would have been filled by the B & M had its application for powers to make a branch from Bedwas to Caerphilly been successful.

By the early years of the present century, especially after the transfer in 1901 of the Rhymney's locomotive works to a site east of the present passenger station, and with five million tons of coal annually passing through Aber marshalling yard and other groups of sidings, the locomotives or railmotors of seven different railways could be seen in and around Caerphilly, making it one of the busiest railway centres in South Wales.

STATIONS AT CAERPHILLY

With the opening of its line to Cardiff in 1871 the RR abandoned its first Caerphilly passenger station behind the pub near the original direct line down to Walnut Tree, although the latter line remained busy because the RR obtained running powers by this route to Radyr for the exchange of Penarth Dock traffic, including that off the LNWR. The new passenger station on the Cardiff line at the south end of Caerphilly town was for many years not much thought of, as it had only two platforms and was quite inadequate to cope with some seventy passenger train departures a day by 1913, as well as a heavy freight traffic. None too soon, and in association with some four-tracking and new signalling, the station was enlarged in 1913 to four through platforms and a bay. The Barry Railway could have had a regular passenger service into Caerphilly had it been agreeable to the Rhymney's demand that the Barry would be admitted only if it subscribed towards the station enlargement, but occasional excursions were in fact run by the Barry beginning with the visit of King Edward VII to Caerphilly in 1907.

In the 1980s two through platforms sufficed for the regular-interval diesel multiple-unit service, and most of the freight traffic

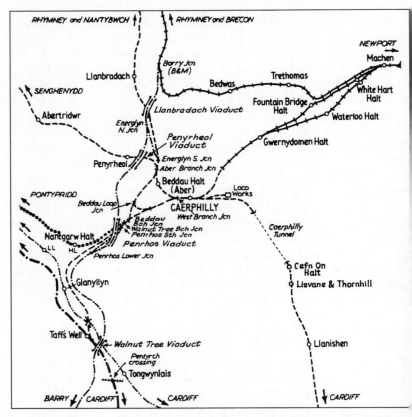

passed via Radyr, the station having been refurbished in the 1970s as
a joint rail-and-bus exchange, with modern passenger facilities.

Within the half-century since the railway grouping, the
Caerphilly network has been progressively reduced by the elimination of connecting curves and junctions, and by the withdrawal of
all services on the Pontypridd-Machen axis, and earlier from the
Barry Railway's route of 1905 across the Rhymney Valley to join the
Brecon & Merthyr. The Railways Act of 1921 swept away a mass of
statutory running powers and restrictive agreements which had
hitherto governed the routing of traffic, the enlarged GWR being
thus free to use what routes it pleased within its system. Adding to
this the decline in coal shipping traffic after World War I, a reported
threat of mining subsidence to the viaducts, and the attraction of
cost savings, the GWR obtained powers in 1926 to abandon nearly
three miles of line between Penrhos Lower Junction and Duffryn

Isaf. This involved the demolition of the viaducts at Penrhos, Penyrheol (over the Rhymney's Senghenydd Branch) and Llanbradach. It was not until 1937, eleven years after obtaining powers of abandonment, that the two latter structures were demolished, the great steel girders being sent crashing to the valley floor to be cut-up where they lay; the GWR stated that Llanbradach alone yielded more than 3,000 tons of steel scrap.

SENGHENYDD

The Rhymney's Senghenydd Branch from Aber Branch Junction up through the Aber Valley to the site of the Cornish *émigré* St Cenydd's ancient retreat at the valley's head below Mynydd Eglwysilan was just over three miles long, rising most of the way at 1 in 49, and single-track above Abertridwr.

The branch, authorised in 1890 and opened on 1 February 1894, lost its passenger service on 15 June 1964, nearly two years after withdrawal of public freight facilities, but remained in use until early 1977 to serve Windsor Colliery, ¾ mile short of Senghenydd (Senghenith until 1904), which closed when the National Coal Board began to wind the Windsor coal up through Nantgarw Colliery in the Taff Vale a few miles to the west. It may be added that in 1896 the Barry Railway had obtained powers, but never exercised them, to make a short connection off its Rhymney Valley line to Senghenydd Branch at Penyrheol.

RHYMNEY VALLEY CONNECTIONS

Resuming its course beyond Caerphilly into the Rhymney Valley, the RR made five important connections with other companies in less than ten miles between Aber Junction and Bargoed. The first, immediately north of Aber Junction, was at Energlyn Junction with a spur off the Barry's Rhymney Branch, used mainly for exchange of coal, coke and pitwood to and from the last-named, and to a small extent for other traffic brought down from the Old Rumney line by Brecon & Merthyr locomotives. From Energlyn to Bargoed, the RR and B & M lines kept company on either side of the valley with the river between them, a situation which could on occasion lead (curves or no curves) to a certain amount of rivalry between respective drivers, there being no station on either line for several miles.

At Penalltau Branch Junction, Ystrad Mynach, the Rhymney in

1871 threw off a short but vitally important connection westward to
the Pontypool-Aberdare-Neath lateral route of the GWR. This
branch, and associated running powers over the GWR, gave access
to the two important GWR/RR joint lines to Dowlais (the Taff-
Bargoed Joint, opened 1876) and to Merthyr (the Quakers' Yard &
Merthyr Joint, opened 1886), both built through alliance of the two
companies in competition with the TVR. A third important advantage which accrued to the RR from this partnership was the grant of
running powers through Middle Duffryn to Hirwain Iron Works at
the far top end of the Aberdare Valley, although in practice these
powers were never exercised west of Middle Duffryn.

With all these important flows of traffic, including the Aberdare
coal trains of the GWR bound for Newport via the Sirhowy Valley –
and probably passing en route LNWR trains bringing coal from the
Monmouthshire pits en route to the RR via Ystrad Mynach! – the
former NA & H line as between Quakers' Yard and the Tredegar
Junctions (Pontllanfraith) became in its heyday one of the most
densely occupied in South Wales.

At Ystrad Mynach the RR also threw off a two-mile branch of its
own, the Cylla Branch, diving under the GWR and going up to
Penrhiwfelin; it was opened in sections between 1906-9, and
remained open until last clearance of coal following closure of
Penallta Colliery on 8 November 1991. At Hengoed, immediately
north of Ystrad Mynach, there were also two other connections with
the GWR.

BARGOED

Beyond Hengoed the RR and the Old Rumney became very close
together (physically but not in any spirit of comradeship), the junction between the two railways – the Old Rumney being by then part
of the B & M – being made immediately south of the RR's Bargoed
Station. At the latter the RR divided, the main line continuing up
the west bank of the river to Rhymney town, whence it continued
under joint ownership with the LNWR on to Rhymney Bridge and
Nantybwch, while the Bargoed Rhymney branch bore left into the
valley of that name to make an end-on junction with the Brecon &
Merthyr's Northern Section coming down from Dowlais. In the
narrow part of the main valley above Bargoed, the RR encountered
heavier gradients than between Caerphilly and Bargoed, the final
approach to Rhymney ($23^3/_4$ miles from Cardiff) being at 1 in 82.

Intermediately near Tirphil the RR managed, like the Barry further south at Duffryn Isaf but in this instance in the face of bitter opposition from the B & M, to penetrate for a few yards on to 'English' soil by means of a short branch across the river to serve the New Tredegar and McLaren pits. Above these collieries the Old Rumney line terminated about a mile lower down the valley than the RR station, at a junction with the Rhymney Iron Company's private line. The ironworks in this area were being phased out by the 1890s and industrial production concentrated on coal.

The Old Rumney on the east bank suffered landslips. During single-line working on 9 October 1928 following a slip near New Tredegar a passenger train collided with a colliers' train; one passenger was killed. Line reinstatement being uneconomic, New Tredegar (excl)–McLaren's Colliery (excl) was closed completely from 14 April 1930 and taken out of use that September. McLaren's Colliery (excl)–Rhymney Lower was lifted after 1 March 1933. From September 1930 the colliery was served from the Tirphil connection (closed November 1976) against which the B & M had fought so strenuously. Passenger and goods services to New Tredegar on the Old Rumney (progressively singled from 1934) ceased with line closure on 31 December 1962.

Returning to Bargoed, the branch up the Bargoed Rhymney Valley towards Dowlais Top, forming part of the B & M through route between Newport and Brecon, was completed on 1 September 1868 as a compromise between the rival aspirations of the former company and the RR to obtain access from the Rhymney Valley to Dowlais and beyond. After much expense and tribulation the Rhymney built the first 2¼ miles from Bargoed North Junction to the end-on junction with the B & M at Deri, and the B & M the remainder northward. The B & M had running powers for through traffic between Deri and the Junction with the Old Rumney section below Bargoed, while the RR enjoyed running powers up to Fochriew and Pantywaun for freight. The competitive confusion in and around Bargoed would have been even greater had the Barry Railway succeeded in its efforts during the first decade of the present century to exploit its good relations with the B & M by making a connecting line from the Old Rumney below Bargoed to by-pass the RR and rejoin the B & M north of Deri Junction, which would have involved major bridgework over both the B & M and the RR, a tunnel at the lower end of the Bargoed Rhymney Valley, and a ruling gradient of 1 in 43. (The Barry's 'good relations' with the B & M stemmed partly from a substantial subvention to the doubling of part of the latter's Rhymney Branch).

Above Bargoed in the main valley, the former RR line between Bargoed North Junction and Rhymney is now singled, while the erstwhile LNWR/RR Joint Line on to Rhymney Bridge was closed on 23 September 1953. The Bargoed–Pant Branch closed to passengers on 31 December 1962, and freight, Pant–Deri Junction, 1 April 1963, and to Bargoed North Junction 23 August 1965; the Ogilvie Colliery line lasted until 3 September 1978. After August 1971 the former B & M (Old Rumney) southwards from Bargoed extended for only 1½ miles to Britannia Colliery, being abandoned down to Bedwas Colliery. This section closed 9 January 1977, coal wound at Britannia being transferred via NCB tracks for loading at Bargoed washery, thence to BR metals at Bargoed Pits Junction, closed 23 May 1982.

RAILWAYS IN TAFF VALE

Thanks to the Walnut Tree Gap through the Southern Outcrop at river level, the Taff Vale Railway enjoyed an easier exit from Cardiff than its neighbour the RR, the gradients rising gently, though steeper towards Merthyr. Engineering features were reverse curves round river bends between Radyr and Treforest and the short Ynyscoi Tunnel ¾-mile above Taff's Well, opened out when Cardiff–Navigation House (Abercynon) was doubled, 1846–48. Works between Navigation House and Quakers' Yard included an easterly sweep to avoid the Glamorganshire Canal, a half-mile inclined plane rising towards Merthyr in almost equal proportions at 1 in 20¾ and 1 in 18, and a 144yd tunnel preceding a 120yd-long masonry viaduct over the Taff. From 21 April 1841 trains left Merthyr twenty minutes after Cardiff departures, arrivals coinciding at top and bottom of the incline, the carriages passing each other by rope haulage, powered by a 50hp stationary engine, on the only double track, except sidings, on the entire railway; three passenger trains ran each way daily (the middle pair also conveying goods vehicles), finishing by mid afternoon, when the mineral traffic started. Incline Top station, opened 1845, closed on opening Quakers' Yard station in January 1858; the tunnel was abolished when by TVR Act of 1857 the line and viaduct were widened by 1863. Responding to increased traffic and competition, which rendered its operation inefficient, the incline was superseded in mid 1867 on opening of an adjacent locomotive-worked line with 1 in 40 gradient, no doubt a relief to the crew of the early morning Cardiff–Merthyr mail on Sundays before the stationary engine was working – the train from Cardiff waited at the bottom while fireman and guard lugged all the mailbags up the hill and loaded them into the train for Merthyr waiting at the top...

There were other problems on the Taff main line, deriving from a combination of geography, early lack of capital to improve capacity, and eventual tremendous increase in train movements. Following line doubling from 1846 onwards, until after the 1857 Act trains ran on the right-hand track. Two particular engines (plus one spare) worked the passenger traffic for the first decade, one being apparently stationed at Merthyr (train crews switched to mineral working in the afternoon/evening); otherwise it seems locomotives were stationed at the Cardiff end. As traffic grew, the main line was quadrupled through to Pontypridd, but the location of Crockherbtown Yard on the Down (east) side, and of the lines to the docks, dictated that the goods lines be on the east side as far as Llandaff, 4¼ miles from Cardiff. Of necessity the 5-mile Roath Branch, authorised by 1885 Act, opened 23 April 1888 round the east side of Cardiff to Roath Dock, also made its junction on the east side. But at Llandaff it was essential to carry the freight lines over the passenger lines on the level, and to connect them by a spur into the Radyr Yards; thereafter, the goods lines remained on the up side all the way to Pontypridd. A working timetable of 1897 shows 190 passenger and freight trains traversing the Llandaff Junctions in a normal working day. The Roath Branch was closed on 6 May 1968, most of its course having since been absorbed by highway development.

AN HISTORIC CROSSING

There was another operating problem in this area. At Pentyrch Crossing, a mile short of Walnut Tree, Taff's Well, all four tracks were intersected diagonally by a private railway, originally built as a tramroad about 1815 to connect industrial plants at Pentyrch and Melingriffith, some two miles apart. The industrial railway continued to be used until about 1959, the level-crossing being taken out in 1962.

Passing through the gap at Walnut Tree, the Barry's great viaduct of that name, 130ft high and 1,548ft long, no longer dwarfs its old enemy on the valley floor; all but one of the piers which had supported the steel girders were demolished in 1973, after the girders themselves had been removed in 1969. The Cardiff Railway on the east side of the TVR survived north of Coryton until 1952 to serve Nantgarw Colliery, but became derelict after the opening of the NCB Nantgarw by-products plant, and of a new connection off the TVR main line, which uses a bit of the old CR formation.

GHOST LINES AT TREFOREST

At Treforest Junction and the L & TV junction, some dozen miles from Cardiff, three railways made connection with the TVR main line. Two of these joined up the Up side and climbed westward out of the valley, the earlier being the nominally independent Llantrissant (sic) & Taff Vale Junction Railway, incorporated 1861 (p173) to develop the territory to the west of the TVR, and to help keep others out! It was opened for freight traffic in 1863 and for passengers two years later, being leased and worked by the Taff Vale Railway. Closely parallel with the L & TVJR in its steep descent to Treforest Junction, was the unwelcome Barry Railway freight connection from Tonteg Junction, opened in 1889.

Into this already busy scene at Treforest – Ammon Beasley was to claim in evidence a line occupation of some 450 movements a day – there intruded in 1909 the Cardiff Railway in pursuit of its authorised junction of 1897, driving up from Heath Junction and through the Walnut Tree Gap, parallel with the TVR on the latter's eastern flank, a double line of railway involving twenty-seven bridges, eleven cuttings, and the 108yd Castell Coch or Tongwynlais Tunnel, in some nine miles. The siting of the junction was disputed by the TVR and Barry on grounds of interference with traffic, there being inadequate room for CR coal trains to split for Cardiff and Barry destinations without shunting on the Taff main line, prohibited under the 1897 Act. The Taff unsuccessfully sought powers in 1902-3 for a connection with the Cardiff near Taff's Well, which would have increased Taff revenue while rendering nugatory the CR to the north. In 1906 the Cardiff obtained an Act which it believed solved the junction problem, only to be warned by its two opponents it did not. When arbitration seemed to favour the CR, the Taff produced a master-stroke. Knowing the Rhymney was not averse to amalgamation, and that the over-stretched CR might also be so disposed, it concluded agreements with them to that purpose. During hearings of the two amalgamation Bills in May 1909, the Taff laid in a temporary junction at Treforest. The engineering climax of the new Cardiff Railway as it approached this junction was a 512ft-long steel girder lattice bridge of two 117ft and two 111ft skew spans across the River Taff and a road, reputed to have cost £30,000. Over this bridge on 15 May, in a show of amity with the Taff, and with the young Marquis of Bute riding triumphantly on his own locomotive ahead of twelve wagons of coal from his collieries for shipment from his docks, there rumbled and hooted the only revenue train to cross the Rhydyfelin or Treforest Viaduct.

For in August the Taff/Cardiff vesting Bill failed and on 12 October 1909 the TVR's engineer was instructed to remove the junction. Despite further negotiations it was not reinstated. No longer financially strong, the Cardiff found marginal consolation with a Cardiff–Rhydyfelin railmotor service, public opening being on 1 March 1911 (p130).

PLOT AND COUNTER-PLOT

All this plot and counter-plot came to a head in the High Court in the summer of 1916, when Mr Justice Astbury decided against the claim of the TVR that the Cardiff's notice to treat for a portion of TVR land, required for the making of the junction at Treforest, was invalid. On the matter being taken by the TVR to appeal in November of the same year, the Master of the Rolls decided that the notice to treat was bad, holding that while the Cardiff's Act allowed it to get across the tracks of the TVR to join the latter's freight lines, he 'was not prepared to hold that the Cardiff Railway could select the more burdensome mode of doing so'. Despite the Government's wartime control of the railways, there was of course nothing to prevent one railway company suing another in the middle of World War I, but while these learned arguments were going on, British Army losses in the deadly Battle of the Somme had exceeded 400,000; over 19,000 British soldiers had died on 1 July alone.

So for the Cardiff Railway, all was to no purpose. The junction at Treforest was never effective, and in the following year E.A. Prosser of the Rhymney became joint general manager of that company and of the Cardiff and Taff Vale as well, C.S. Denniss, the Cardiff's general manager, resigning.

It took the demand for steel in another World War a quarter-century later to bring about the demolition of the Cardiff Railway's Rhydyfelin Viaduct, producing 1,150 tons of metal, to write *finis* to this story of yet another railway that never really got there. Only a crumbling embankment and a line of trees now mark the site of this abortive junction at Treforest, but there are ghosts on the other side of the tracks, too. In 1930 the GWR made a connection between the former Barry main line and the TVR Llantrisant Branch where the former passed under the latter near Tonteg Junction, enabling the Barry line solely to be used down to Treforest Junction, and abandoning the former TVR connection at Llantrisant Branch Junction. The Barry passenger trains, Cadoxton–Porth, and Cardiff (via St Fagans)–Pontypridd, went by the TVR route from 10 July 1930, the stations at Treforest (High Level) and Pontypridd (Graig) closing concurrently. The Llantrisant–Pontypridd passenger service was withdrawn on 31 March 1952, and the former Barry services on 10 September 1962. Following the burning down of Tynycaeau North signal box, Tynycaeau North–Walnut Tree West and Cadoxton South–Tonteg Junction closed on 31 March 1963, freight being diverted via Radyr and Penarth. The final end to the Treforest junctions came on 28 September 1964 with the taking out of use of the line to Cwm Colliery.

PONTYPRIDD

Thirteen miles distant from Cardiff and situated at the confluence of the Taff and Rhondda rivers, this was both geographically and in terms of railway operation, the nub and focal point of the TVR system, where the mineral flow from the Rhondda Valley was phased into those from the Aberdare Valley and the Merthyr-Dowlais areas, bound variously for Cardiff, Penarth, Newport and Barry. Yet it was never a great marshalling centre; there was no room to spare for yards where the valleys joined, and the sensible pattern was to make up through trains to and from these three principal sources. Nor when the need for one arose was there room for a locomotive shed, which was established a mile up the Rhondda Valley at Coke Ovens.

It was at Pontypridd on 16 August 1837 that the life of the TVR began with the ceremonial laying of the first stone by Lady Charlotte Guest, wife of the company chairman, – a pleasant variation on the traditional sod-cutting – at the site of Brunel's skew

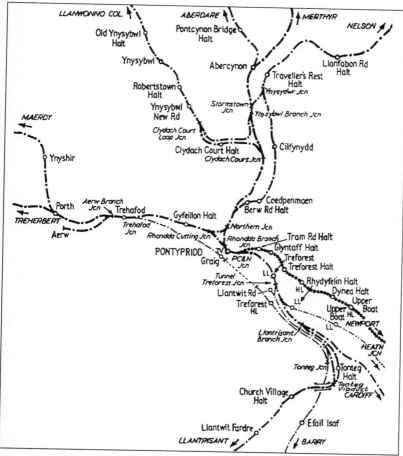

stone arch bridge at 110ft span, over the River Rhondda. Pontypridd station (Newbridge Junction until March 1866) developed from, initially, two platforms and two trains each way daily (three from 24 October 1840) until, following its 1907 reconstruction, it dealt with some 11,000 passengers a day at seven platform faces: a main island platform and five inset bays for local branch services. The total area was 8,205sq yd of which all but 835sq yd was roofed over; points and signals required 230 levers. With frequent through trains and constant interchange with branch services, it was always busy, and on Saturday nights (especially after big football matches) proceedings tended to become uproariously vocal, with the English tongue a poor second...

With the new pattern of diesel multiple-unit services and the general 'rationalisation' in the Cardiff Valleys, the use of the station (excluding the separate goods lines still on the Up side) was reduced in 1970 to the Up (west) face of the island platform only, for passenger trains in either direction; for some years it was the longest platform in the Western Region of British Railways. In conjunction with colour-light re-signalling under the control of a single box at Pontypridd, a tidying-up of station passenger facilities was carried out between 1970–76, embracing not only Pontypridd but most of the forty-six stations on the various lines from Cardiff into the valleys, and along the coast to Barry and Penarth. (See also Chapter XII).

A feature of traffic operation at Pontypridd from October 1872 was a triangle formed by the diverging Rhondda and Merthyr routes in conjunction with a short connecting line between them (the North Curve, linking Rhondda Cutting Junction on the Rhondda Branch with Pontypridd North Junction on the main line). This not only catered for direct freight movements between the Rhondda and the Aberdare and Merthyr routes (not all the coal traffic necessarily went to the sea), but to ease the working at Pontypridd passenger station, was used for reversing branch passenger trains. It was in the course of one such operation on 19 October 1878 that an empty passenger train which was backing on the wrong road from the North Junction to Rhondda Cutting Junction (whence it would be in the right direction to return to the passenger station, locomotive leading) collided at the Cutting Junction with a Down Rhondda passenger train, causing thirteen fatal casualties. The North Curve was finally closed on 5 August 1968.

Only half a-mile or so north of Rhondda Cutting Junction there occurred another serious collision, at Coke Ovens on 23 January 1911, when a Down passenger train ran into the rear of a loaded coal train, and eleven people were killed.

Two other pre-grouping railways had passenger stations at Pontypridd. Until 1922, when the GWR having taken over began to admit users of the former PC & N and ADR Caerphilly local service to the main station, they had to cross the river to the latter's previous terminal at Tram Road Motor Halt, which was accordingly closed on 10 July 1922. More important was the Pontypridd (Graig) Station of the Barry Railway, a simple two-platform affair tucked away in the hilly part of the town at the north end of the 1,323yd Treforest (or Pontypridd) Tunnel. This station was used both by the

Barry-Porth service introduced on 16 March 1896 with running powers into the TVR station at Porth (Rhondda), and by the Barry's trains begun on 7 June of the following year between Pontypridd and Cardiff (Clarence Road); the running powers into Porth were not applicable to this latter service, whose existence was a source of great irritation to the TVR, hence the following anecdote. This was related to me by a GWR official, whose father was the TVR station-master at Pontypridd at the time. In order to monitor the Barry's traffic between Pontypridd and Cardiff the schoolboy son was required each Monday morning to pass by the Barry Station and (with money from the TVR till, duly accounted for on the appropriate form), purchase a ticket to Cardiff which was never used but put in an envelope to the TVR head office at Queen Street. This ploy worked very well until the Barry folk rumbled it, and were provided by their own head office each week with a specially-numbered ticket, conveying a highly inflated impression of the Barry's volume of traffic, which was duly kept on one side for the schoolboy who was well known as buying a ticket but never using it.

THE RHONDDA VALLEYS

For more than a century 'the Rhondda' has been synonymous with the whole ethos of the mining valleys: the despoliation of rural life by the Industrial Revolution, the alternating boom and slump of the traditional staple industry, its strikes, lockouts, disasters and even occasional riots, the long struggles for union recognition, living standards and social welfare. Emerging through this pattern there grew also a strong religious fervour, and a notable cultural tradition of its own.

RHONDDA'S SUPREMACY

Essentially the two Rhondda valleys in their long prosperity were coal-mining valleys soon eclipsing all other districts, and achieving before World War I a total annual production of over nine million tons, equal to more than a sixth of the total South Wales output. Although there were factories in the Rhondda which fabricated iron, manufactured cables, colliery machinery and so on, these were subsidiary industries; there was no major iron-making centre in the Rhondda as there was aplenty at Merthyr, Dowlais and in the Aberdare Valley. The Taff Vale was originally very much an ironmasters' railway and the directors, faced in the company's early years with heavy demands for capital, were probably happy to be mindful of Brunel's opinion that railways were not likely to be profitably built to carry only coal; sinking pits was inevitably a risky business, both physically and commercially, especially with the deep seams in the Upper Rhondda.

Nevertheless, about a month after opening of the second section of main line in 1841, mineral traffic started over the branch authorised in 1836 'to communicate with the Tramroad leading to the Collieries called Dinas'. Some two miles in length, from Newbridge to a place called Aerw by the Taff Vale (Eirw by the Great Western and British Rail), it was the railway's first tentative thrust into the lower part of the *Rhondda Fawr* (Big Rhondda). The tramroad with which this branch connected had been built in two stages between 1809-12 from the canal at Treforest to Hafod Colliery and thence on to Dinas; the latter section belonged to Walter Coffin, an original TVR director, who seems to have been somewhat obstructive when other colliery owners wanted to use his tramroad. Pressure to extend the railway further up the main valley and into the *Rhondda Fach* (Little Rhondda), now became very strong from commercial interests anxious to exploit the mineral rights, but while the directors obtained powers in the TVR Act of 1846 for extensions including to Treherbert and Maerdy, they were inhibited by the financial crisis following the Railway Mania of 1845, and by their own anxiety not to land the company in heavy expenditure until it should be clear that the coal in the upper valley would be there for haulage in profitable quantity.

So the rails crept up the Rhondda, extending through Porth to Dinas in the main valley in spring 1849 and into the *Rhondda Fach* to Ynyshir in December that year. With the successful proving of deep-level steam coal seams at Ystrad and Treherbert (Bute Merthyr Colliery) in the mid-1850s, the railway was pushed on by stages to reach Treherbert, 10¾ miles from Pontypridd, on 7 August 1856. In the same year, the *Rhondda Fach* branch reached Ferndale and later Maerdy, 6½ miles from Porth, by the acquisition of a private railway. Maerdy, situated at a fairly lofty 900ft above sea level, was the highest point on the Taff Vale system; in 1979 Maerdy Colliery was still producing coal, the very last in the whole Rhondda to do so. Whereas the Pontypridd-Treherbert line is moderately graded, with a steepening in tendency to 1 in 100 through Treherbert, gradients on the *Rhondda Fach* are brutal: from 1 in 60 at Ynyshir to 1 in 55 through Tylorstown to Ferndale, and 1 in 41/52 to Maerdy.

Passenger services came rather tardily to the Rhondda. In the main valley they began between Pontypridd and Ystrad on 4 February 1861, and were extended to Treherbert 7 January 1863; in the *Rhondda Fach* they did not officially begin between Porth and Ferndale until the middle of 1876, being extended to Maerdy thirteen years later. The Maerdy passenger service was withdrawn on 15 June 1964, after which the branch was reduced to single track throughout.

RHONDDA BRANCHES

Apart from the Maerdy line, the TVR had four purely mineral branches in the main valley. The oldest, the single-line Aerw Branch, led off the original branch of 1841 at Aerw Branch Junction, being opened in 1854 for just under a mile to serve collieries; it kept open until 1977 for the clearance of stocks from the last of these, the Lewis Merthyr. Much more interesting was the Pwllyrhebog ('Hawk's Dell') Branch further up the valley, extending for two miles from just above Tonypandy up Clydach Vale to the colliery of that name, where it terminated on top of a mountain and close to the Llantrisant-Penygraig Branch of the GWR. The interest of the Pwllyrhebog Branch, which was partly opened to Blaenclydach Goods in 1863, and thence to the colliery by acquisition of the latter's private railway in 1889, lay in its ruling gradient of 1 in 13 for half-a-mile immediately below Blaenclydach Goods. This was worked by three TVR 0–6–0 tank engines designed by T. Hurry Riches in 1884, which had sloping boilers to maintain a safe water level while on the incline, together with coupled wheels 5ft 3in diameter to enable the axles to clear the sheaves of the winding cable; the incline was worked by balancing with a braking apparatus at the top. Sadly, this fascinating railway was closed on 1 July 1951, and the Clydach Vale coal brought down via Penygraig to Llantrisant.

At the top of the valley where the mountains close in, the railway split into three immediately beyond Treherbert. The oldest of these lines, extending two miles beyond Treherbert to Blaenrhondda Colliery near the head of the Rhondda River, was the rump of the abortive Rhondda Valley & Hirwain Junction Railway, incorporated 12 August 1867 to cross the intervening mountains into the head of the Aberdare Valley at Hirwain (Hirwaun from 1926), there joining the Vale of Neath line with the opportunity to open a route for Rhondda coal to Swansea; a later Act of 1872 authorised a branch into Aberdare. The only portion constructed was that from Blaenrhondda Branch Junction to the colliery of that name, opened in 1873 and worked by the Taff Vale. The latter being vigorously opposed to any other railway seeking to exploit the Rhondda, secured a lease of the RV & HJR from the date of opening, and the remainder of the scheme was abandoned; by Act of 1889 the TVR swallowed the minnow completely. British Rail wrote the end of the chapter with closure of the surviving piece, to Fernhill Colliery, at the end of 1966. Also gone is a short spur from Blaenrhondda Branch Junction to Blaencwm Colliery.

Less successful than its smothering tactics against the RV & HJR was the Taff Vale's opposition to the Rhondda & Swansea Bay Railway, incorporated 10 August 1882 to connect the Rhondda down through the Afan Valley to Port Talbot, Briton Ferry, Neath and Swansea. It reached Treherbert through the Rhondda Tunnel of 1m 1,683yd in 1890 – the story of which belongs to an ensuing chapter – but never succeeded in diverting to the western ports as much of the Rhondda coal traffic as its promoters had hoped; this was due to the better free-on-board (FOB) price obtainable at Cardiff, the higher rail rates to Swansea, and the limited extent to which Rhondda steam coal was required to be mixed with other coals from the western part of the coalfield, as against the bituminous coals from Monmouthshire and the Lower Rhondda.

THE 'BARRY OCTOPUS'

Finally of Rhondda railways, the Barry: the coal-hungry invader, the octopus, 'sordid and greedy... the spoiled child of Parliament', as learned counsel described it before Parliamentary Committees. The reverse of the medal had been the high rates charged by the TVR from the stronghold of its monopoly position in conjunction with the Bute Dock interests, and the congestion and delays which on many occasions led to the actual stoppage of collieries through there being no empty wagons available at the screens. So, after its Parliamentary triumph of 1884 the Barry Railway emerged from its tunnel at Pontypridd, slipped along the west bank of the river, and effected its junction with the TVR at Hafod (Barry) Junction, 1¾ miles beyond Pontypridd, crossing over the river to do so. As the Barry had been compelled to take the high ground to pass west of

Pontypridd, it had to climb away from Trehafod to reach the tunnel, so while a TVR Down mineral train with its '50 of coal on' could drift gently down the 1 in 175 past Trehafod, a Barry train going in the same direction on the other side of the river might be seen being vigorously assisted up the 1 in 220 past Maesycoed Goods Depot.

Despite several efforts to extend further up the Rhondda, the Barry never got beyond Hafod for mineral traffic, but as a result of some pressure by the local authorities, the TVR did agree to give the Barry passenger running powers from Trehafod into Porth, where connection was made with the TVR trains. This service began on 16 March 1896, and as already recorded earlier in this Chapter, was diverted over the former TVR route in 1930. Between 11 October 1943 and 7 September 1944 Tonteg–Pontypridd Tunnel (excl) Up line was used for storage of 119 (total) USA locomotives (p270). Though double track working was resumed, after World War II any coal traffic from the Rhondda to Barry could readily be accommodated by the Taff Vale route. From June 1951 Tonteg Junction–Pontypridd Pwllgwaun closed to all traffic. Trehafod Junction–Pontypridd Maescoed Goods remained open until closure of that depot on 4 June 1956.

Apart from competition by other railways, the Taff Vale suffered from 1905 onwards through the development of electric tramways under powers obtained by the local authorities; by 1908 these services extended right through the main valley parallel with the railway from Pontypridd to Treherbert, while four years later they reached Maerdy. It is perhaps amusing to recall that the tramcars suffered at times from pitfall subsidences, a trouble more usually associated with railways! The trams were abandoned in favour of buses during the 1930s, the Taff Vale having sought to meet the competition by introducing from the early 1900s a service of steam railmotors, for which half-a-dozen halts or platforms were provided in the *Rhondda Fawr;* as late as 1908 this service was still described in the timetable as 'provisional and experimental, and may not be continued… horses, corpses, carriages and other traffic requiring a special vehicle will not be conveyed by the cars.'

Let us leave the Rhondda now, even the main valley line singled beyond Cwmparc since 1973 and Porth since 1981, with the reflection that at the turn of the century, there were no fewer than thirty-one signalboxes, six branch line connections, and nineteen major sidings (apart from those in public goods yards) in less than eleven miles between Pontypridd and Treherbert; in the course of a normal working day, more than 150 goods and mineral trains were booked over it.

BRANCHES TO NELSON

North of Pontypridd along the Taff main line the next major branch was that from Navigation House (Abercynon) to Aberdare, but the intervening 3½ miles saw five other junctions. The TVR's Llancaiach Branch, authorised 1836, with inclined plane, horse-worked, opened to the north-east in November 1841, initially bringing coal down from Duncan & Company's Llancaiach Collieries but later making a west-trailing junction with the NA & HR's Taff Vale Extension line. In 1887 a 1½-mile branch was made from Pont Shon Norton Junction nearer Pontypridd to serve the Albion Colliery at Cilfynydd, and thirteen years later this second branch was extended for a further mile northward to join the original Llancaiach Branch at Ynysdwr Junction. On 1 June 1900 the TVR began a passenger service from Pontypridd via the Pont Shon Norton connection to its own station named Nelson, just short of the junction with the GWR at Llancaiach, later renamed Nelson & Llancaiach. In 1930 the GWR decided to adapt the quarter-mile between the two stations for passenger working and to extend the Pontypridd service to the junction station, but evidently there was a change of heart as the branch passenger service was withdrawn on 12 September 1932 and six years later the track was lifted north of Cilfynydd, though the Pont Shon Norton connection remained open until September 1970 to serve Albion Colliery.

THE YNYSYBWL BRANCH

This was one of the most picturesque and one of the steepest of the Glamorganshire branches, winding up the wooded Cwm Clydach valley for some 4¾ miles from the TVR main line. Opened for coal traffic in 1886 to serve the new Lady Windsor Colliery the branch originally connected with the main line by a northward-facing junction at Stormstown, but in 1900 a direct connection towards Pontypridd was effected at Clydach Court Junction, the two separate connections with the branch joining at Windsor Passing Siding Box just below the colliery. Thence the railway climbed the valley past Robertstown to Old Ynysbwl (2½ miles from Clydach Court

Junction) on gradients of between 1 in 47 and 1 in 66, a considerable challenge to the TVR steam railmotors introduced between Pontypridd and Old Ynysbwl Platform on 17 October 1904. Between the passenger terminus the branch continued on a ruling gradient of 1 in 30 past Mynachdy Colliery to Llanwonno Colliery near the hamlet of that name (and, like Senghenydd, the reputed retreat of a saint). Llanwonno Colliery was closed in or before 1938 and the track lifted down to Mynachdy; thence down to Old Ynysybwl Halt was formally closed on 22 September 1949, although no traffic had passed since 1944. Passenger service was withdrawn on 28 July 1952, and public goods traffic in November 1959. Though Lady Windsor Colliery kept the line in use for some time, the final working before closure was a railtour on 15 October 1988.

THE ABERDARE VALLEY

Running parallel with and a few miles to the north of the Rhondda, the Aberdare Valley through which flows the Cynon River, differs from the two Rhondda Valleys both in some geographical respects and in the pattern of its industrial growth: both factors which affected the history of their respective railways. Whereas for example the *Rhondda Fawr* ends against a mountain wall which involved the Rhondda & Swansea Bay Railway in expensive tunnelling, the Aberdare Valley leads more gently at its western end on to a plateau some 700ft above sea level at Hirwaun, affording a steep if practicable course for what became the important cross-valley trunk railway between Pontypool and Neath. Secondly, whereas the Rhondda possessed no traditional iron-making industry to tempt early railway promoters, the conjunction of the necessary ingredients near the head of the Aberdare Valley led to the establishment of ironworks at Hirwaun as early as 1757, followed by others at Abernant, Aberdare and Aberaman. Moreover, the veins of steam coal were proved much earlier, and at more accessible depths in the Aberdare district than was the case in the Rhondda. Thus between about 1840–55, before the iron industry began to decline, the population of the Aberdare district increased from around 7,000 to nearly 40,000, and sixteen steam coal pits went into production. By the end of this period the Aberdare district was producing in excess of a million tons a year, and although this total was more than doubled by the 1880s, that of the Rhondda was by then more than twice the Aberdare figure;

together, they formed the greatest concentration of high-grade steam coal in the world.

The six-mile Aberdare Canal, from the Glamorganshire Canal at Navigation House to Aberdare, was authorised by Act of 1793 and included powers for tramroads within eight miles of the canal. Several were built, in connection with those of the ironmasters, even before the canal opened in 1812. By this time quite a network of tramroads extended through the upper part of the valley towards and beyond Hirwaun.

Promoted principally by Sir John Guest and Crawshay Bailey (of Aberaman Ironworks), the Aberdare Railway Company was incorporated by Act of 31 July 1845 for an eight-mile line from Aberdare to join the TVR at Navigation House (Aberdare Junction, June 1849; Abercynon, December 1896), together with the ¾-mile Cwmbach Branch from Cwmbach Junction below Aberaman towards the north side of the valley, serving collieries and connecting with the Aberdare Iron Company's converted tramroad to Abernant. Railway and branch opened for minerals in July, and the railway to passengers on 6 August 1846, after an inaugural ceremony the previous day. Mill Street, ¾-mile north of Aberdare station, briefly served as terminus (*Bradshaw*, May 1847–November 1852), reopening as a platform, 1905–1912. All but a short length at Aberdare (then worked for passengers only by separate engine) of the single track was doubled in December 1856. Largely to resist eastward penetration by the Vale of Neath Railway the TVR leased the Aberdare from 1 January 1847, absorbing it by Act of 31 July 1902.

VALE OF NEATH RAILWAY

The second entrant into the Aberdare Valley was the Vale of Neath Railway Company. Its incorporation Act of 3 August 1846 authorised the building of a railway up through the Glyn Neath Valley for fifteen miles, past Hirwaun to a junction at Gelli Tarw 1¼ miles further on, whence one arm would turn left down to Merthyr and the other straight on down to Aberdare, nineteen miles from Neath. The Vale of Neath had a strong element of affiliation with both the GWR and the South Wales Railway, the latter injecting substantial capital and thereby obtaining representation on the board. Brunel acted as engineer until 1858, when he became consultant, being succeeded as head of the engineering department by a strong character named Joshua Williams, whose original job on the company had been that of secretary, but who progressively assumed responsibility for traffic management, locomotives, and civil engineering. Joshua thus became a sort of Welsh railway Pooh-Bah like Cornelius Lundie of the Rhymney; if ever there had been a row between them it would have been worth listening to.

Its connection with the South Wales Railway at Neath of necessity made the Vale of Neath a broad gauge railway, the construction of which involved some heavy climbing towards Hirwaun, including over five miles at 1 in 47-57 above Glyn Neath; the descent from Gelli Tarw into Aberdare conversely required two miles down at 1 in 50. The TVR having already occupied the valley floor, the Vale of Neath kept to the north side of it: in their final forms, the two railways ran closely parallel for six miles from just above Aberdare, where their passenger stations adjoined, to the west end of Quakers' Yard Tunnel.

Owing to constructional troubles on the Merthyr section, the Aberdare Branch of the V of N was opened first, for passengers on 24 September 1851, and for goods that December. June 1853 saw extension to the basin at the canal head half-a-mile further on, with the objects of attracting traffic from the collieries lower down, and of loading to barge iron from Hirwaun. The exchange arrangements between the two modes were not satisfactory, however, so in 1855 the V of N sponsored a minuscule Aberdare Valley Railway Company to bridge the gap of 1½ miles between the canal basin and Middle Duffryn Colliery, one of the nuclei of the immense and powerful Powell Duffryn concern. The chairman of the little company was Henry Austin Bruce (later the first Lord Aberdare), Joshua Williams acting as secretary from the V of N office at Neath. This small but important railway was authorised 2 July 1855 and opened in November of the following year, being worked by and leased to the Vale of Neath, which absorbed it from 1 January 1864.

Meanwhile, in order to enable through running between Pontypool, Neath and beyond when the West Midland should join it at Middle Duffryn, the Vale of Neath decided in 1862 to add a third rail throughout. This became available at the end of 1863, and on 18 April 1864 the West Midland (by then part of the GWR) completed the remaining five miles through Quakers' Yard Tunnel to Middle Duffryn, thus enabling GWR narrow gauge trains to run through from Pontypool, also for a short period those of the LNWR, and even later those of the Rhymney Railway en route to and from Middle Duffryn. Connections existed between the GWR and TVR and vice-versa at both Mountain Ash and Gadlys Junction (Aberdare), both completed in 1864, but whereas the former was little used and was taken out in 1913, Gadlys was the main exchange-point between the two railways in this once immensely busy valley. The whole route between Pontypool, Neath and Swansea came under the control of the GWR by virtue of an agreement that the Vale of Neath should be worked as part of the GWR on and from 1 February 1865, an arrangement ratified by Parliament in the following year.

MINERAL BRANCHES

In order to serve colliery developments in the narrow Dare and Aman Valleys lying to the west of Aberdare, three short and steep single-line mineral branches were built around the middle of the century, two by the Vale of Neath and one by the Taff Vale. The V of N Dare Valley Branch left the Aberdare line at Gelli Tarw and ran parallel with it for 2½ miles to Dare Junction, which originally was a reversing junction, the line turning back to enter the Dare Valley and reach Nantmelyn Colliery, 1¼ miles from the junction. These two sections were opened for minerals on 7 November 1854, the Nantmelyn line being extended in June 1857 for a quarter-of-a-mile to Bwlffa Dare Colliery at the head of the little valley. Meanwhile in November 1856 the original piece was pushed straight on from Dare Junction for almost three miles to Cwmaman Colliery in the Aman Valley; between Dare Junction and Cwmaman there were until 1924 six 'halts' used by workmen's trains. The principal features of interest on the Dare Branch, however, were Brunel's two timber viaducts, both standing 70ft above the valley floor: the Gamlyn Viaduct 600ft in length across the Cynon just below Gelli Tarw Junction, and the Dare Viaduct of 450ft across the valley of that name. When finally demolished in 1947, both branches having become redundant, the two viaducts had outlived by thirteen years the last of Brunel's Cornish viaducts.

The Taff Vale's mineral branch into the same area was separately promoted as the Dare Valley Railway Company, incorporated 21 July 1863 to build 2¼ miles of line from the TVR at Dare Valley Junction (immediately north of Aberdare passenger station), with a short branch which was not proceeded with towards Hirwaun. The Dare

Valley line passed under the older Vale of Neath Dare Branch line (Gelli Tarw-Dare Junction), and the latter ran parallel with the V of N's Nantmelyn and Bwlffa Dare line all the way, but at a lower level, to the last-named colliery. From its opening in 1866 until vested in the Taff Vale by Act of 1889, the Dare Valley was worked by and leased to the sponsor company; it had in fact been constructed by George Fisher, the Taff Vale engineer. A service of workmen's trains was run by the TVR between Aberdare and Nantmelyn Platform, weekly season tickets *only* being issued at a uniform fare of ten old pence for the week. The TVR ran so many workmen's-only trains that its 1914 time-table devoted three separate pages to them.

With the cessation of coal production in the Dare and Aman Valleys, the two ex-V of N branches were lifted between 1947 and 1955, but the former TVR branch to Bwlffa Dare was not closed until May 1962 and removed in August 1963.

PRIVATE RAILWAYS

In addition to the Great Western and Taff Vale Railways, the Aberdare Valley was intersected by numerous private railways, some of which had originated in the tramroad era. Whereas in the Rhondda similar private lines had been absorbed in the Taff Vale system (eg Ferndale-Maerdy, and part of the Pwllyrhebog) the two principal private systems in the Aberdare Valley were owned by the important Powell Duffryn and Nixon's Navigation interests, for whom the ownership of their own railways connecting with both the GWR and the TVR conferred a strong bargaining position as between one railway company and another. Nixon's Private Railway served the group's collieries in the lower part of the valley around Mountain Ash, and enjoyed two separate connections with the GWR route, known as Nixon's East Junction and Nixon's West Junction respectively At Navigation Colliery Siding, where there was a fouling point between the connections off the two 'main line' railways, there was an unusual arrangement in the form of a signal post with two semaphore arms, one controlling the approach from the GWR and the other arm the approach from the TVR; whichever guard got his train there first, cleared the signal for his own train and raised to 'stop' the arm applicable to the other train. He then stood on a specially erected platform and gave the right-away to his own train.

Further up the valley the Powell Duffryn Private Railway extended from Middle Duffryn Colliery on the GWR, over the top of the TVR, joined another line from Aberaman, and went up into the Aman Valley. These two private railways, Nixon's and Powell Duffryn, were to have been connected to form the northern end of the first unsuccessful scheme (1883) for a Pontypridd, Caerphilly & Newport Railway which, as mentioned in Chapter V, was got up by the two coal combines in conjunction with the Newport dock interests (several of the leading personalities being common to both parties) so as to form an independent route between the Aberdare Valley and Newport. The PD branch from the Aman Valley would have been joined to Nixon's Railway from Lower Duffryn Colliery by a new line, which would then have used an extension of Nixon's Railway eastward towards Abercynon, passing under the TVR Merthyr line and running down the east side of Taff Vale to join at Glyntaff, across the river, east of Pontypridd, the PC & N route as eventually built. With the failure of the 1883 scheme and the cutting-down of the PC & N to Pontypridd, Nixon's line from Lower Duffryn was left suspended in mid-valley, but was eventually connected to the TVR Aberdare Branch at Pontycynon Junction. Incidentally, the railway geography of the area between Pontypridd and Abercynon would have been almost incredibly congested if the PC & N scheme of 1883, and the Cardiff Railway's authorised branch of 1897 from below Treforest to Coedpenmaen, and two short TVR branches of 1896 in the same area, had all been constructed.

The Aberdare Valley had its share of other railways that were never built, local schemes promoted during the 'Second Railway Mania' of the mid 1860s. The Rhondda Valley & Hirwain Junction Railway of 1867 has already been mentioned. The Aberdare & Central Wales Junction, Royal Assent 30 July 1866, was another, rival of a rejected Aberdare Northern of the same session, for projection northwards into a wilderness inhabited principally by the Neath & Brecon Railway and lots of sheep. Another failure was the Aberdare Valley & Caerphilly Junction of 1866, an earlier version of the PC & N scheme of the 1880s. More grandiose than any of these, but just as improbable as the first two, was the North Pembrokeshire & Fishguard's proposed eastward extension of 1897, which was intended (*inter* very much *alia*) to come across the mountains from the Neath & Brecon at Colbren Junction to Hirwaun, make an end-on junction with the TVR at Mill Street above Aberdare, and obtain running powers through Gelli Tarw to both Merthyr and Quakers' Yard.

The Aberdare district has been heavily hit by the rundown of both collieries and railways. Pontypool-Neath was closed as a through route on 15 June 1964, and Glyn Neath–Hirwaun Pond closed entirely on 2 October 1967, followed on 29 November 1971 by Aberdare High Level–Middle Duffryn (with Middle Duffryn–Mountain Ash (Cardiff Road) being concurrently sold to the NCB). Subjected to intensive parallel road competition from Aberdare UDC electric tramcars since 1913, replaced by buses from March 1935, the TVR line, Abercynon–Aberdare Low Level, closed to passengers on 16 March 1964. Most of this line, singled from 20 October 1968 except for Abercwmboi passing loop, survived for freight and occasional excursions until restoration of the passenger service. For this, and subsequent developments associated with the coal trade as remained in 1980 (Penrhiwceiber Colliery, Abercwmboi phurnacite plant, a washery and Tower Colliery) see Chapter XII. Meanwhile, in order to reach Tower Colliery at the very top of the valley, using the old Vale of Neath between Aberdare and Hirwaun Pond, a new spur opened on 29 July 1973 between the site of Cwmbach Junction and the V of N line, itself reopened thence to Aberdare on the same day. This operation, financed by the local council, enabled the site of the former TVR above Cwmbach Junction to be cleared for redevelopment and included closure of the level crossing, for long unpopular, in the middle of the town. It required a new rail crossing of the Cynon River, for which a steel girder bridge was imported from the closed branch between Oxford and Princes Risborough, and re-erected in this Welsh valley. The Aberdare Canal was closed to navigation about 1900, and most traces of it have now disappeared.

MERTHYR AND DOWLAIS

Over eleven miles by rail above Pontypridd, nearly twenty-five from Cardiff, at the confluence of the Taff River with its tributary the *Taf Fechan*, Merthyr Tydfil lies below limestone hills of the coalfield's Northern Outcrop, frowned upon from the north east by the steep escarpment of the Cwm Bargoed and the Gibraltarian slag-heaps of Merthyr's industrial twin, Dowlais. Here during the second half of the eighteenth century and the early decades of the nineteenth, there evolved in a miasma of toil, sweat, tears and fumes, the archetype of all South Wales industrial towns, with its four great works: Crawshay's Cyfarthfa along the river north-west of the town;

Hill's Plymouth Works to the south; Homfray's Penydarren on the slope towards Dowlais; and finally Guest's Dowlais Ironworks in Dowlais itself, at a height of 900ft above sea level, 350ft higher than Merthyr. By 1840 this was the largest group of ironworks in the world, Dowlais alone employing over 5,000 people, while the population of Merthyr, then the largest town in Wales, exceeded those of Newport, Cardiff and Swansea combined. It was no wonder that railways proper came to Merthyr close behind the Glamorganshire Canal and the Penydarren Tramroad of 1802. Their order of arrival was TVR 1841, Vale of Neath 1853, Brecon & Merthyr (Dowlais 1863, Merthyr 1868), LNWR (Dowlais 1873, Merthyr 1879), and

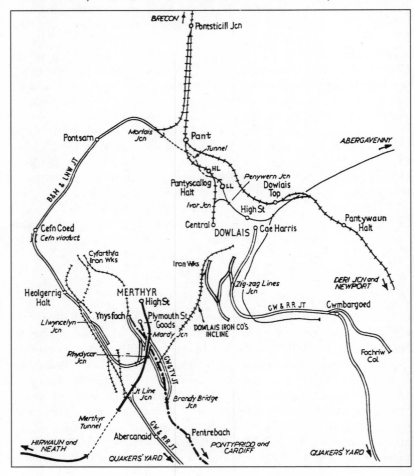

Great Western & Rhymney Joint (Dowlais 1876, Merthyr 1886). Additionally, the locomotives of the Cambrian Railways could be seen in Merthyr from about 1900 onwards, on through passenger workings from Aberystwyth over the Mid Wales and B & M Railways. But some of the railway companies which spent so much money in fighting their way into Merthyr arrived to find that the great days of the old iron industry were already on the wane. Penydarren closed in 1858, Plymouth gave up producing iron in 1880, and Cyfarthfa was closed between 1875-79, and despite the construction of a new steel-making plant at Ynysfach, never really recovered its old importance. Dowlais on the other hand had turned successfully to steel production in the 1860s and in 1891 established a new steelworks on East Moors, Cardiff, reducing the importance of the Dowlais Works. Coal to some extent succeeded iron in the Merthyr area, but being so close to the outcrop was never produced on the scale achieved in Aberdare and the Rhondda. The collapse of heavy industry and of employment after World War I is part of a later story.

THE DOWLAIS INCLINE

The TVR, on its opening on 21 April 1841 to a rather inconvenient Plymouth Street Station near the river in Merthyr, found itself in the midst of a network of industrial tramroads between the various works and the Glamorganshire Canal, the Penydarren Tramroad, and the limestone quarries, ironstone and coal workings on the hills above the town. The TVR sought to make its own connections with the more important of these installations, notably in 1837 with proposals for branches to Cyfarthfa, Plymouth, Penydarren and Dowlais. From I.K. Brunel's evidence before the House of Lords Committee the last three works named were to be served by the same self-acting incline off the TVR main line, rising for 1¼ miles in three stages of 1 in 10, 1 in 20, and 1 in 10; a witness for the Dowlais Iron Company stated that the latter then had fourteen iron furnaces, and that the incline would be required to carry 40,000 tons of ore and 44,000 tons of iron annually. These branches were authorised by the TVR Act of 30 June 1837, but difficulties still arose with the ironmasters, particularly with John Guest who was conscious of his embarrassing position as both head of Dowlais and chairman of the TVR, leading to his resignation from the latter appointment in 1847 when the clash of interests became crucial. By 1840 the Dowlais Iron Company, which was suffering from the inad-

equacy of its existing steep and tortuous tramroad connection with
Merthyr, compelled the TVR to concede in its Act of that year a
provision that 'should the TVR not proceed after passing of this Act
to construct the Dowlais Branch, or should there be a lapse of 30
days in its construction, the Dowlais Iron Company be empowered,
subject to giving seven days' notice, to enter upon the lands and
construct the branch, charging expense of same to the TV
Company'.

This in fact is precisely what the DIC eventually did, although not
until after the company had obtained its own Act of 28 July 1849.
The Dowlais Railway, 1¾ miles in length, was opened from the main
gates of the ironworks (with a branch to the furnaces) down to a
junction with the TVR on 21 August 1851; there was a winding-
engine house about half-way up, beyond which the DIC locomotives
worked to and from the ironworks. Between 1851-54 passengers
were carried (the view from the incline must have been awe-
inspiring!) and the incline continued to be used for freight traffic
until the virtual closure of the Dowlais Works during the great
depression in the 1930s.

In the event the TVR did not build any of its contemplated
mineral branches at Merthyr except the half-mile Ynysfach Branch
from Plymouth Street, which originally connected with Crawshay's
private railway to Cyfarthfa Ironworks, and later to the same firm's
steelworks. The latter were sold for dismantling in 1919, since when
no traffic had passed over the branch except slag for railway ballast,
and when this ceased, the branch was officially closed on 23 March
1950.

MERTHYR TUNNEL

The impending entry into Merthyr of the Vale of Neath Railway, and
of others which might follow it, was one of the reasons which led to
difficulty between the DIC and the monopolistic ideas of the TVR.
The Vale of Neath opened its broad gauge Merthyr extension from
Gelli Tarw Junction on 2 November 1853, the 6¼ miles having taken
six years to complete. This was almost wholly due to contractors'
troubles in boring the Merthyr Tunnel through which the railway
approached the town on falling gradients of 1 in 80 and 1 in 50; this
tunnel, at 1m 737yd, was the third longest in Wales. Entering
Merthyr, the line crossed over the river and the TVR by a long
viaduct to its station at Merthyr (High Street), which eventually

became the passenger terminus for all the railways at Merthyr. The TVR transferred its passenger trains to High Street on 1 August 1877, requiring the making of a joint half-mile connection from Brandy Bridge Junction on the TVR to Mardy Junction with the Vale of Neath on the approach to High Street; this connection was joint GWR-TVR property. Plymouth Street then became a goods station, which it remained until its closure on 27 November 1967, after a working life of 126 years. A short connection between the Dowlais Incline and the Vale of Neath was opened about 1858.

QUAKERS' YARD & MERTHYR

One further railway remains to be mentioned as completing the access to Merthyr from the south. This was the Quakers' Yard & Merthyr Joint Railway (GW & Rhymney Joint) opened 1 April 1886.

It is symbolic of South Wales inter-railway politics a century ago, that the course of the QY & M Joint Line closely followed that proposed by the Brecon & Merthyr Railway for its Southern Extension of 1865, which both the GWR and RR had contended to be impracticable! From its junction with the Pontypool-Neath line at Quakers' Yard the Joint Line crossed over the TVR and the river, and running parallel with the TVR all the way but on the west side of the river, extended for 6½ miles to junctions with the Cyfarthfa private railway and the GWR Vale of Neath section. Its ruling gradient was 1 in 51 out of Merthyr towards Abercanaid, but further south there was a bank of 1 in 80 rising from Quakers' Yard, past Aberfan, of tragic memory. The Joint line had one very short branch across the river to Merthyr Vale Colliery, this connection being closed in 1951 when the traffic was concentrated on the former Taff Vale route.

THE BRECON & MERTHYR

Except for the Vale of Neath with its long tunnel and steep descent, the southern routes into Merthyr already described presented few difficulties compared with the alternative access to Merthyr via Dowlais (adopted by the Brecon & Merthyr and LNW Railways) or to Dowlais only (GW and Rhymney Railways), but in the spirit of the age, they all struggled and squandered to get there.

First in the field for access from the north was the little Brecon & Merthyr, substantially supported by the Brecon bankers, the de

Wintons, and other local interests, which canvassed several alternative schemes before depositing in 1858 its Bill for a Brecon-Dowlais railway (connecting at the latter place with the Dowlais Railway), for which they obtained the support of G.T. Clark of the Dowlais Iron Company and (for the time being) John Boyle of the Rhymney. Two proposed branches were to connect with the Rhymney Iron Works and with the Bargoed Rhymney branch of the RR respectively. After a series of flirtations and skirmishes with rival neighbours, and two further applications to Parliament, the company opened its initial nineteen miles of railway on 1 May 1863 from Brecon to Pant on the outskirts of Dowlais. It was not until 23 June 1869 that the line was extended for 1¼ miles into the Dowlais (Lloyd Street) terminus (later 'Central') adjoining the Ivor Ironworks (named after Sir John Guest's heir, who later became the first Lord Wimborne). The engineer for the B & M was Henry Conybeare, who characterised the new railway as 'a good locomotive road throughout', notwithstanding that from crossing the River Usk at Talybont, the line climbed southward through the Brecon Beacons by the notorious Seven Mile Bank rising 925ft in this distance, including 6½ miles at 1 in 38, and culminating in the 667yd Torpantau or Beacon (summit) Tunnel at an altitude of 1,313ft at its west end.

Even before the B & M had achieved its initial opening to Pant, the company had run into a series of troubles, self-aggravated by its own costly and frustrating exertions to break through to the seaboard at Newport, in which as we have seen in Chapter V, it eventually succeeded in 1868. Even this was subject to a two-years' delay because the TVR secured a legal restriction that the B & M's Junction with the RR in the Bargoed Rhymney Valley could not be made effective until the B & M had fulfilled a prior obligation to complete its authorised connection with the Dowlais Railway, or in lieu thereof such junction as Parliament might authorise with the TVR at Merthyr. Being thus caught between its two powerful neighbours was not the little company's only worry, however; the LNWR was thrusting across its path towards Merthyr, while among those overwhelmed by the financial crisis of 1866 was the company's principal contractor, Thomas Savin, who was not merely building the railway but was also working it with his own locomotives and guaranteeing a five per cent dividend. This crisis found the company with its Merthyr extension unfinished, with the Bargoed Rhymney line to connect with the Old Rumney and with Newport legally incapable of being opened until the Merthyr branch should be opened, with a legal/financial morass of creditors' petitions, threats to seize the locomotives without which the line could not be worked, and the appointment of a receiver by the Court of Chancery.

By 1870 the company had somewhat miraculously got its affairs into better order, through revision of its capital structure and a scheme of arrangement approved by Parliament and the court; by this time also the Merthyr extension was finished, being opened throughout on 1 August 1868. This was a remarkable and spectacular piece of railway, engineered mainly by Alexander Sutherland, who took over from Conybeare when the latter became consulting engineer. Leaving the original Brecon–Pant line at Pontsticill Junction a few miles below the summit at Torpantau, it followed the bends of the *Taf Fechan* (Little Taff) River in a wide sweep to the west, and then from Cefn descended into Merthyr, 6¾ miles from Pontsticill, on almost continuous downhill gradients of 1 in 45/50. Within this short distance the railway completely reversed direction, so that one's first glimpse of the home signal for Merthyr was of the back of the semaphore arm. Two other features of the extension were the Pontsarn and Cefn masonry viaducts over the converging arms of the Taff; the fifteen-arch, curved, Cefn Coed Viaduct was the larger, 725ft long and 122ft above the *Taf Fawr*.

THE LNWR REACHES MERTHYR

Meanwhile the B & M had been engaged in a kind of Khyber Pass mountain warfare with the LNWR between Merthyr-Dowlais and Rhymney Bridge, the little Welsh Dai promoting lines to Rhymney and Nantybwch in the face of the invader Goliath. Compromise eventually prevailed, the B & M allowing the LNWR (in consideration of some virtually meaningless, face-saving running powers) to press on westwards through Dowlais Top to Ivor Junction, Dowlais, opened 1 January 1873, whence it acquired access to the B & M's Lloyd Street station and the Dowlais Iron Company's traffic. But the LNWR was never content to sit on the hilltop at Dowlais and merely gaze down into the lucrative industrial reek in the Merthyr bowl. As early as 1865 Euston had supported a grand design of John Gardner's for a spectacular ski-run descent from Dowlais into Merthyr, the sweeping curves of which would have twice intersected the Dowlais Company's incline. November 1873, therefore, saw an LNWR Bill for connecting lines at Merthyr, to the B & M, the Vale of Neath, and the Gethin Railway, a private colliery line providing access as far down the Vale of Taff as Troedyrhiw; also running powers over the DIC lines. The B & M capitulated: on 18 May 1874, during committee stage, agreement was reached that Euston would withdraw all but the 1¼-mile link (and short loop not made) from Penywern Junction (where the new line would leave the existing one to Ivor Junction) to the B & M's Merthyr Extension at Morlais, 1½ miles from Pontsticill, in exchange for the B & M thence to Merthyr becoming joint, Euston retrospectively subsidising its cost at £25,000 a mile. The new connection was authorised by the LNWR Act of 16 July 1874, the agreement being scheduled to an LNWR Act of 1875. Morlais tunnel, on the new line, by which the LNWR passed under the original B & M to Dowlais and its extension towards the Bargoed Rhymney Valley, was 1,040yd long; its completion, to celebrations reported in the *Merthyr Express* of 14 June, enabled LNWR trains to run into Merthyr from Monday 9 June 1879, and soon LNWR locomotives were working Crawshay's private railway to nearby pits and works. About a month later LNWR through trains ceased using the B & M's Dowlais station on opening of the LNWR's 'Dowlais Top', though a connecting service was retained at Lloyd Street until the nearer 'Dowlais High Street' was opened on 4 May 1885, when Dowlais Top was closed. the LNWR/B & M agreement thus implemented wrote *diwedd* (finis) to the aspirations of the Midland Railway to enter the area.

A FIVE-COMPANY STATION.

The arrival of the LNWR in Merthyr completed the five-company representation at High Street passenger station where, as at Brecon (Free Street), each was entitled to separate booking office and other accommodation. At the outbreak of World War I in 1914, over fifty weekday passenger train departures were scheduled, including through services to and from Newport via the QY & M Joint and the LNWR Sirhowy Line, and a daily express service to Neath and Swansea via Hirwaun. The station then comprised five platforms under a timber roof, the main part of which was designed by Brunel and lasted until 1953.

The High Street station was the scene of a spectacular accident on 16 May 1874 when part of a Vale of Neath mineral train broke loose on the ascent to Merthyr Tunnel, ran back into the station, and forced a B & M passenger train and its locomotive on to the concourse; one person was killed and about fifty injured. Such runaways were an endemic accident risk on these lines. There were several bad ones on the Seven Mile Bank of the B & M north of Torpantau, the worst on 2 December 1878 when a northbound goods train, thirty-six wagons and brake-van with two locomotives in front and one behind, failed to stop for brakes to be pinned-down at the top of the incline – the brakesman had been on duty thirteen hours already in freezing weather – and thundered to destruction down the 1 in 38, scattering pieces of valve-gear, connecting rods and other bits disintegrated from the vainly-reversed locomotives, until the whole train went off the rails near the bottom, killing most of the crew.

STEEP CLIMBS TO DOWLAIS

East of Taff Vale, two railways climbed to Dowlais through the parallel narrow valleys of the Bargoed Rhymney and the Bargoed Taff. From its end-on junction with the RR at Deri, the B & M ascended the former valley on a ruling grade of 1 in 38 to a summit level of 1,314ft near Pantywaen, while a few miles further west the Great Western & Rhymney Railways' Taff Bargoed Joint Line rose for much of its 9¼ miles from Nelson & Llancaiach at 1 in 40 or so to the desolate Cwmbargoed plateau. The LNWR also had a mineral branch, its maximum length two miles, opened to Cwmbargoed (LNWR) on 14 February 1881, from Cwmbargoed Junction (between Dowlais Top and Dowlais (High Street)); it finally closed by 1937. At Cwmbargoed, with both railways at about the 1,250ft datum, the Taff Bargoed Joint Line also projected eastward over a DIC statutory railway worked by the two partners by arrangement, to Fochriw Colliery which also had siding connection to the B & M at Fochriw Junction. From Cwmbargoed, the Joint Line went on to Dowlais Zig-Zag Lines Junction, where it divided, one line going on for ¾-mile to the passenger station at Dowlais (Cae Harris) – a building more chapel-like in appearance than many chapels – and thence across a public road into the Ivor Works. The other arm descended very steeply from Zig-Zag Lines Junction in three sections and through two reversing junctions (Furnace Tops and Ffos-y-Fran) to its termination at the steelworks.

SURVIVORS

Of all the railways to Merthyr and Dowlais, only two survive; the former TVR main line, which since 1971 has been singled north of Abercynon except for a passing loop at Black Lion, and the Taff Bargoed Joint (also partly singled) to Dowlais; this line lost its passenger service as long ago as 15 June 1964, but gained some traffic from the making of a short link line from Treharris to the Ocean and Taff Merthyr collieries when the Pontypool–Neath route closed.

With the withdrawal of passenger services between Merthyr and Quakers' Yard (12 February 1951), Abergavenny (6 January 1958), Pontsticill Junction (13 November 1961) and Hirwaun (31 December 1962), the historic old station at High Street became redundant, and was replaced in 1971 by a small modern affair with a single island platform and car park. On the north side, the ex-LNWR through freight services were diverted to ex-GWR routes from 22 November 1954; the Dowlais Central branch closed for passengers 2 May 1960, and Brecon–Newport 31 December 1962; the last section of the old B & M to be kept open for freight at the northern end was between Merthyr and Vaynor Quarry, closed October 1966. Subsequently, however, the former B & M trackbed between Pant and Torpantau was acquired by the Brecon Mountain Railway Company Ltd (Rheilffordd Mynydd Brecheiniog) for conversion into a pleasure railway of 1ft 11¾in gauge, the first section of which, Pant–Pontsticill, was subject of a Light Railway Order which came into effect on 18 May 1980.

Page 169 (Top) In the bleak canyon of the Upper Avon Valley in 1950, between Cymmer and the western portal of the Rhondda Tunnel at Blaengwynfi, an Abergwynfi–Bridgend passenger train *(right)* scores a near miss on a solitary mountain sheep, photographed from an eastbound train on the ex-R & SB line; *(bottom)* On the original route of the Merthyr, Tredegar and Abergavenny Railway an ex-GWR 0-6-0PT heads a push-and-pull train over the spidery bridge crossing the River Usk, shortly after leaving Abergavenny. *R. J. Doran; W. A. Camwell)*

Page 170 (Top)   Taff Vale Railway 4-4-2T No 175 decorated to work the Prince of Wales' special train in connection with the Cardiff Exhibition of 1898. Mr T. Hurry Riches stands on the right in the central top-hatted group; *(bottom)* Displaying on its saddle tank the coronet of the Marquis of Bute, 0-6-0T No 24 served the Marquis, the Bute Docks Company, and the Cardiff Railway Company, being withdrawn by the GWR in 1922. *(Trefor L. Jones collection; Author's collection)*

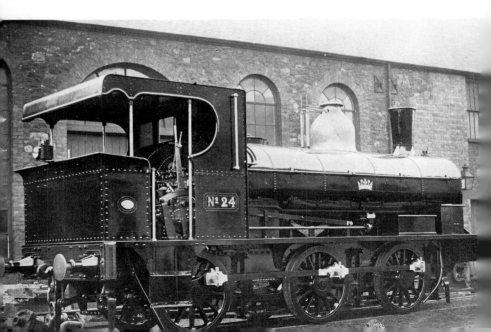

CHAPTER VIII

Westward
from Cardiff

South of the great mining valleys described in the previous chapter, the thirty-eight miles of the South Wales main railway westward from Cardiff to Neath lie roughly along the southern outcrop of the coalfield. Through Llantrisant and Bridgend nearly to Port Talbot the railway thus forms a boundary between the largely rural stretch of the Vale of Glamorgan to the south, and the industrially developed valleys of the Ely, Ogmore, Garw and Llynvi. Within this area, no fewer than twenty-one separately incorporated railway companies contributed at various times to the build-up of a close and historically confusing network of local railways, serving a mixed mining territory of dry steam and coking coals, with anthracite becoming predominant further westward.

THE ELY VALLEY

From Cardiff the South Wales main line follows the River Ely for eleven miles to Llantrisant – in the railway sense a misnomer, the station being two miles distant at Pontyclun. Here the river, turning northwards towards the mountain barrier forming the southern slope of the *Rhondda Fawr*, compelled Brunel to maintain his westward course at the expense of sharp undulations over Llanharan and Stormy Down. From 2 August 1860 Llantrisant became a junction with the opening for minerals of one of three lines authorised by the incorporation Act on 13 July 1857 of the broad gauge Ely Valley Railway – a successor to part of territory claimed by the abortive broad gauge Rhondda & Ely Valleys Junction Railway of 1845, from Llantrisant through Penygraig and over the mountains to the head of *Rhondda Fawr*. After a further

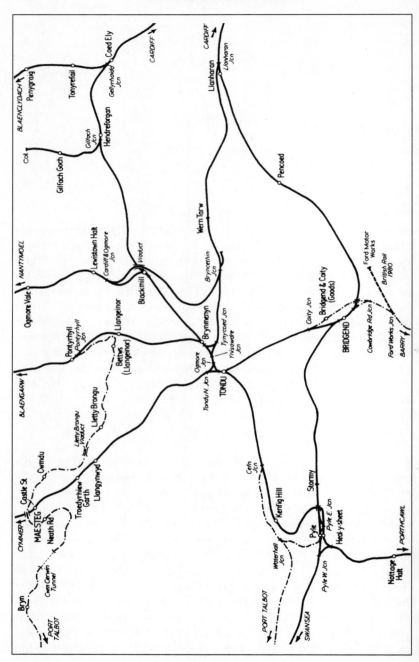

Act of 14 June 1858 authorising the Mwyndy Branch, the EVR, on the other hand, was content initially with local mineral lines, one reaching Mwyndy Ironworks, thence to Brofiskin limeworks, another Gellyrhaidd Colliery, both in January 1862, and an extension from Tonyrefail serving Penygraig Colliery from December 1862.

From its inception the Ely Valley was worked by the GWR, which took a 999-year lease in 1861, an arrangement hastened by the smaller company's declared wish to change to the narrow gauge, and by the Great Western's acquisition of Cilely Colliery near Tonyrefail. The Ely Valley's unsuccessful flirtation with the narrow gauge was also motivated by the impending incursion into its territory of the TVR which, in its anxiety to forestall any further penetration by the GWR eastward from Llantrisant, obtained the support of colliery interests for its satellite Llantrissant (sic) & Taff Vale Junction Railway. Incorporated by Act of 7 June 1861 this company obtained powers for a 5¼-mile railway from the TVR main line at Llantrisant Branch Junction, Treforest (p142) to a junction with the EVR's Mwyndy Branch (over which the TVR had running powers) at Maesaraul, bringing Mwyndy iron ore much closer to Dowlais. By a third rail laid from Maesaraul within the broad gauge Mwyndy Branch, TVR freight working began in January 1865 to Llantrisant; this had already started along a 2¼-mile mineral branch from Common Branch Junction north of Maesaraul Junction, across country to the Ely Valley 'main line' at Llantrisant Common Junction, about half-way between Llantrisant and Tonyrefail. This last-named branch in its turn acquired a sub-branch with the opening for goods and minerals in April 1883 of the Treferig Valley Railway, incorporated as a separate company by Act of 21 July 1879 and extending for 2¾ miles from Treferig Junction on the Common Branch, up the Nant Mychydd defile to Glyn Colliery. As there was also a Gelynog Branch Junction with a private colliery line a little lower down, the relatively small triangle formed by these railways north of Llantrisant involved no fewer than seven junctions.

The last TVR route in this area, authorised by the L & TVJR Act of 23 July 1866, opened on 11 September 1886 after extensions of time granted by Parliament: the 7-mile 'Llantrisant No 1 Branch' ran from the junction of that name to the Radyr-Penarth line at Waterhall Junction. It gave a more direct route between the Ely district collieries and Penarth Dock and its eleventh-hour comple-

tion owed much to impending competition from the Barry's
Llantrisant–Peterston–Drope Junction route (opened in 1889).

Having served their purpose, the L & TVJ and the Treferig
Companies became amalgamated with the TVR in 1889, a year in
which the parent company found it convenient to sweep these and
other subsidiaries into a capital reconstruction.

PASSENGER SERVICES

The TVR Pontypridd–Llantrisant–Cowbridge (p175) passenger
service started on 18 September 1865; within six years additional
stations opened at Llantwit, Cross Inn, Llanharry Platform, and
Ystradowen. A serious accident occurred to a Pontypridd train near
Llantrisant on 12 August 1893 when a broken spring fell off 4–4–2T
No 173 causing derailment down an embankment with the loss of
thirteen lives. GWR passenger services up the Ely Valley started as
late as 1 May 1901, between Llantrisant and Penygraig, twenty-
three years after the branch had been extended on 10 August 1878
for two miles from Penygraig to the Cambrian Colliery on top of
the mountain, alongside the TVR's Pwllyrhebog Branch, and 9¾
miles from Llantrisant. This extension was built by yet another
'independent' company, the Ely & Clydach Valleys, incorporated
by Act of 5 August 1873. A curious historical quirk is that whereas
this extension company became amalgamated into the GWR under
the latter's Act of 1880, the original EVR Company remained
under lease to the GWR until absorbed as late as 1903.

The Penygraig train afforded a ride which in places was notably
picturesque, and typical also of other valley lines lying further to
the west. From Llantrisant the uphill climb steepened progressively
from 1 in 100 to 1 in 60, and then 1 in 50. As far as Coed Ely the
scenery was well wooded, but then the valley as it narrowed became
bleak and bitter, especially if as it happened on a trip I made in
1942 behind GWR 2–4–0T No 3594 hauling only two trailers, that a
thin curtain of rain was hissing across the valley. Leaving Tonyrefail
the locomotive had to get away on 1 in 50 and a wet rail, and then
climbed into the neck of the valley at 1 in 44, the Up and Down
lines being on separate alignments to ease the grade. Finally the
train passed through a wet, narrow gorge in a rock cutting to breast
the summit into Penygraig station, high above the town, where at
least the cheerful presence of a lady signalman imparted some alle-
viation of the weeping day…

After the withdrawal of the Penygraig passenger service on 9 June 1958, the upper part of the branch remained open principally to serve Cambrian Colliery, but was closed above Coed Ely on 3 April 1967; Llantrisant–Coed Ely remained in use for important colliery and washery traffic at the latter place until closed above Mwyndy Junction from 30 November 1983. Both branches from Common Branch Junction, to Treferig and Llantrisant Common Junction respectively, were early casualties of the grouping in 1924-30, except that about a mile at the Llantrisant Common Junction end remained open until the early 1950s for wagon storage and because the junction signalbox was needed for access to colliery sidings. The official document proposing the abandonment of the surviving mile included, most properly under the rules, a statement that '… there is no traffic passing over this line and the only revenue is £9 per annum in respect of a tenancy for the grazing of goats'. (The second version of the Taff Vale Company's armorial device included a goat, proper, suspicious of dragons).

After the withdrawal of the Pontypridd-Llantrisant passenger service on 31 March 1952, the four miles between Treforest Junction and Cwm Colliery, Llantwit Vardre, were closed in 1964, leaving Cwm Colliery and coke ovens to be served from the Llantrisant end. The Common Branch-Waterhall Junction line was also closed in 1964, except for access to Creigiau Quarry via Common Branch Junction, closed 31 January 1978. The Brofiskin Branch closed finally in October 1968.

THE VALE OF GLAMORGAN

Only three railways penetrated the wide, rural Vale of Glamorgan south of the Cardiff–Swansea main line: the Llantrisant and Tondu branches to coastal Aberthaw and Porthcawl respectively, and the later, coastwise, Vale of Glamorgan Railway, the only survivor of the trio.

The Llantrisant–Cowbridge–Aberthaw Branch represented the TVR's most southerly penetration. A local venture, supported by the TVR, with which relations were not always harmonious, the Cowbridge Railway Company was incorporated by Act of 29 July 1862 for a standard gauge line from the country town of Cowbridge to the L & TVJR at Maesaraul passing over the GWR to which a spur dropped at Llantrisant. By agreement with Paddington in June 1863, however, the Cowbridge terminated at Llantrisant, abandoning the northern section, the L & TVJ being reached instead by a third rail laid along the Mwyndy Branch to Maesaraul Junction. With hired TVR motive power, the Cowbridge officially opened to freight on 30 January 1865; passengers waited until September for the TVR service (p174) of three daily return trips (two through to Pontypridd, reversing at Llantrisant before crossing over the GWR). Not far distant from the roaring Rhondda, but a world apart in its placid countrified atmosphere, working itself from April 1870, the Cowbridge pottered along peacefully, getting so out of repair as to need a fortnight's recuperative closure to passengers before being leased to the TVR from 1 January 1876. In 1880 promotion under Barry Railway auspices of the Vale of Glamorgan Railway impelled the TVR to thrust across the intruder's path. This virtually meaningless gesture involved incorporation by Act of 12 August 1889 of the Cowbridge & Aberthaw Railway, whereby the branch, from a resited Cowbridge station, was extended for all traffic on 1 October 1892 for a further 6½ miles down the Thaw Valley to the ancient but little-used port of Aberthaw. The Cowbridge vested in the TVR in the latter's consolidation of 1889, the C&A being absorbed in 1895. The extension served only a few quarries and limeworks, but its history might have been very different had the CEGB Generating Station at Aberthaw been built earlier. As it was, the exiguous Cowbridge–Aberthaw passenger service was withdrawn on 5 May 1930, freight 1 November 1932, and the track recovered in 1947. The Llantrisant–Cowbridge passenger service, latterly worked by diesel railcar, lingered until withdrawn on 26 November 1951, freight remaining until 1 February 1965 when the track was lifted south of Llanharry where the last rail-served South Wales ironstone mine kept the branch stub-end in use until production ceased in 1975, the rails to Llantrisant being lifted after June 1977. Llantrisant station, which in 1920 had dealt with over thirty passenger train departures daily, closed to passengers on 2 November 1964 and freight in February 1988.

BARRY TO BRIDGEND

The Vale of Glamorgan Railway Company, incorporated by Act of 26 August 1889, represented compromise between the Barry's ambition to thrust westwards into the coal-bearing valleys of the Llynvi & Ogmore district, and those of the coalowners, seeking a more direct outlet for shipment in competition with docks at Port Talbot and Swansea. The 20¼-mile V of G extended from an end-on junction with the Barry, through the Vale to Bridgend. Though aspiring to go further, it nevertheless took three extensions of time granted by Parliament before completion. Agreement being reached for the Barry Company to work the railway for sixty per cent of the gross receipts, with a guaranteed four per cent dividend, the Vale of Glamorgan became virtually a Barry subsidiary, but survived to become separately amalgamated with the GWR under the Railways Act, 1921.

With ruling gradient of 1 in 81, engineering included limestone cuttings and a 110ft-high, 374yd-long, 16-arch masonry viaduct above Porthkerry Park, between tunnels of 73yd and 545yd, east of which the line joined the working company immediately west of Barry Town station. When in autumn 1897 Lt-Col Yorke of the Railway Inspectorate reported on the line, he had misgivings about the viaduct, which had already encountered settlement problems, so that he imposed a 20mph limit and required continuous employment of watchmen. Minerals and passenger traffic started on 1 December 1897. On 10 January 1898 one of the piers began to sink, causing immediate closure of the structure until 8 January 1900, while a hastily-constructed northerly 'shoo-fly' diversion was used (retrospectively authorised in 1899). Col Yorke's subsequent scathing report revealed he had been misled during his inspection: trial bores reportedly implied foundations on rock, whereas several piers rested on clay. As late as 1965 one farmer at least was ploughing up fishplates from the site of the diversion!

At Cowbridge Road Junction, half a mile south of Bridgend GWR station, the Vale of Glamorgan route divided, one spur going off into the station, where the local passenger service from Barry terminated, while the other spur passed above the GWR main line and through a deep cutting to join the GWR Bridgend–Tondu line at Coity Junction, 1¼ miles north east of Bridgend. Running powers into Tondu having been refused by Parliament, Coity Junction became the exchange point for Barry Docks traffic, and locomotive facilities were maintained there. The Cowbridge Road-Coity Junction line was closed on 15 June 1964, except for half-a-mile between Coity Junction and the Bridgend & Coity goods depot, which survived until 28 November 1977.

Even while the Vale of Glamorgan line was still under construction, it was drawn by a faction of South Wales industrialists and the

Barry Railway interests into the grandiose wildcat scheme (as the contemporary railway press described it) of 1895 for a London & South Wales Railway from Cogan at the Barry's Junction with the TVR south west of Cardiff, far into England to join the Metropolitan Railway at Great Missenden and the Midland at Welsh Harp, Hendon. But this immense project, estimated to cost nearly £6 million, was really no more than a ploy to push the GWR into hastening its own South Wales Direct Railway (Wootton Bassett-Patchway) which, in consideration of the London & South Wales Bill being withdrawn and some commercial concessions to the South Wales interests, was duly authorised in 1896.

The role of the Vale of Glamorgan in this great project would have been an extension line from Ewenny, south of Bridgend, westward across the moors and dunes to connect up with the Port Talbot and the Rhondda & Swansea Bay Railways near Port Talbot. Although the London & South Wales Railway scheme was abandoned, the idea of such a westward penetration lingered for another decade or so in the Barry Railway's strategic philosophy, and was only finally extinguished when the GWR forestalled it by taking the Port Talbot and the R & SB companies under its control some years before World War I.

Local passenger services were withdrawn between Barry and Bridgend on 15 June 1964 and local freight 1963–67, but in 1980 the V of G remained opened for through freight, notably coal to the CEGB Aberthaw Generating Station, and was used for major diversions of main line trains in the event of engineering occupations between Cardiff and Bridgend. An important addition to its usefulness was the opening on 15 January 1980 of a 1¼-mile single-track branch from near Ewenny to serve the Ford Motor Company's Bridgend engine plant, with an anticipated 170,000 tonnes of traffic per year. (See Chapter XII).

LLYNVI AND OGMORE

In geographical sequence from east to west, the rivers Ogmore, Garw and Llynvi combine into the River Ogwr (Ogmore) at Tondu, three miles above Bridgend. Equally the local railways serving these industrialised valleys came together at Tondu, which became the headquarters of the Llynvi & Ogmore Railway Company, with its workshops, a substantial locomotive shed (nearly fifty steam locomotives stationed there even after World War II) and in 1889 after the GWR take-over, an L & O District Superintendent. Within a five-mile radius of Bridgend, there were nearly twenty junctions, excluding those with or within the network of colliery private lines.

The genesis of this once intensive local complex comprised two tramroads, both oddly of 4ft 7in gauge: the Duffryn Llynvi & Porthcawl Railway incorporated 1825 to make a line nearly seventeen miles long from Duffryn Llynvi north of Maesteg to the Bristol Channel at Porthcawl, with powers to make a pier and other works at the last-named place, and the Bridgend Railway, incorporated on 19 June 1828 to make a connecting line from Bridgend (on the site of the present bus station) to join the DL & PR west of Tondu. The DL & PR was thus one of the earliest examples of the incorporation of a company combining rail transport with its own trade harbour.

These horse tramroads were open by 1828 and 1834 respectively, but soon becoming inadequate to the developing traffic in iron, coal, bricks, tinplate and spelter from the Llynvi Valley, the Porthcawl was taken over in 1847 by the Llynvi Valley Railway Company, incorporated 7 August 1846, and the Bridgend by the LVR's re-incorporation Act of 15 June 1855, when conversion to broad gauge locomotive line was authorised. It opened for minerals on 10 August 1861, and passengers (Bridgend–Maesteg) 25 February 1864. The Ogmore Valley Railways Company, however, incorporated 13 July 1863, had perversely decided upon the standard gauge for its 7¼-mile Nantymoel–Tondu line, with powers for a third rail over the LVR between Tondu and Porthcawl, thus reproducing the contentious elements of the Ely Valley–TVR situation a few miles to the east. The OVR opened on 1 August 1865, having sold a locomotive to the LVR, probably for working OVR standard gauge passenger trains over the mixed gauge to Porthcawl. That day the LVR started a passenger service to Porthcawl in addition to that already operating to Bridgend over the new line from Tondu, largely superseding the tramway alignment. At Bridgend the LVR built its own little station on the north side of the GWR's main line station; until the nineteen seventies its distinctive building survived withdrawal of local valley services.

A FAMILY BUSINESS

The fact that the OVR adopted a different gauge to that of its neighbour the LVR betokened no dispute between them; they were in fact interlocked through mutual interests of the Brogdens, a family of industrialists from Lancashire. John Brogden & Sons had acquired ironworks in the Maesteg-Tondu district in 1854; the LVR directorate included Alexander Brogden of Ulverston, who was also a director of the Lancaster & Carlisle and of the Solway Junction companies, while of six members of the Ogmore Valley board in 1865, not only Alexander but also John, Henry and James were all Brogdens! In the same year (1865) the OVR obtained powers to acquire, for strategic reasons which emerge later, the Ely Valley Extension Railway Company, incorporated 28 July 1863 for 2½ miles of broad gauge line from termination of the Gellyrhaidd (later Hendreforgan) Branch to Gilfach Goch; opened in October 1865, it was worked by the GWR as part of the EVR (p173). The Taff Vale's Treferig Railway had been intended to push westward to connect with the Ely Valley Extension at both Hendreforgan and Gilfach Goch, but nothing came of this in the ambitious form originally proposed.

The Llynvi Valley and the Ogmore Valley companies had also been authorised in 1864 to undertake jointly improvements to Porthcawl Harbour, and it was logical for the two companies to amalgamate as the Llynvi & Ogmore Railway Company by Act of 28 June 1866; by 1868 the third rail had been laid throughout the system, although broad gauge rails where they existed remained until 1872 for traffic exchange with the GWR. Spurred on by its customers' growing revolt against the Broad Gauge, and encouraged by the machinations of the LNWR seeking a westward outlet from the Rhymney Railway at Caerphilly towards the Llynvi group of valleys and Port Talbot, the L & O brought forward in 1871 a bold project – to which no doubt the Euston coffers might be expected to contribute – for a new railway from Brynmenyn near Tondu, eastward past Treferig to cross the Vale of Taff near Taff's Well by an eighteen-arch viaduct more than 400yd long and 120ft high, and so to join up with the RR at Nantgarw. Although the L & O on withdrawing the proposal claimed that this was because the GWR had agreed to lay down the narrow gauge... 'over the whole of their system in South Wales', it was at least one of the factors in the latter decision. Thence to another inevitability: the GWR agreed to take-over the working and management of the L & O from 1 July 1873, by which time the local system embraced over twenty-seven miles of railway, serving some twenty-six collieries.

COMPLETING THE NETWORK

Between the GWR's assumption of management and formal amalgamation ten years later, some further extensions of the network were made. On 1 September 1875 a link-up was effected between Blackmill, at the foot of the Ogmore Valley, and the Ely Valley Extension Railway, hitherto detached from the owning system, at Hendreforgan. In the following year, the Cardiff & Ogmore Valley Railway Company, incorporated 21 July 1873 and three years later technically amalgamated with the L & O although the latter never worked it, was opened for freight traffic on 2 October 1876. It left the Ogmore Valley line at C & O Junction, about a mile above Blackmill, and curved eastward past several collieries to join the South Wales main line at Llanharan, the first station west of Llantrisant. The C & O line became linked to Tondu by a two-mile addition (Bryncethin Junction-Ynysawdre Junction) on 1 May in the following year. The effect of these additions was to afford a direct route for valleys traffic towards Cardiff, and from 1889, via Llanharan, Peterston and Drope Junction to Barry Docks. Although it served other collieries as well as those of David Davies' Ocean Coal at Blaengarw and elsewhere it was clearly intended to secure a shorter journey, and thus lower rates, than going round by Tondu. Also, in the event of the GWR main line being blocked by engineering operations between Llantrisant and Pyle or Port Talbot, another diversionary route became available via Llanharan-Tondu.

Two major developments which completed the GWR network in this area were the opening of the 5¾-mile Garw Branch (Brynmenyn Junction, Tondu to Blaengarw, in the central valley of the trio, for freight on 25 October 1876) and the extension of the original Llynvi Valley line from Nantyffyllon to Cymmer in the Afan Valley, through the single-line Cymmer Tunnel, nearly a mile long, on 1 July 1878 (for passenger traffic on 16 July 1880); the original name of Nantyffyllon was Tywith, meaning 'left-sided house'.

All three parallel valley lines were steeply graded, with maximum limitations of 1 in 37 at Caerau in the Llynvi, 1 in 32 in the Ogmore, and 1 in 34 in the Garw, with 1 in 18 beyond the limit of passenger working in the last-named. This was the scene of a sad accident in 1950, when a freight train of nine wagons ran away for over three miles to Llangeinor, the fireman being killed in the ensuing derailment.

PENETRATION FROM PORT TALBOT

From the completion by 1878 of the Llynvi & Ogmore network, having already taken over the management of that company five years before, the GWR enjoyed a complete monopoly of the developing local coalfield and its other industries, of which Maesteg and Tondu were the principal centres, for the next twenty years. When competition arose, it was with the incorporation on 31 July 1894 of the Port Talbot Railway & Docks Company for the purposes of acquiring the existing harbour and docks at the mouth of the River Avon, and constructing a connecting railway eastward into the coalfield. The first section, opened for freight traffic on 31 August 1897, extended for just under eleven miles from Port Talbot through Maesteg (where it crossed over the top of the GWR) to Lletty Brongu on the eastern slope of the Llynvi Valley. On 17 January of the following year, the PTR was extended for three miles from Lletty Brongu to a junction at Pontyrhyll with the Garw Branch. The PTR had running powers for passenger traffic from this junction up to Blaengarw but had to exchange freight at Pontyrhyll.

A further penetration of the coalfield by the Port Talbot Company was authorised by its Ogmore Valleys Extension Act of 7 August 1896. Opened on 19 December 1898, this left the Port Talbot dock lines at Copper Works Junction, ran parallel with and on the seaward side of the GWR main line for some four miles across Margam Moors and then turned inland over the top of the GWR, to terminate at Cefn Junction with the Pyle-Tondu line. Intermediately at Waterhall Junction (the second of that name in South Wales) was a mile-long spur, which made an eastern-facing junction with the GWR main line at Pyle, and which never seemed to enjoy much use. The building of this extension involved the acquisition of two private railways, the Cefn & Pyle and the Morfa, at the eastern and western ends respectively, the Cefn & Pyle giving access to the group of collieries on its north side including Bryndu, Aberbaiden, and Ton Phillip. Altogether in the boom years, the railway group comprising the former L & O system, the Blaengarw Branch and the PTR penetrating lines served more than fifty collieries.

PORTHCAWL

Although its role as a port to serve hinterland industry formed part of the basic concept of the local rail system first authorised in 1825, Porthcawl ceased to perform this function just before the end of the last century. The ensuing period of some seventy years down to the ultimate, controversial, extinction of the branch in 1965, witnessed the railway performing the quite different function of serving a growing residential and holiday seaside resort, affording a fascinating case-study of local and social history which can only be summarised here.

The DL & P having constructed a breakwater and tidal harbour under its initial powers, the Llynvi Valley and the Ogmore Valley companies combined in the 1860s to provide an inner wet dock of 1½ acres, capable of handling ships of up to 2,000 tons and equipped with coal tips and other appliances; this dock was constructed by James Brogden & Sons. The port shipped out coal, iron including rails and chairs, receiving timber pit-props and other cargoes in return. There was even a shipbuilding firm based there, together with shipping agents, ship chandlers and so on, some of whose former offices are identifiable to this day. Porthcawl's shipping prosperity was comparatively short-lived, however, its relative lack of capacity and limited seaward access making it impossible in later years to compete economically with the superior facilities of Port Talbot and Barry, especially in view of the improved rail access which became available to those ports. The GWR, which until the Railways Act of 1921 was more interested in serving ports than in working them, therefore closed the docks in 1898, and they were filled in during the 1920s to provide an esplanade and car park for the increasing number of residents and visitors. The ¾-mile Porthcawl Branch enjoyed successive improved connections with the main line at Pyle: from 13 November 1876 the GWR and L & O level-crossing was replaced by an underpass and westerly spur; 1882 saw the L & O realigned, with its station closer to the GWR; the latter, from 1 July 1886, closed its own station to the west, resiting it with staggered platforms opposite the L & O establishment; direct junctions giving through running, Porthcawl–Cardiff and Tondu– Port Talbot, opened July 1900; and further alterations linking the two stations followed in November 1912. After closure of the branch, freight traffic continued from Tondu through Pyle to Port Talbot as well as via Cefn Junction and the PTR; from 1974 only the latter continued in use.

The original station at Porthcawl, immediately north of the main road level-crossing, was superseded on 6 March 1916 by a new one of three terminal platforms on the site of the old dock lines beyond the crossing. After being held up by World War II, the GWR brought into operation in early March 1947 a new curve from the branch towards Port Talbot at Pyle West Loop Junction on the main line. This was used by stone trains from Cornelly Sidings on the branch for the Abbey Steel Works at Port Talbot, by excursions from the Swansea district, and by residential trains worked with diesel railcars, between Porthcawl, Port Talbot and Swansea. These had a long-standing counterpart in a residential express, run for the convenience of local residents working in Cardiff, which ran to the capital city in the morning and returned in the evening. The morning service, four or five coaches and non-stop from Bridgend, could provide on occasion some surprisingly sprightly running by a six-coupled pannier tank with 4ft 7½in wheels, spinning along past Llantrisant and Peterston at around a mile a minute... In the 1950s, there was even a scheme approved for another new station at Porthcawl, on the north side of the level-crossing so as to relieve the road congestion; this would have had no fewer than six platforms, mostly for excursion traffic. But restriction of capital expenditure and the looming imminence of 're-shaping', doomed all this within a decade or so. Porthcawl lost all its passenger trains on 9 September 1963 and the branch was completely closed on 1 February 1965. Pyle station on the main line closed to passengers on 2 November 1964 (the Pyle-Tondu service having officially ceased at the same time as Pyle-Porthcawl), leaving Bridgend and Port Talbot as the first two stations open from Cardiff, respectively twenty and 32¼ miles from the capital.

WITHDRAWALS

The pattern of service withdrawals in the L & O district was common to that of other mining areas, the passenger services succumbing to the advance of motors, public and private, while freight lines were carved up piecemeal as individual pits and plants became extinguished. In the Garw Valley, the ex-PTR passenger service was an early casualty, GWR trains to Bridgend being more convenient for main line connections and recreation than the circuitous route to Port Talbot. This service, Port Talbot–Pontycymmer, began on 14 February 1898 (four weeks after opening to Pontyrhyll). According to *Bradshaw*, along with the GWR service terminating at Pontycymmer, it extended to

Blaengarw from 3 May 1902. It was cut back, Port Talbot–Maesteg (Neath Road), from 12 September 1932, surviving only until 11 September 1933, though freight lasted until 31 August 1964. The GWR Blaengarw service, however, operated until 9 February 1953. In neighbouring Ogmore Vale the Nantymoel trains ceased on 5 May 1958. Both latter branches closed to freight on 22 March 1965 but remained for coal in 1980.

Passenger service on what in railway terms was the oldest valley, the Llynvi (often Llynfi, sometimes Llwynfi!) outlasted the other two, mainly because it afforded connection through the Cymmer and Rhondda Tunnels with the Rhondda Valley at Treherbert, and there were difficulties in arranging alternative bus services over the intervening mountains: difficulties had also been encountered by Sir Daniel Gooch in 1876, when he rode on pony-back from Treherbert to Abergwynfi to inspect the Avon Colliery, then being sunk at the latter place as a source of locomotive coal for the GWR. So the passenger service between Bridgend and Treherbert via the Rhondda Tunnel was reprieved until 22 June 1970, while school trains continued to run between Cymmer and Llangynwyd until 14 July. Between Tondu and Nantyffyllon the branch continued to deal with NCB traffic from the Maesteg area, having been similarly open up to Caerau until 7 March 1977; lower down the valley, traffic has also been lost following the closure in 1977 of the CEGB Llynfi generating station, opened in 1943. Also in the same valley, the PTR line between Maesteg and Pontyrhyll Junction was progressively abandoned from about 1948 onwards, a mile or so eastward of the former PTR station at Maesteg (Neath Road) to Cwmdu being transferred to NCB ownership in 1964 and absorbed into the latter's rail system.

In the eastern part of the district, the passenger service between Blackmill, Hendreforgan and Gilfach Goch was an early casualty, being finally withdrawn on 22 September 1930, while from the eastern end Gellyrhaidd Junction-Gilfach Goch was closed completely on 5 June 1961. The former Cardiff & Ogmore Valley Railway, C & O Junction–Bryncethin Junction, closed 28 July 1938, the massive viaduct (seven steel spans on masonry piers and abutments) over the River Ogmore and Ely Valley Extension line being demolished during World War II. On 3 December 1962 Llanharan Junction was severed and the C & OV cut back to tap, via Bryncethin Junction and the Pencoed Branch, coal around Wern Tarw. Known thereafter as the Raglan Branch, Ogmore

Junction–Wern Tarw had been closed and lifted by September 1983.

PORT TALBOT

Racing downhill from Stormy, past the Margam marshalling yard completed in 1960, the traveller finds the mountains closing in on the right to press the main railway and trunk road against the eastern shores of Swansea Bay between the Rivers Avon (Afan) and Neath, forming an industrial belt some six miles long in which prior to 1922 were located three nominally independent railways in addition to the GWR.

By 1980 there was little diversity of heavy industry in this area beyond the huge complex layouts of the British Steel Corporation at Port Talbot, the BP chemicals plant a few miles to the west on Baglan Burrows, and the coal production of the Dulais Valley above Neath. During the Industrial Revolution the district blossomed rapidly with the production of iron, coal, tinplate, and particularly copper. With ore brought by sea from Cornwall, this was smelted at the Cwmavon Copper Works above Port Talbot, established in 1776 by the Governor & Company of Copper Miners in England, who laid out the original dock at Port Talbot (then known as Aberavon) in 1837, and to whom Airey's map of 1876 attributes the ownership of the original local railways thence to Cwmavon, succeeding much earlier tramroads. Aberavon and Neath were soon eclipsed in the smelting of copper by Swansea and in 1870, just two decades after the opening of the South Wales Railway through Port Talbot and Neath to Swansea, the company went into liquidation. Its interest was taken-over by a local personality of great energy and drive, C.R.M. Talbot of Margam Abbey, who had been chairman of the South Wales Railway Company prior to its amalgamation with the GWR, and who continued for many years as a director of the latter, having given the family name to 'Port Talbot'.

It was not until the formation of the Port Talbot Railway & Docks Company in 1894, however, that there began the establishment of dock facilities adequate for the expansion of shipping trade based upon the rapid growth of the coalfields of the Avon Valley and the L & O district to the east. By 1900 the trade of the port had risen to over half-a-million tons; coal exports increased to 2.3 million tons by 1916, and total trade to a peak of 3.2 million tons (2.7 million tons of coal) in 1923. Provision of railway facilities was equally

Page 187 (Top) GWR outside-framed Aberdare Class 2-6-0 No 2625, in its final form, at Aberdare shed *circa* 1930; *(centre)* The ultimate TVR 0-6-2T design by John Cameron, the A Class of 1914. Depicted is No 149, built by Hawthorn Leslie in 1920; *(bottom)* Barry Railway 0-6-4T No 143, as built by Hawthorn Leslie in 1914. *(Author; Locomotive Publishing Co/Ian Allan)*

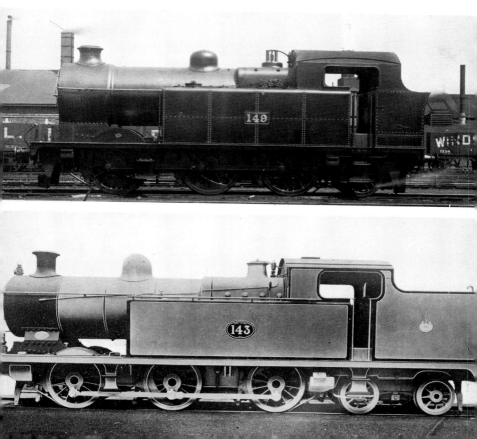

Page 188 (Top) Rhymney Railway steam railmotor No 1 at Senghenydd in 1908; (centre) Basic railway – ex-GWR railmotor trailer, propelled by an ex-GWR 0-6-0PT, at Treforest Halt on a Caerphilly – Pontypridd service in 1952; (bottom) Train of tramcar-type trailers hauled by steam locomotive on the Swansea & Mumbles line, around the turn of the century. (E. R. Mountford collection; T. B. Sands; Locomotive Publishing Co/Ian Allan)

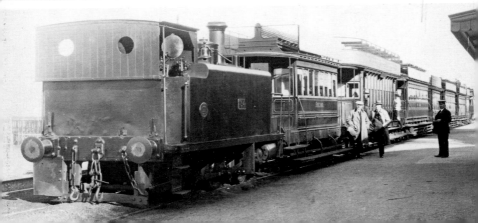

rapid: within four-and-a-half years of its incorporation, the PTR had opened not only the east-ward branches to the Garw Valley and the Ogmore Valley already described, but also on 14 November 1898 a northwards line from Port Talbot through Cwmavon into the coalfield at Tonmawr (nearly six miles), plus the Blaenavon and Whitworth mineral branches (2½ miles), together with dock lines in Port Talbot, a system mileage of 33½ miles. In Port Talbot the PTR offices were architecturally a compromise between a munic-ipal building and a chapel. A short distance away, across the main street from the GWR station, was the PTR's simple, wooden Central station, unusual in featuring at the single platform end not a starting signal but the distant for Tonygroes Junction, whence

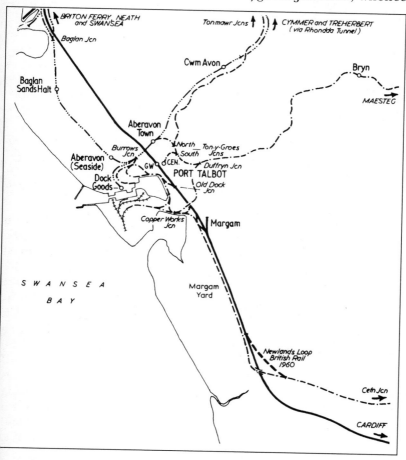

connections diverged to both Tonmawr (PTR) and the Rhondda & Swansea Bay Railway. But keeping eastward from Tonygroes, the PTR main line led past the main traffic yard and locomotive depot at Duffryn Junction towards Maesteg, up through the Cwm Duffryn Valley on fierce grades of some four miles at 1 in 40 into the ¾-mile long Cwm Cerwyn Tunnel, in the middle of which the gradient suddenly changed from 1 in 70 rising to level; thence past Maesteg (7½ miles) was all downhill. To work this fearsome line the PTR introduced in 1899 two 0–8–2 tank engines, Nos 20 and 21, built by the Cooke Locomotive Works of USA, and three more built by Sharp, Stewart in 1901. The former two were referred to in the 1907 working timetable as the 'Yankee Engines', and were slightly less powerful than the Sharp, Stewart locomotives, which were expected to take a greater number of empties up to the tunnel with a banker on as well, either type was expected to take fifty-five empties out of Duffryn Yard! Except on Saturdays when demand could exceed its capacity, during 1907–20 the Port Talbot–Blaengarw passenger service was mainly worked by the largest (76ft 9in overall) British steam railmotor, a sixty-six seater longer than most coaches, and electrically lit. It boasted a tractive effort of 9,520lbs and a unique 0–6–0 driving unit. This dramatic route closed, Duffryn Junction–Maesteg, from 31 August 1964. The NCB length (p185) was lifted in 1989.

SOUTH WALES MINERAL RAILWAY

Although its control of the docks and its impressive concentration of industrial traffic within a relatively short radius established the PTR in a special position around Port Talbot, it was in age the most junior of the three railways (other than the GWR) which served the Afan Valley district, the other two being the Rhondda & Swansea Bay and the South Wales Mineral Railways; the last-named was in fact the oldest of the trio. Encouraged by the advent of the South Wales and Vale of Neath Railways, 1850–51, the prospective coalowners of the upper Afan Valley and minor side valleys to the north of it, secured by Act of 15 August 1853 the incorporation of the South Wales Mineral Railway Company for a mountainous cross-country line some thirteen miles long between the remote Glyncorrwg Valley north of Cymmer and a junction with the South Wales Railway at Briton Ferry between Aberavon (Port Talbot) and Neath. The SWMR was laid out by Brunel, later succeeded by R.

Brereton, and in the circumstances of the time was of necessity broad gauge. To overcome an acute difference in level at the Western end, Brunel's route descended to the South Wales Railway at Briton Ferry by a double-track cable-worked incline about 1½ miles long, the rest of the railway being single track. At Briton Ferry, the SWMR connected with the Briton Ferry Floating Dock Company, incorporated by Act of 3 July 1851 to provide dock facilities for Neath; the lock gates were designed by Brunel. The dock opened on 23 August 1861, followed on 1 September by the initial 5¾ miles of the SWMR between Briton Ferry and the west end of the 1,109yd Gyfylcha Tunnel at Tonmawr, by which the railway passed through the mountain ridge into the main Afan Valley. Two short colliery branches were brought into use in 1862, and on 10 March 1863 the railway was completed through the tunnel and on to Glyncorrwg, a further 7¼ miles. The whole line was converted to standard gauge in May 1872.

The SWMR Company was leased from before its opening to the Glyncorrwg Coal Company and later to the latter's successor, but was never financially successful, and a receiver was appointed by the Court of Chancery. In 1895 there were debit balances on both capital and revenue accounts. The company's troubles included unrealised expectations of the growth of coal traffic, high working costs including the incline working, and from 1898 onwards, the diversion of traffic to the superior facilities of Port Talbot over the PTR's new line from Tonygroes Junction to Tonmawr and thence to the Blaenavon and Whitworth branches. The PTR Tonmawr branch only carried a public passenger service between 1898 and 22 September 1930. Eventually the working and management of the SWMR was taken over by the GWR with effect from 1 January 1908, the Briton Ferry incline being closed two years later; the Briton Ferry Floating Dock Company had already vested in the GWR in 1873, eight years after the Vale of Neath (February 1865, confirmed by GWR Act of August 1866), which was a mortgagee of the dock company.

HARD SLOG TO GLYNCORRWG

Later designated by the GWR as the North Rhondda Branch, the northernmost three miles of the SWMR between Cymmer Corrwg (the SWMR's single platform on the opposite side of the Afan Gorge to the GWR station) and North Rhondda Halt and Colliery represented the only section of the SWMR over which passenger services operated. A more difficult venue could hardly have been imagined, the single track winding through the narrow defile of the Glyn Corrwg and rising for most of the way at 1 in 28/22. The public service which started on 28 March 1918 went only two miles to the lonely township of Glyncorrwg, the population of which – at one time over 10,000 – was afflicted by the heaviest annual rainfall in Glamorgan. After the public service was withdrawn on 22 September 1930, workmen's trains continued to run through to North Rhondda Halt until the closure of the collieries. The colliers' train comprised several four-wheeled coaches, which must have been among the last of this wheel arrangement to be regularly used on British Railways, and which were propelled all the way up the valley to the accompaniment of almost continuous hooting and occasional slipping. Conversely, a mineral train coming down from North Rhondda to Port Talbot had to halt at eight stop boards in some twelve miles.

On 13 July 1947, the SWMR line through Gyfylcha Tunnel was closed through landslip, and coal traffic from North Rhondda was diverted via Cymmer and Tondu, utilising the connection effected between the GWR and the SWMR, by means of a high steel-girder bridge across the gorge, as part of the extension of the Llynvi Valley line through the 1,595yd Cymmer Tunnel into the Afan Valley, opened on 1 July 1878. The North Rhondda Branch was finally closed in August 1970.

THE RHONDDA & SWANSEA BAY

Descending the whole course of the Afan Valley from Blaengwynfi to Port Talbot, and thence westward through Briton Ferry and past Neath eventually to reach its ultimate goal at Swansea, the Rhondda & Swansea Bay Railway was promoted in the 1880s to connect the Rhondda and Afan coalfields with the port of Swansea. Among the routes surveyed in early planning was one from Treherbert towards Glyncorrwg and thence over the South Wales Mineral Railway to Briton Ferry, but fortunately this was dropped and the alternative was adopted and authorised by the incorporating Act of 10 August 1882, of tunnelling straight through the mountain from the junction with the Taff Valley Railway above Treherbert, thence from Blaengwynfi down the Afan Valley to Pontrhydyfen, four miles above Port Talbot. Originally the main line was to cut through the high ground to Briton Ferry, with a branch to Port Talbot via Cwmavon. In 1883 powers were obtained to extend from Briton Ferry to Prince of Wales Dock, Swansea, but agreement with the GWR for traffic facilities led to abandonment of the extension and part of the authorised 1882 line between Pontrhydyfen and Briton Ferry. Never consummated, the agreement was annulled by Act of 1891, with powers revived for the Briton Ferry line, and in 1892 to extend thence over the Neath to Swansea. There followed four Acts between 1893 and 1898, too complex for space here, which authorised abandonments, substitutions, new lines and extensions of time.

Though Aberavon–Cymmer opened on 2 November 1885, it was not until 2 June 1890 that trains reached Blaengwynfi and 2 July 1890 before the 3,443yd Rhondda Tunnel, longest wholly in South Wales, was pierced and the Rhondda coalfield tapped by the R & SB. In the following year, having crossed the GWR (to the latter's chagrin) on the level, west of Port Talbot station, the R & SB was able to begin passenger traffic to and from the Docks Station at Port Talbot, where it established a wharf. The Docks station closed for passenger traffic on 14 March 1895, with the extension of passenger service through to Swansea, mineral traffic between Aberavon and Briton Ferry having already started on 30 December 1893. Between Port Talbot and Briton Ferry, the R & SB kept away from the GWR main line on its seaward side across Baglan Burrows, throwing off at Baglan Junction a short spur into Briton Ferry Dock.

A WET WELSH TUNNEL

My personal recollection of the R & SB route is of damp journeys through the Rhondda Tunnel, with icy douches of water descending at intervals into the locomotive cab, and of mountain sheep hazardously hiding from the rain inside either portal. Emerging from the western end, with the single line from Abergwynfi descending alongside from its terminus at a slightly higher level, the two single lines ran side-by-side through the barren valley to Cymmer, where the line from Abergwynfi bore left into the GWR station (Cymmer Afan, formerly Cymmer General), the R & SB using its own station in the centre – Cwm Corrwg, SWMR, lay on the north-western slope across the gorge. A feature of the R & SB station was a refreshment building with four separate entrances, all of which led to a single long room.

On 18 April 1946 the 5.47am workmen's train from Treherbert to Duffryn Rhondda, consisting of 0-6-2T No 356 (ex-TVR) and four coaches became derailed 340ft from the Blaengwynfi end of Cymmer Viaduct, the locomotive and leading coach falling over the embankment; mercifully none of the eighty-five passengers was seriously hurt. In order to avoid repairs to the 167yd Gelli Tunnel and the Groeserw Viaduct on the R & SB section, both of which were liable to mining subsidence, 1½ miles of the R & SB line between Cymmer and Blaengwynfi were closed and traffic diverted over the relevant portion of the GWR Bridgend (Llynvi Valley) line, from which most of the Bridgend trains were diverted into Blaengwynfi. This scheme came into operation on 13 June 1960 but only three years later, on 3 December 1962, the Swansea-Treherbert passenger service was withdrawn. This was partially replaced by a service between Bridgend and Treherbert via the Llynvi and Afan Valleys, but this in its turn was cut back to Cymmer on 26 February 1968 by the temporary closure (which ultimately proved to be permanent) of the Rhondda Tunnel due to serious earth movement.

Below Cymmer, the R & SB was on falling grades as steep as 1 in 39 down to Aberavon; on 24 November 1960 a descending unfitted freight train of twenty-six wagons and brake hauled by a 57XX pannier tank got out of control on the descent, over-ran Pontrhydyfen station, and collided head-on with an ascending diesel multiple-unit working through from Swansea to Barry Island, causing two fatal casualties and a number of injured. It was near the scene of this accident that in 1954 the PTR Port Talbot-Tonmawr branch of 1898, which for some three miles ran closely parallel with the R & SB through the valley, was closed between Margam Forge, Cwmavon and Oakwood below Pontryhdyfen, and traffic diverted over a new connection with the R & SB section. Between 1954–64, however, the Tonmawr–Blaenavon–Whitworth branches all closed.

The R & SB had two passenger stations in the Port Talbot area, Aberavon (Town) and Aberavon (Seaside) respectively north and south of the level-crossing of the GWR main line; the former station had for some years a few PTR connecting trains from and to the Central station, while 'Seaside', the site of which is now covered by building development, enjoyed in its time considerable popularity with summer day trippers.

THE GWR TAKE-OVER

Although the three local companies just described retained their separate corporate status until the Railways Act of 1921, their working and management was taken-over by the GWR more than a decade earlier. This was a sharp counter-move by Paddington to a threat by the Barry Railway to expand westward from the Vale of Glamorgan Railway to join up with the proposed Neath, Pontardawe & Brynamman Railway. The last-named company had been incorporated in 1895 and ten years later was still dormant, until the GWR was alerted by the election of T.R. Thompson, a Barry director, as chairman, and by the Barry seeking powers to subscribe to the NP & B Company. The GWR therefore made agreements whereby the working and management of the R & SB came under its direction, with full running powers, with effect from 1 January 1906, in return for financial guarantees to the shareholders, and similarly with the PTR from 1 January 1908, except that in the latter case the dock undertaking was left under the management of the owning company. Also on I January 1908 an agreement was implemented between the GWR, PTR and the South Wales Mineral Railway whereby the former took over the working of the SWMR for 67½% of the gross receipts, subject to a minimum-revenue guarantee which was underwritten in the tripartite agreement.

Apart from the defensive value of these agreements against the Barry, the GWR made excellent use of them for traffic working, being able to work with its own locomotives and men all traffic from the Tondu area for Port Talbot and Swansea via the Ogmore Valleys Extension Railway (PTR) through Margam, and using the R & SB route to Swansea.

With the local collieries running down and the decline in shipment traffic, Briton Ferry Dock was closed as a trade harbour in 1940, being made tidal in 1954. At Port Talbot, where coal shipments had declined from the 1923 peak of 2.7m tons to 147,000 tons by 1958, and where a major new harbour was completed by the British Transport Docks Board in 1970 to accommodate bulk carriers of 100,000 tons deadweight, the old docks were closed for public commercial traffic on 1 January 1972. Port Talbot is now classified as a tidal harbour, and in 1980 remained busy with annual inwards shipments of iron ore and coking coal in excess of 6m tonnes through the modern Ore Terminal, nearly 69,000 tonnes of ore having been discharged for onward rail movement to Llanwern

during a single 24-hour period; scope existed for further development of bulk cargoes. On the north side of Port Talbot, almost the
whole inland network of the three former local companies (the ex-
GWR main line of course excluded) has been progressively closed
down. (See Chapter XII).

CHAPTER IX

Neath and Swansea

The ancient town of Neath is situated 5½ miles north of Port Talbot and eight miles east of Swansea. It was an industrial and transport centre long before it became the railway gateway to Swansea. Smelting of copper began at Neath as early as the mid-sixteenth century until superseded by Swansea. Canal communication with the hinterland began before 1800, while the famous Neath Abbey Ironworks built not only iron ships, but also steam locomotives for early customers such as the Penydarren Tramroad and the Dowlais Iron Company.

Five railways contributed to development of Neath: the South Wales (opened 1850), Vale of Neath (1851), Swansea & Neath (1863), Neath & Brecon (1864) and Rhondda & Swansea Bay (1894). In avoiding Crymlyn bog, between Neath and Swansea, both the SWR and R & SB would have liked to bridge the river nearer its mouth, in order to follow low-level routes into Swansea across Crymlyn Burrows, between bog and sea, but were frustrated by the objections of the Neath Harbour Commissioners, bedazzled by the prospect of tall ships stemming the tide into visionary docks which never amounted to more than a few up-river wharves plus the docks at Briton Ferry. Thus baulked, Brunel took the SWR right into the town before making a full U-turn over the river and then striking towards Swansea on a ruling grade of 1 in 88 through Skewen. Brunel's crossing over both the river and the Tennant canal was by a timber viaduct just west of Neath Station, replaced in 1906 by steel-girder spans.

By Act of 6 August 1861 the Swansea & Neath Railway Company was incorporated, being one of the few to be authorised in the changing climate of the period to adopt mixed gauge, for a more direct line from a junction with the Vale of Neath north-west of the town through to the North Dock at Swansea along the Crymlyn

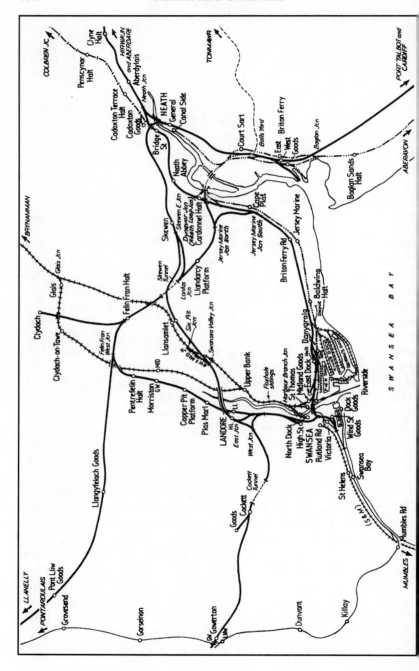

Burrows. After a sharp battle between the Vale of Neath and the South Wales, with Big Brother Paddington supporting the latter, the Vale of Neath acquired it in 1863 and worked it from its opening on 15 July 1863.

Next, the town was reached by the Neath & Brecon Railway, incorporated by Act of 29 July 1862 as the Dulas (sic) Valley Mineral Railway for a line from Neath into the Dulais Valley, diverging from the Neath Valley proper at Aberdulais 1¾ miles above the town, and opening up a coalfield between Neath and Onllwyn, still served during the 1980s. These initial ten miles were opened on 2 October 1864. By Act of 13 July 1863 the company changed its name to that of Neath & Brecon Railway, with powers to extend over the mountains to Brecon in order to become part of a through route between Swansea, Central Wales and the Midlands (p205).

Last comer to Neath was the Rhondda & Swansea Bay Railway, which in 1883 had proposed to circumvent the Neath Harbour Commissioners' objections to a down-river bridge by driving a 1,490yd tunnel under the river. This project was abandoned however in the light of engineering difficulties and the abortive agreement with the GWR to convey R & SB traffic to Swansea; the annulment of this agreement in 1891 was followed by the R & SB acquiring powers (Act of 27 June 1892) for a fresh extension to the Prince of Wales' Dock, Swansea, crossing the river below Brunel's bridge by means of its own remarkable Neath River Swing Bridge – the only one in the country to be built both on the skew and on a curve. Its total length is 388ft, the swing portion being of 170ft, with five fixed spans, and a gross weight of 1,400 tons. The engineer, S. H. Yockney, had been a pupil of Brunel's. To reach the bridge, the R & SB line after following the coastline between Aberavon and Baglan, passed under the GWR main line at Baglan Junction and thence ran parallel with it on the inland side to burrow under the GWR main line again at Court Sart; in 1935 the R & SB line was abandoned for through traffic, this being concentrated on the GWR main line by means of track alterations at either end. The R & SB line was extended from Aberavon to Briton Ferry Dock on 30 December 1893 and thence across the swing bridge towards Swansea on 14 December of the following year.

STATIONS AT NEATH

Of various passenger stations which have served Neath since 1850, that still in use is the GWR station, formerly Neath (General). The first station here was replaced in 1865 by a 'High Level' structure on the curve above the Neath & Brecon, itself superseded from 4 June 1877 by a third station reverting to the first location. Platforms were extended in 1896 and modernised buildings opened on 6 March 1978.

Although the GWR main line afforded a direct northward connection to and from the former Vale of Neath Aberdare and Merthyr route immediately north of this station, traffic to and from the Swansea & Neath and the Neath & Brecon lines could only be exchanged by a back-shunt and reversal at Neath Junction, west of which the N & B joined the Swansea & Neath at Cadoxton (later N & B) Junction, almost beneath Brunel's bridge over the river. The Neath & Brecon goods station, yard and workshops were situated north of the passenger station, originally the property of the Swansea & Neath, and known successively as 'Low Level', 'Bridge Street' from July 1924, and 'Riverside' from September 1926, where the N & B local passenger service also terminated from December 1892, and where as a tenant its general offices were also situated; the N & B had no running powers on to Swansea. Riverside closed for passenger traffic on 15 July 1964, the N & B local service having been withdrawn from 15 October 1962.

The last railway to open a passenger station at Neath was the Rhondda & Swansea Bay which, concurrently with extending towards Swansea, opened a 1¼-mile branch from Neath Branch Junction alongside firstly the river's and then the canal's east bank to a terminus close to the GWR main line station. The R & SB station, opened 14 March 1895, was initially 'Neath', became Neath (Canal Bridge) in July 1924, and Neath (Canal Side) in September 1926; it closed to passengers on 16 September 1935 and freight 6 September 1965, but part of the branch remained for private siding traffic until 30 November 1983.

SWANSEA

Second in population only to Cardiff and, by 1980, exceeding it as the premier port in South Wales in aggregate docks tonnages and numbers of shipping movements, Swansea from the earliest days of maritime trade was assured of an important future by its relatively sheltered position under the Gower Peninsula towards the western arm of Swansea Bay, and by the great industrial potential of its hinterland. In particular, its trade was stimulated by the development of copper smelting in the eighteenth century, reaching its peak about 1860, and although this trade was in due course lost to overseas development copper refining continued. The anthracite coalfield north of the city expanded; a substantial and still growing industry in petrol refining was established in the 1920s, while the iron, steel, chemical and tinplate industries, dispersed among a multitude of relatively small works, were by 1980 represented by huge modern plants. Unlike some other ports which had to reach out into the hinterland to feed their docks with traffic, Swansea from the outset had large resources for industry on its very doorstep.

Swansea lies along the valley of the River Tawe, the major growth of the city being to the west of it, the east bank of the river having been largely the area of development and desecration by the copper industry, the despoiled legacy of which is now being sympathetically overtaken by specialist landscaping. Initially the transport link between hinterland and port was the Swansea Canal, completed between Ystradgynlais and the river mouth in 1798, acquired by the GWR in 1872 and finally closed to navigation in 1921. In the middle of the century the docks and railways developed concurrently, beginning with the advent of the South Wales Railway in 1850 and the incorporation of the Swansea Harbour Trustees in 1857, until Swansea enjoyed a comprehensive dock system comprising the North Dock(1852), the South Dock (1859), the Prince of Wales' (1881), the King's (1909), and the Queen's (1920), the last-named being used mainly for petroleum. The early North and South Docks were sited on the west bank of the Tawe, the later ones on the east side, with the various railway companies having connections either over their own lines, or in connection with the Trustees' private railway network. After the railway grouping, the Trustees' dock and railway system was transferred to the GWR by separate voluntary legislation, the GWR (Swansea Harbour Vesting) Act of 18 July 1923, retrospectively effective from 1 July 1923.

Meanwhile, through enterprise, diplomacy or sheer cunning, Swansea had become ringed by railways on all three landward quarters. Ten different railway companies in all were involved in providing access to the port, but boiling down in the 1922-23 analysis to the GWR and LMS, plus the purely local Swansea & Mumbles Of these, only the GWR and its satellites penetrated through the area from east to west, the LMS faction entering from west and north.

SOUTH WALES RAILWAY

Brunel, having to take an inland approach to Swansea, crossed the
Tawe Valley with (according to Proceedings of the Institution of
Civil Engineers, 1855) a 587yd timber viaduct with 110ft complex
bowstring centre span, 75ft above the river, and thirty-six approach
spans. Rebuilding in 1886 resulted in a 389yd structure with twenty-
one varied approach spans of wrought iron girders and timber
decking on masonry piers and a 147ft centre span (strengthened
1960). The approaches were reconstructed during 1978–79, 1,500
tons of steelwork replacing 640 tons of wrought iron and over 500
tons of timber, raising permitted speed from 20 to 40mph and
allowing heavier loads to be carried..

While the South Wales Railway as first opened on 18 June 1850
terminated at the High Street passenger station in Swansea, this – a
simple wooden structure of two platforms with an overall roof,
under which nearly 700 people sat down to celebrate the SWR's
opening – became in effect a dead-end branch 1¼ miles from
Landore once the main line was extended from the latter place to
Carmarthen two years later. High Street was first enlarged in 1879,
but although the opening of the Swansea West Loop in 1906
allowed through working between High Street and the Carmarthen
direction, it was not until High Street was completely modernised
between 1923-32, that the station became adequate for increasing
traffic and longer trains. The station now bears the simple name
'Swansea (Abertawe)' being the sole survivor of seven passenger
termini at one time extant in the city. The once busy Landore,
although still the location of the principal motive power depot in
the area, was closed to passengers on 2 November 1964.

Arriving in Swansea the SWR lost no time in reaching the docks,
opening a branch of under ½ mile southwards from North Dock
Branch Junction (¼ mile north of High Street) in June 1852, to the
North Dock opened that year, the rails being extended ¼ mile in
September 1859. Vale of Neath coal traffic was initially worked to
this dock by the GWR (on behalf of the SWR) between Neath and
Swansea, but the V of N succeeded, after mutual asperities with
Paddington, in working this traffic with its own locomotives from
1861. In the following year the smaller company obtained a lease of
the Swansea Harbour Railway, built by the Trustees to extend the
North Dock Branch to the 1859 South Dock. Again a year later, on
15 July 1863, the Vale of Neath brought into use its mixed gauge
satellite, the Swansea & Neath, over the 7¾ miles from Neath

Junction to Wind Street Junction, between the North and South Docks, thus depriving the SWR/GWR of the haulage revenue between Neath and Swansea. On 1 August 1863 the Vale of Neath opened a passenger station at Wind Street, which in the following year welcomed a service of narrow (or standard) gauge passenger trains between Hereford and Swansea.

By 1865 the GWR had become fully possessed of the SWR, the Vale of Neath, and along with the latter the Swansea & Neath. November of that year was marked by a bad accident at the North Dock, which was crossed by one of two opening bridges on the Swansea & Neath, the other being over the New Cut of the River Tawe: the locomotive and thirty wagons of coal plunged disastrously and with fatal results through the open bridge into the dock, leading to the imprisonment for six months of the allegedly negligent signalman. The incidence of these two bridges close together, in the context of continuously increasing railway and marine movements, was doubtless one of the reasons for closing Wind Street for passengers on 1 March 1873, the coastal service diverting via the SWR line to Swansea, but reverting from October 1880 to a new terminus at East Dock on the other side of the river, close to Prince of Wales' or East Dock. In 1928 the GWR obtained powers to close the North Dock; railways to the South Dock closed in 1964–65.

THE R & SB IN SWANSEA

Last entrant to Swansea from eastward was the Rhondda & Swansea Bay Railway, running parallel with and mostly on the shoreward side of the GWR (the old Swansea & Neath line) from its own Neath River Bridge up to the east bank of the Tawe, almost opposite the entrance to North Dock Basin. The R & SB was opened for freight traffic on 14 December 1894 and for passengers to its new station at Swansea (Riverside) on 14 March 1895, although until 7 May 1899 R & SB trains used the mile of Trustees' dock lines between Danygraig and Riverside. A mile east of Danygraig station were the R & SB works and engine shed (1896–1964); the site of the nearby carriage shed became part of the Swansea Freightliner Terminal, opened 24 February 1969. Otherwise, the former R & SB line west of Jersey Marine South had been reduced to dock traffic use under the 1935 scheme, and was closed up to Danygraig exclusive in December 1967. Riverside in pre-grouping days was fascinating for the spectacle, thus far west, of Taff Vale Railway coaches: the two companies had a mutual arrangement whereby some of their trains worked through between Swansea and Cardiff and vice-versa, with alternating carriage sets. But both East Dock and Riverside Stations are gone; the service between Riverside and Treherbert was diverted to East Dock from 11 September 1933, Riverside being closed, but from 30 September 1935 some of the surviving local trains began to use High Street, until East Dock finally closed to passengers on 28 September 1936.

THE MIDLAND'S ENTRY

Meanwhile, through the acquisition of or arrangements with smaller companies, the LNWR and Midland Railways had been busily seeking routes of their own from the North and Midlands to Swansea, independently of the somewhat exiguous running powers via Middle Duffryn to which they had been entitled since 1864. In the event, both these big companies were to accomplish their objective within a few years of one another, and to finish up in confrontation across Swansea Docks.

For access to Swansea, the Midland used first its running powers from Worcester to Hereford, then the Hereford, Hay & Brecon, the Mid-Wales, the Brecon & Merthyr, the Neath & Brecon, and finally the Swansea Vale Railways. Between Hereford and Brecon the ancient Hay Railway, a horse tramroad originating in 1811, was partitioned in 1860 between the HH & B (Hay to Three Cocks Junction with the Mid-Wales Railway), the Mid-Wales (Three Cocks to Talyllyn), and the B & M (Talyllyn to Brecon, through the Talyllyn Tunnel, 674yd and one of the oldest in the British Isles). The B & M began to operate at Brecon in 1863, the Mid-Wales and the HH & B a year later; both were worked and dividends guaranteed by the contractor, Thomas Savin, whose financial collapse in 1866 led to virtual failure of the B & M. By Act of 5 July 1865 the HH & B and B & M were empowered to enter into agreement for amalgamation, but such agreement reached that August was later pronounced by the Court of Chancery to have been illegally processed and was cancelled by Act of 1868. From October 1868 the HH & B was worked by the Mid-Wales. HH & B running powers between Three Cocks and Brecon were granted by Act of 1869; on 1 October 1869, despite GWR opposition, the Midland Railway began working the HH & B, first vital step in its march on Swansea. Leased from July 1874, the HH & B was fully absorbed by Midland Acts of 1885–86.

Meanwhile the Neath & Brecon had extended its line, physically arduous and commercially precarious, over some 23 miles of largely barren mountain, from Onllwyn to Brecon, climbing for six miles mostly at 1 in 50 to the 1,267ft summit at Bwlch Siding, then descending for 7½ miles with almost equal severity to cross the Usk at Devynock & Senny Bridge, where the B & M carefully sought to obstruct further progress with foundations of a bridge intended to carry a B & M line, never built, to Llandovery. Eventually the N & B reached Brecon on 3 June 1867; undismayed by the refusal of the Board of Trade Inspector to approve for passenger traffic the end-on connection with the B & M over a bridge of marked fragility, the N & B used to detach the engine (which thus became a light engine and not a passenger train) and crowd the passengers upon it to convey them to a point nearer the B & M station. Eventually the B & M's new passenger station at Free Street (finally closed to passengers at the end of 1962) became available to all the using companies in 1871, complete with separate booking offices for each! Two years later, from mid July 1873, the Midland had begun to run through coaches between Birmingham and Brecon, and was poised to press on to Swansea over the three further small railways with which it was to conclude its 82-mile route march from Hereford.

THE SWANSEA VALE RAILWAY

This railway, which was to help the Midland over the last lap of its long haul to Swansea, had a most curious history. Formed from early tramroads extending inland up the east bank of the Tawe, near whose mouth its terminus was most favourably situated, it was built on land owned or leased by its several proprietors without Parliamentary powers. Joining in the 'Mania' of the 1845–46 session, it unsuccessfully sought to build a railway to Pontardawe, eight miles from Swansea, there to join the proposed Welsh Midland Railway (a line from Worcester to Leominster, Hay, Brecon and Swansea) which, however, failed in Parliament. The directors then decided to offer to sell their 'Swansea Valley Railway' (sic) to the South Wales Company, payment to be in shares of the latter. This was on the assumption that the South Wales would develop the Swansea Valley in order to tap the growing industrial outlets of the valley itself but as happened elsewhere in South Wales, the SWR was hell-bent for Fishguard, and its only immediate interest in the SVR seemed to be to get rid of the level-crossing of the two routes between Llansamlet and Landore, the local company being already on the ground and in a situation, which as at Stormy, Llanelly and elsewhere, threatened to become a serious operating obstacle to the newcomer. The South Wales, however, lacking powers to purchase the company, secured incorporation by the Swansea Valley Railway Act of 2 July 1847 of what was virtually a dummy company, with powers for a railway from Swansea to near Ystradgynlais and, subject to conditions which proved incapable of fulfilment, to acquire the original SVR. The outcome was a fiasco: the new SVR was unable to afford the old SVR, and the SWR had no powers to subscribe to the new company and provide the purchase money itself. Thus the private company considered itself relieved of its 1846 agreement to sell out to the South Wales, and after lengthy legal wrangles it stayed independent. A new registered joint stock company was formed in January 1850 to acquire the old SVR which opened to freight between Swansea and Glais in 1852, with two second-hand engines, *Bat* (later renamed *Raven* (?)), and *Eclipse*.

The company became sufficiently confident of its independence to convert to a statutory undertaking by Act of 15 June 1855; renamed Swansea Vale Railway, it was to maintain a standard gauge line, conceding to the South Wales an obligation to provide broad gauge where required. Further construction Acts of 14 July 1856 and 22 July 1861 resulted in completion to Pontardawe by 21 February 1860, the start of passenger services from Swansea (St Thomas), these extending to Ynisygeinon 21 January 1861 and Ystalyfera 20 November 1861 (both reported in *The Cambrian*). Brynamman, in the heart of the coalfield, was reached on 1 January 1864 (passenger, March 1868). Meanwhile the problem of the contentious level-crossing with the South Wales (by now GWR) had been resolved by agreement, the latter's main line being carried over the top of the SVR, and exchange sidings established and served by a short section of joint line at Six Pit Junction. The SVR conceded running powers down to the wharves which it served near the Swansea terminus, using the third rail which the SVR had agreed to provide. As an historical freak, the junction and signalbox from the GWR main line towards Six Pit and the Swansea Vale line was officially known throughout its life as 'Swansea *Valley* Junction', perpetuating the name of a statutory railway that was never built. The LMS preserved the name 'Swansea Vale' in the relevant pages of its working timetables.

The link between the SVR and the N & B was initiated by Act of

29 July 1864 with the incorporation of the impressively-titled 'Swansea Vale and Neath & Brecon Junction Railway Company', with more words to its name than the 7½ miles which eventually connected the SVR at Ynisygeinon Junction, twelve miles above Swansea, with Colbren Junction one mile beyond Onllwyn on the N & B, near the headwaters of the Tawe. It was an expensive railway to construct, rising the whole way at 1 in 48/55, and the contractor failed. The N & B leased it for 999 years from January 1867 and by Act of 26 July 1869 the SV and N & BJ was dissolved and amalgamated with the N & B. Perhaps the most crucial factor was that under the 1864 Act the SVR had obtained running powers not only to Colbren but all the way on to Brecon over the N & B.

THE MIDLAND TAKES OVER

By the time the SV/N & BJ was opened, on 10 November 1873, the Swansea Vale chairman Starling Benson, who had taken a leading part in the company's affairs from the very beginning and who seems to have been more than a match for Brunel himself in the rows with the South Wales, was responsive as were his colleagues to Midland overtures for a take-over. The Midland accordingly became lessees of the SVR from 1 July 1874, followed by full absorption by Act of 11 August 1876.

The system of which the Midland took possession on 1 September 1874 comprised a main line 18½ miles long by the original route, opened in stages to Brynamman in 1864. A diversion closer to the Tawe, the Morriston Loop, opened from Upper Bank to Morriston on 2 October 1871 and on to Glais on 1 March 1875, when all passenger trains were diverted from the main line. The loop served principally the growing suburb of Morriston (named after John Morris of the Forest Copper Works) and local industries. (It was not until 9 May 1881 that the GWR also reached Morriston direct, by a two-mile northward extension from Hafod Junction, Landore). Total extent of the SVR system at the time of its acquisition amounted to over twenty-six route miles, including some small branches, of which one crossed the Tawe New Cut to a railway-owned wharf on the North Dock.

With the SVR in hand, from 2 July 1877 the MR implemented an agreement with the N & B to work the latter between Brecon and Ynysygeinon, leaving the local company with only the 11¼ miles of its system between Colbren Junction and Neath – probably the only profitable part! Meanwhile, by 1876 the Midland was working through goods trains twice daily each way to Swansea, and also Birmingham–Swansea through coaches, taking about 7½ hours, but affording the traveller a scenic spectacular. The N & B agreement provided that between Colbren Junction and Ynysygeinon, the Midland not only worked the traffic, but provided the staff and physical maintenance. The N & B was in grave trouble through having over-extended its financial commitments on unprofitable lines, and having drifted into receivership by 1874 was glad enough to have this particular liability off-loaded, so the agreement continued until 1889. In that year Sir Edward Watkin took over as chairman of the N & B, supported on the board by another Manchester, Sheffield & Lincolnshire director, J. W. Maclure, MP. Watkin with his MS & L associations was full of ideas for developing through traffic between Lancashire-Cheshire and South Wales via the Wrexham, Mold & Connah's Quay, the Wrexham & Ellesmere, and the Cambrian (which in 1904 was to absorb the Mid-Wales), leading to the Welsh Railways Union Bill, the Welsh Railways Through Traffic Act of 1889, etc. For whatever immediate reason, the MR summarily removed its plant and materials from the Colbren-Ynysygeinon section upon the expiry of the agreement on 30 June 1889, leaving the N & B to improvise a service with whatever resources it could muster. Describing Derby's action as 'unique in the worst history of railway obstruction,' Watkin – who was not without experience in matters of this kind – took the Midland to court; the arbitrator awarded the N & B damages in excess of £6,000, and the MR restored the service from 22 July 1889.

CLOSURES

Except that the Birmingham through coaches were withdrawn as a wartime measure in 1916 the Midland, and from 1 January 1923 the LMS, continued to work the Hereford-Swansea services for over half-a-century. On 1 January 1931 the LMS withdrew from all traffic working between Brecon and Ynysygeinon, the GWR taking over the local freight working (through LMS goods traffic being diverted to other routes, principally the Central Wales) and GWR local passenger services being substituted between Neath Riverside and Brecon, with a connecting passenger shuttle between Colbren Junction and Ystradgynlais. The last-named was so little used that it lasted only until 12 September 1932, but coal traffic from

Abercrave, towards the top end of the branch, enabled it to be kept open until 3 November 1969. The final closure of the erstwhile Swansea Vale and Neath & Brecon Junction Railway thus came five years after the centenary of the promoters' Parliamentary aspirations not only to reach Swansea Docks over their own metals, but also to acquire and connect with the oldest local railway of all, the Oystermouth (Swansea & Mumbles).

Towards the end of 1962 all passenger service ceased between Hereford and Neath, the official dates of withdrawal being Brecon-Neath on 15 October, and Hereford-Brecon on 31 December; the latter date also saw the end of freight service on the HH & B section, except at Eardisley and Credenhill, which remained served from Hereford until 28 September 1964. Public freight traffic ceased between Onllwyn (excl) and Brecon during 1962 and 1963, but on 1 July 1964 the line was reopened to Craig-y-Nos (Penwyllt) for Messrs Hobbs (Quarries) Ltd traffic. This firm generously restored the private waiting room (silver taps in the toilet and all) used by Mme Adelina Patti, the famous singer, who until 1919 lived nearby at Craig-y-Nos Castle, now a hospital. At Craig-y-Nos only the waiting room was private, but between Devynock and Brecon were two private platforms known as Penpont and Abercamlais, provided by the N & B for local landowners when the line was built.

THE LNWR AND SWANSEA

In its competitive and largely parallel drive into the Swansea area, the LNWR management found itself in much the same strategically complex position as the Midland, until the two rivals arrived within a year or so of one another. The North Western's Central Wales route of 95¾ miles from Craven Arms (itself on a joint line some twenty miles south of Shrewsbury) drew upon a somewhat stronger catchment area in the north, while eventually all but twenty-four miles of the whole route was in the direct ownership of the LNWR, the remainder being partly joint, and partly covered by running powers over the GWR.

Initially the first link in Euston's chain was the little Knighton Railway, incorporated 1858, opened over the 12¼ miles Craven Arms-Knighton by 1861, and worked by the LNWR from 1862. The Central Wales Railway, incorporated 1859, opened Knighton–Llandrindod (19¾ miles) in 1865, handing on the torch to the Central Wales Extension Railway, incorporated 1860, to reach

Llandovery, 27¼ miles from Llandrindod, worked by the LNWR, in October 1868. Meanwhile, by the LNWR (Knighton, Central Wales, and Central Wales Extension Railways Transfer) Act of 25 June 1868, the three companies had been gathered into the Euston fold – but south of Llandovery the LNWR was in what on the Scottish border would have been termed 'debatable lands'.

THE LLANELLY RAILWAY

Historical analogy between the rival routes of the Midland and the LNWR to Swansea applies particularly to the respective final stages of entry to the port, both companies using local companies whose origins went back to the tramroad era. In this respect, the LNWR route between Llandovery and Swansea was much the senior, the originator having been the Llanelly Railway & Dock Company, incorporated 1828 for making a wet dock at Llanelly (now Llanelli), eleven miles west of Swansea, and a horse tramroad in connection. To this undertaking there has often been ascribed the distinction of being the first dock-and-railway venture in South Wales, but actually the Duffryn Llynvi & Porthcawl – *vide* Chapter VIII – was senior by some three years as to authorisation and five in opening.

All the same, the Llanelly Railway & Dock Company pressed ahead rapidly to develop its basically standard gauge system, from Llanelly to Pontardulais 1 June 1839, and thence by stages through Pantyffynnon and Tirydail (then called Duffryn Junction, one of several such in South Wales) until reaching Llandilo on 24 January 1857. By its lease of the separate Vale of Towy Railway, incorporated in 1854, the Llanelly arrived at Llandovery on 1 April 1858, where it had to sit down for ten years to await the arrival from the north of the Central Wales Extension. Meanwhile, on 14 November 1864 the Llanelly had opened its 13¼-mile Carmarthen Branch from Carmarthen Valley Junction to Abergwili Junction with the Carmarthen & Cardigan Railway (p236), and on 14 December 1867 the critical 12½ miles between Pontardulais and Swansea. By this time the Llanelly operated 72¾ route miles, including the Vale of Towy worked by agreement, and some branches yet to be mentioned.

The Pontardulais-Swansea extension was originally single-track throughout – the LNWR was to double it by 1892 – passing above the GWR South Wales main line six miles to the east of Llanelly, climbing thence at 1 in 72 to Dunvant and then descending the

Clyne Valley on the eastern flank of the Gower Peninsula on gradients of 1 in 70–80 to cross over the Swansea & Mumbles Railway (the ancient Oystermouth Tramroad) at Mumbles Road. Thence it ran parallel with the latter on its seaward side, along the shores of Swansea Bay to terminate at Swansea (Victoria), with important adjacent connections to the North and South Docks and to the GWR near High Street station. From Gower Road, later Gowerton, 7½ miles from Swansea, the Llanelly opened at the same time as the Swansea line, a branch three miles long to Penclawdd; although its primary function was to serve local collieries and later the Elba Steel Works, this branch was known as 'the Cockle Line' because of the profusion of this delicacy gathered nearby. The LNWR extended the branch a further 1¾ miles to Llanmorlais in 1884, but it lost its modest passenger service as early as 5 January 1931, and was closed altogether on 2 September 1957.

The Llanelly Railway was not only expansionist in thought but in some ways advanced in practice, including for instance an early form of interlocking signals with points; ostensibly it also paid reasonable dividends; the latter, though would appear to have been paid at the expense of adequate maintenance. Although its passenger terminus in Swansea was opened for traffic in 1867, it was structurally unfinished until after the LNWR took over. The local company was in fact ripe for the picking as the LNWR advanced into the south-west. In 1868, the same year as Euston's influence was extended to Llandovery, the LNWR by astute diplomacy not only persuaded the Llanelly to become its partner in a renewal of the latter's lease of the Vale of Towy, but also to grant running powers over the whole of the Llanelly system, affording the LNWR access to Swansea, Llanelly, and Carmarthen. With overdue hindsight of the consequences of thus opening the door, the Llanelly Company unsuccessfully contested these powers right up to the House of Lords. Moreover, Euston engineered re-incorporation of the Llanelly's Swansea and Carmarthen lines by Act of 16 June 1871 as the Swansea & Carmarthen Railway, worked by the LNWR from 1 July that year. Changed by 1873 Act to 'Central Wales & Carmarthen Junction Railway', following outright purchase by Euston of the Swansea line and Llanmorlais branch for £310,000, and comprising the Llandilo–Carmarthen line, the CW & CJ vested in the LNWR by Act of 21 July 1891.

Left with its total mileage halved after its damaging flirtation with Euston, the Llanelly did not do too badly to become worked under

acceptable terms by the GWR from 1 January 1873, leading to amal-
gamation of the veteran local company with the GWR by Act of 24
June 1899. Paddington also succeeded to the Llanelly's lease in the
Vale of Towy (Llandovery–Llandilo) which thus became a joint line,
remaining so until nationalisation. The LNWR's running rights
over the Llanelly guaranteed continued passage between
Pontardulais and Vale of Towy Junction, Llandilo, over 12½ miles of
GWR metals.

EUSTON TO SWANSEA!

After taking virtually full control of the Central Wales route in 1873,
and completing the Victoria terminus at Swansea in 1882 (nothing
to write home about, but a palace after the Llanelly's unfinished
shack) the LNWR put great efforts into traffic development. The
business was really in three parts: mineral and general freight with
collieries and industrial plants around the Pontardulais area and
with Swansea Docks, local passenger business in the same area,
conducted mainly by push-and-pull sets with Webb tank engines,
and the long-distance passenger traffic on the heavily-graded route
between Swansea and Shrewsbury over the 820ft summit at Sugar
Loaf Tunnel, between Llanwrtyd and Llandovery, approached by 1
in 80 southbound and 1 in 60 northbound, and with only a few short
double-line sections in the fifty-six miles between Pantyffynnon and
Knighton. Growth of the passenger business was linked with
increasing popularity of the Central Wales spas at and on either side
of Llandrindod Wells, and led to the appearance at Swansea of
through coaches not only from Birmingham, Manchester and
Liverpool, but also from York (mainly for mails) and Euston; until
after nationalisation, the through Swansea fares from Euston, St
Pancras and Paddington were identical! Until World War II there
was even a Saturday-only through coach between Liverpool and
Pembroke Dock, via Llandilo and the Carmarthen Branch,
although this catered mainly for holiday-makers at Tenby.

On the freight side, Swansea originated about six through trains
a day to Shrewsbury, some of which penetrated as far as Garston on
the Mersey, and Burton-on-Trent, the latter being the return
empties of a highly competitive (in the brewery sense) train which
brought supplies of famous Burton beers to Swansea. Fish from
Swansea Bay went daily northward by special train to Llandilo,
where the Swansea wagons were married-up with Milford Haven fish

brought by GWR to Carmarthen, and thence by LNWR/LMS. A cattle special also ran daily if required but was mandatory, as the pundits now call it, on Wednesday market days at Carmarthen.

These are the days that are gone, as we say too often now in Wales. The Central Wales route did more than its bit in World War II as in World War I, and although the final LMS timetable for 1947 showed much the same number of trains as in 1939, with nationalisation, many more motor cars, and foreign holidays, the Marples-Beeching writing was on the wall. Although the Western Region which had now taken over the Central Wales route proposed to keep it open by introducing Centralised Traffic Control, it was later decided in accordance with central policy to submit a closure proposal. After the appropriate Transport Users' Consultative Committee had made recommendation about hardship, the Minister agreed to a scheme whereby the Craven Arms-Swansea service was diverted at the bottom end from Pontardulais over the former Llanelly Railway line into Llanelli, reversing there to run into and out of Swansea (High Street) over the South Wales main line. This took effect with the closure of the Swansea end to passenger traffic from Victoria to Pontardulais (exclusive) on 15 June 1964, while on 10 August of the same year, the Central Wales line closed to through freight traffic, and to local freight 1964–68. Despite a second closure proposal, the Shrewsbury–Llanelli–Swansea passenger service of four diesel multiple-unit trains each weekday still operated in 1980, the journey taking three hours twenty minutes, the same as the average of the former LMS steam trains, which had heavier loads but did not have to go into and out of Llanelli. There had also developed a keen demand for excursion traffic, although this was hampered by a single line block section of 30½ miles between Craven Arms and Llandrindod, reputed to be the longest in operation on British Railways The Llandilo Carmarthen branch had already closed in 1963.

Following these closures, the 3½-mile section southwards from Pontardulais remained to serve an important coal depot at Gorseinon. On 22 September 1974, however, a short chord opened, linking this line, via Grovesend Colliery Loop, with the Swansea District Line (former GWR), and enabling the remaining former LNWR line between the new connection and Pontardulais to be concurrently reduced to the oblivion which had already overtaken the section between Swansea Victoria and Gorseinon.

THE SWANSEA & MUMBLES

Although in its final role the Swansea & Mumbles Railway was virtu-ally a residential-cum-recreational electric tramway running along the shores of Swansea Bay for some six miles between its Swansea passenger station terminus and the Pier Station at Mumbles Head, its history was in many respects unique. It was the first railway to provide a public passenger service; it employed at various times horse, steam, petrol, diesel and electric traction (the last three in conjunction), and when its service ended on 5 January 1960, the oldest public railway closed after a life of over 155 years.

The Oystermouth Railway or Tramroad Company was incorpo-rated by Act of 29 June 1804, which included a generously worded section providing for haulage 'by men, horses, or otherwise', thus apparently covering the variety of traction agencies actually employed over the years! The authorised tramroad, of unspecified gauge but probably 4ft 0in or 4ft 2in, was to extend from the Swansea Canal near the subsequent site of High Street Station, down to near the site of Victoria Station (which the Swansea & Mumbles' eventual passenger terminus at Rutland Street closely adjoined) to Oystermouth, with a branch from Black Pill to quarries in the Clyne Valley. This branch took-off close to the later Mumbles Road station of the LNWR, and was extended about 1855 to a colliery which also became served by the Llanelly and LNWR Railways. The year 1855, when the Oystermouth track was relaid for the colliery traffic, also probably marked the conversion from tram-road gauge to the standard 4ft 8½ in.

Although some goods traffic continued to pass over the Swansea & Mumbles at least until World War II it seems that this never fulfilled expectations, but the railway was in the passenger business, with some later blank periods, from 25 March 1807 when a regular service was begun between Swansea and Oystermouth by a licensee, Benjamin French, until 1960. In 1808, the company was in such straits that it had to borrow £1,500 on mortgage, and seven years later the mortgagees took possession, leading to an extraordinary and bewildering succession of legal proceedings, in which a variety of interested parties besieged the courts and the Railway & Canal Commission in pursuance of rival claims. There was for instance the Llanelly Company, whose agents in building its line into Swansea sought to interfere physically with the Oystermouth's right-of-way. Two years later John Dickson, the contractor for the Swansea Vale and Neath & Brecon Junction, secured an agreement to acquire the

Oystermouth as part of his unsuccessful scheme for extending the N & B to docks at the Mumbles, but when Dickson filed his petition in bankruptcy, G. B. Morris as current mortgagee of the Oystermouth evidently concluded that the sale to Dickson was null and void, like that of the Swansea Valley line to the SWR earlier in this chapter. Morris, who had been running the horse-drawn passenger service to Oystermouth since 1860, therefore arranged with the Swansea Improvements & Tramways Company, which had been formed in 1874 to provide horse tramways in Swansea, to take-over the working of the Oystermouth under a grant of running powers, with powers for lease or purchase. The SI & T took-over on 1 July 1877, and on 17 August of the same year introduced steam trams. Dickson through his trustee in bankruptcy successfully contested in the courts his right to implement the purchase agreed with Morris in 1865, so the Oystermouth was put up for sale at auction, bought for £31,000 by Dickson's associates, and re-mortgaged to one of them for £15,000.

Dickson being discharged from bankruptcy was enabled to start his own steam-worked service over the line, forming in 1879 the Swansea & Mumbles Railway Co. Ltd., and meanwhile making every effort to eject the SI & T altogether. He had succeeded in the previous year in stopping the latter's steam trams, on the grounds that the SI & T had no powers to use steam traction. The Tramways Company was determined to fight for its statutory running powers, and eventually in 1880 after hearings before two courts, a vacation judge, and the Railway Commissioners, the Court of Appeal decided that the SI & T was fully entitled to running powers, but endorsed the award of the Railway Commission that these could be exercised only by horse traction, and that one such horse-drawn tram or trams should fill the interval between each steam tram or trams!

Legal difficulties nevertheless went on during the 1890s, after the Swansea & Mumbles Railway Company had been conveyed to new lessors. This period also coincided with some physical extension of the system, following the incorporation in 1889 of the Mumbles Railway & Pier Company. This extended the line 1¼ miles from Oystermouth to Mumbles Pier on 10 May 1898, while on 26 August 1900 it opened a 1½ mile diversion between Oystermouth and Black Pill, along the shore instead of beside the highway. By this time the differences between the two companies (of which the Mumbles Railway & Pier Company was responsible for working) and the

SI & T had seemingly been composed, and the last-named had been granted a 999-year lease of the joint undertaking from 1 July 1899. The SI & T had already itself come under the control of the British Electric Traction group (BET), and although the Swansea street trams began to be converted to electric traction in 1900, it was not until 2 March 1929 that this medium came into public operation on the S & M, using 660V DC with overhead wires. The 'Oystermouth' thus entered its final phase as an electric tramway using smart double-deck cars, though in 1936 it acquired for the diminishing freight traffic a four-wheeled Fowler diesel locomotive emblazoned 'The Mumbles Railway'; in 1929 the company had obtained a petrol locomotive, mainly for shunting dead tramcars around the depot. Thus in its lifetime it had run the full gamut of traction methods.

By 1958 with Swansea's electric trams gone and with the Swansea & Mumbles losing money in a bus-orientated area, there was no place for an electric seaside tramway, and the South Wales Transport Company (the local BET bus subsidiary) to which the SI & T's lease had been assigned in 1929, took over the assets by arrangement with the Swansea & Mumbles and the Mumbles Railway & Pier Companies. In 1959 an Act of Abandonment was obtained, the system closing to public traffic on 5 January 1960.

There remains to be mentioned only the short section of the original Oystermouth line, never used for passenger traffic, which extended from between Rutland Street and Victoria stations to the Swansea Canal near High Street Station. In 1897 this was leased to the Swansea Harbour Trust as part of the docks rail network; with the take-over of the SHT by the GWR in 1923 it became part of the last-named system, but most of it appears to have been disused for many years.

[In respect of the complex changes of ownership and organisation in the history of the Swansea & Mumbles line, the author acknowledges the help provided by *The Swansea & Mumbles Railway*, by Charles E. Lee – Oakwood Press, 1970.] [rep. 1988]

THE SWANSEA HINTERLAND

The hinterland of coal-bearing valleys lying between Swansea and the Black Mountains has been and to an extent still is penetrated by railways built to bring coal to Swansea and to Llanelli also. But this was only one of the objectives of the GWR in obtaining powers by Act of 15 August 1904 for its 'Swansea District Lines' between junctions with the existing main line at Skewen, west of Neath, and at Llandilo Junction, 1½ miles east of Llanelli. Although the new route would pass clear to the north of Swansea, it would afford a springboard for penetration of the developing coalfield immediately to the north. It would also enable existing coal traffic from the Amman Valley coalfield to be worked more directly to the Eastern Docks by means of a triangular junction with the former Llanelly Railway line below Pontardulais, in conjunction with a direct connection at its eastern end to the old Swansea & Neath Railway at Jersey Marine South. Almost more importantly in view of the growth of traffic following the opening of the Fishguard shipping route in 1906, it would enable through trains not only to avoid Swansea altogether, but would increase line capacity through Swansea, not least from the reduction in banking-engine moves both ways up to Cockett Tunnel.

With the exception of the Westbury and Frome Avoiding Lines of 1933, this was the last of the GWR's famous 'cut-offs', following closely upon Ashendon-Aynho on the London-Birmingham route (1910). It was brought into use between Skewen East Junction on the main line to Felin Fran, also the Swansea-facing loop from Lonlas Junction to Jersey Marine South, on 18 February 1912; the remainder from Felin Fran, where a marshalling yard comprising four miles of track and holding over 1,000 wagons was laid out, through to the junctions at Morlais and Hendy below Pontardulais, came into use on 14 July 1913. It is a heavily-engineered line, with three tunnels (Lonlas, Llangyfelach, and Penllergaer, of which Llangyfelach is much the longest at 1,953yd), a major viaduct over the Tawe, and another over the Loughor near Morlais Junction East. The summit at Llangyfelach is approached at 1 in 120 in both directions, albeit a great improvement on the 1 in 50/52 up to Cockett. Between Neath and Llanelli the gain in distance is marginal, advantages in other directions having been stated.

Following the opening of the District Lines, the GWR on 8 May 1914 extended its Swansea-Morriston service to Felin Fran Halt, and at various times eastward beyond the latter, even as far as East Dock via Llandarcy, but the service ceased on 11 June 1956, when there was only one train left in each direction. A more important development had occurred on 9 May 1915, when the Neath Loop was opened between Dynevor Junction North and Jersey Marine Junction North, enabling through trains to be diverted on to the District Line at Court Sart Junction over the R & SB swing bridge instead of via Skewen–Lonlas. In 1917, the big Llandarcy petrol refinery was opened, served off the Jersey Marine-Lonlas Junction loop, and a workers' halt existed there between 1924–47. Much later, in 1956, the establishment of the Velindre Llangyfelach Steelworks added an important source of traffic to the route, but compared with the steam age passenger usage seems to have declined somewhat. In 1939 there was an 'Irish Goods', specifically so designated in the working timetable, running nightly in each direction over the Swansea District Line between Paddington and Fishguard, one of almost continuous freight movements. In 1914 the GWR obtained powers to extend the cut-off from Llangennech, on the Pontardulais-Llanelly section of the old Llanelly Railway, to Pembrey further west on the main line but, wisely, these powers were not exercised (p249).

THE NORTHERN COALFIELD

Rail penetration of the mainly anthracite measures of the Amman Valley, a score or so miles north of Swansea, began in April 1840 when the Llanelly Railway opened the first five miles of its branch from Pantyffynnon up the valley to Cwmamman (later Garnant). This was extended in June 1842 to Brynamman, involving a continuous ascent at 1 in 63 for 1¾ miles. In the meanwhile, there had also been brought into use in May 1841 a two-mile extension from Garnant Junction to the Gwaun-cae-Gurwen and other collieries to the south of Brynamman; from the initials 'GCG on the private wagons of the colliery company, this branch and its successors became known, even in the austere pages of the GWR working timetables, as the 'GCG branches'. The original GCG line involved an inclined plane and, renamed 'Cawdor Branch', was largely superseded from 4 November 1907 by a new alignment (authorised by 1904 Act), with 1 in 40 ruling gradient, over which GWR steam railmotors worked a passenger service between 1 January 1908 and 4 May 1926.

The Swansea Vale (later Midland) Railway had also reached Brynamman from Gurnos Junction, Ystalyfera, in 1864, having a separate valuable connection at Cwmllynfell with the GCG Colliery's private line. Between Swansea and Gurnos the Midland gradients were not exceptional, but in ascending the Cwm Twrch Valley it had to climb at 1 in 67 from Gurnos, and then at 1 in 45 with even a short pitch at 1 in 29 towards Cwmllynfell. On a still, clear day it would just be possible to hear the laboured but evocative approach of rival GW and Midland trains being banked from opposite directions towards Brynamman, where the two companies connected, but with separate adjacent passenger stations, the MR one being a terminus. Here after nationalisation, there existed a positive galaxy of signals of varying design: GWR, Midland, LNWR, and LMS.

In the last decade before World War I, both the GWR and the MR were concerned not only to meet the expected expansion of the coalfield between Swansea and Brynamman, and the shift of emphasis towards the Eastern Docks for the shipment of coal, but also the continuing threat – in the event successfully resisted – of the Neath, Pontardawe & Brynamman scheme, supported by the Barry rail and dock interest, to gain access to the Brynamman area. In 1911, when the Midland was shifting a million tons of coal a year through Gurnos Junction, and was obtaining a goodly share of the inward movement of a similar quantity of pitwood imported through Swansea, the Midland obtained powers to make a new line a little more than four miles long from the vicinity of Llansamlet to the King's Dock, and to provide shipping appliances of its own at that dock. The by-pass would have cut out the congestion between Upper Bank and the docks at the expense of tunnelling under Kilvey Hill, in the shadow of which the MR reached St Thomas, but although the powers were kept alive until about 1917, this line was never built. The MR was content to obtain improved facilities to the Eastern Docks over the GW and SHT lines, and to enjoy its own shipping equipment at the Coaling Arm of King's Dock, reached over the SHT dock lines and thence by an otherwise entirely isolated quarter-mile of Midland track: an interesting parallel to the LNWR's similar mode of access to its Tyndall Street depot in Cardiff.

The GWR project, as authorised in 1911-12, was much more extensive, comprising a ten-mile link between the Swansea District Line at Felin Fran and Gwaun-cae-Gurwen, together with a branch (never built) into the Egel Valley, the main purpose of which seems to have been to frustrate part of the NP & B programme. Apart from this political manoeuvre, another purpose of the Felin Fran-GCG line would have been to provide a shorter route between the Amman Valley district and Swansea Docks. It would have involved heavy gradients and constructional engineering, and although the whole of the route was fenced and some 'phantom' passenger

stations built intermediately, the only portions opened were from
GCG southwards to Duke Colliery, known as the Cwmgorse Branch,
in September 1922, and at the southern end, from Felin Fran in
sections between 1923 and 1930 through to Trebanos (Graig or
Daren Colliery). In 1980 the northern section terminated at
Abernant Colliery, opened 1960, 2¼ miles from Abernant (late
Cwmgorse) Junction; a new rail-connected colliery at Betws, near
Ammanford, opened in 1978, potential weekly throughput being
16,000 tons. The southern end, Mond–Trebanos, closed on 1
September 1965; in 1980 an improved connection went in to Mond
Nickel Works.

Brynamman itself is now isolated from rail. The ex-Midland
passenger service from Swansea ceased on 25 September 1950, and
that of the former GWR from Pantyffynnon (excl) on 18 August
1958. With the closure of collieries both lines closed to Brynamman
on 28 September 1964, thought while Glanamman remained for
freight until 30 January 1965, the ex-MR line closed entirely to
Gurnos, and from 30 April 1968 terminated at Six Pit, cut back to
Upper Bank over a decade later (see Chapter XII). With Clydach-
–Morriston having closed on 1 September 1965, this left from
Swansea Docks to Morriston East as the only section surviving in
1980 of the Swansea Vale lines of the former Midland Railway.

CHAPTER X

The South West Corner

Today Swansea is the most westerly of the Principality's great cargo ports. Between it and the end of Brunel's handiwork at the busy packet port of Fishguard still lie seventy miles of main line, but as the westbound express surges into speed down-grade out of Cockett Tunnel, it is entering the last dozen miles of the virtually straight kind of railway that Brunel loved to build.

Cutting behind the neck of the Gower Peninsula, the old South Wales Railway crossed the River Loughor just above its entry into the Burry Inlet of Carmarthen Bay; Brunel spanned the river in 1852 by a timber viaduct, rebuilt in steel in 1908–9. While approaching this viaduct on 3 October 1904 disaster overtook the Up New Milford boat train, with fatalities and injuries, by derailment at speed, a contributory factor being water-surge in the saddle tanks of 0–6–0 No 1674 piloting 4–4–0 No 3460 *Montreal*.

LLANELLI

The Loughor marks the beginning, and the mouth of the Gwendraeth at Kidwelly, thirteen miles further on, symbolises the farther limit of the westernmost part of South Wales to have shared in the opening stages of the Industrial Revolution. It was area which in the late eighteenth century, and the greater part of the nineteenth, became dotted with collieries and manufactures of iron, copper, tinplate (at one time over eighty tinning plants), brick works and so on, mostly clustering between the shore and the high ground immediately north of it, though a few ventured into deeper mountainous country. This development brought with it and was fostered by the archetypal pattern of small canals, tramroads and latterly railways proper. The focal point of these activities was Llanelly (now Llanelli), still a vital centre of industrial activity, but

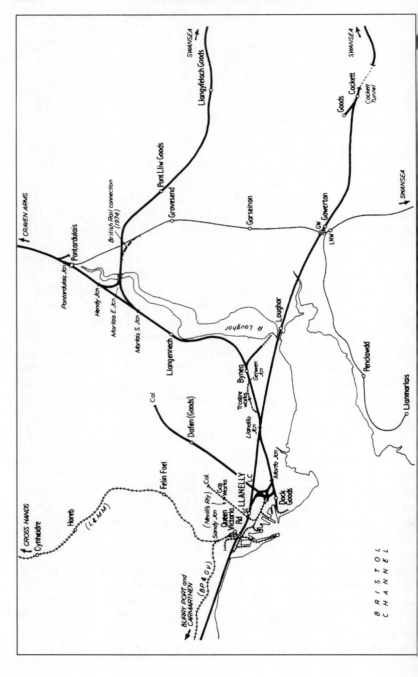

in a more modern image.

Earliest rail transportation at Llanelly was Alexander Raby's Tramroad, 1½ miles, opened 1799 between Raby's Dock and iron-works at Cwmddyche. The tramroad was acquired for extension to Gorslas, Cross Hands, by the Carmarthenshire Railway or Tramroad Company (Act of 3 June 1802), 12 miles long, horse-worked, 4ft gauge flange rails on stone blocks, opened between May 1803 and late 1805. The company ceased trading in 1844 and the rails were lifted, though annual coal exports through Llanelly then exceeded 115,000 tons. The reconstructed 'Carmarthenshire Dock', which the company had obtained powers to acquire and improve under its Act of 1802, was sold to the Llanelly Harbour Commissioners. In addition to this dock, there was the Llanelly Railway & Dock Company's dock opened 1835, and Nevill's or the Copperworks Dock, owned by Nevill, Druce & Company which had started copper smelting in Llanelly as early as 1792, and built its own dock to import copper ore from Cornwall. This firm set up Nevill's Dock & Railway Company Ltd, which like the Harbour Commissioners' lines served a number of private sidings in the dock area. Following the closure of Nevill's Copperworks Dock in 1951, and of many of the private sidings, Nevill's Dock & Railway Company was acquired in 1961 by Bachelor Robinson Metals & Chemicals Ltd, the only part of the company's former rail system still in use being that from the junction with British Rail into Messrs Bachelor Robinson's works. Then, too, there was Mansell Lewis's private railway (later the Stradey Estate Railway) which ran from the docks to serve the Old Castle Iron & Steel Works and other works on the western side of the town.

Apart from its contributory traffic value, the significance of this local network to the SWR/GWR was that when the former opened through Llanelly in 1852 it encountered a succession of level-crossings by other railways. First there was the diagonal crossing at Llandilo (now Llandeilo) Junction with the Llanelly Company's line of 1839 from Llanelly Dock station to Pontardulais; after the acquisition of this part of the LR by the GWR, this embarrassment was partially mitigated by the opening in 1879 of a short connection to Llandilo Junction East, enabling the Pontardulais passenger service to use the GWR's Llanelly station. In July 1913 a new connection opened between Genwen Junction and Llandeilo Junction. Since completion of the giant Trostre tinplate plant in 1957, the former Llanelly Down line between those junctions became bi-directional, while the Up gave access to the plant. Nevill's Dock & Railway Company formerly enjoyed running powers between Dolau Junction in the dock area and Genwen Junction, in order to serve customers reached through the latter

The next level-crossing was that of the Dafen Branch (in some GWR publications 'St David's Railway'), opened in 1833 with horse traction as the oldest piece of the Llanelly Railway, it served various collieries and was extended in 1903 from its original length of just under two miles to 2¾ miles, closing St David's incline and reaching new collieries, but closed altogether from 4 March 1963, while Llandeilo Junction–Morfa Junction in the dock area, together with most other dock lines, closed from 24 January 1966.

The SWR/GWR station at Llanelly had to be located between this pair of level-crossings and another pair beyond it At the height of the port's prosperity the traffic working here must have been pretty hectic, because in addition to the main line trains, the Llanelly Railway in 1853 arrived on the Down side of the GWR station with a standard-gauge branch ¾-mile in length from Morfa Junction in the dock area for the exchange of passengers and transhipment of goods. This was inadequate and cumbrous, so a broad-gauge connection was also made a few years later, having a short life until the gauge conversion in the area (1872). From 1 July 1875 the LNWR worked freight to Llanelly Docks and from 1 June 1889 its goods trains ran into the GWR main line station.

West of the passenger station there were two further rail crossings on the level. Controlled from Llanelly West Signal Box, one of Nevill's Dock & Railway Company's lines served pits and a gasworks; this crossing was removed in March 1961. At Old Castle, there crossed the Mansel Lewis/Stradey Estate line between the docks and Old Castle Tinplate Works and other plants, worked by Nevill Company engines.

LLANELLY & MYNYDD MAWR

Incorporated by Act of 19 July 1875, the Llanelly & Mynydd Mawr Railway Company acquired the 'old' Carmarthenshire's rights and remains for the purpose of laying a standard gauge line. (A second Carmarthenshire Railway Company, supported by the Llanelly Railway, incorporated by Act of 1864 and co-existing with the still-existing first company of that name, had come to nothing.) As the Mansel Lewis/Stradey Estate Railway had taken the former

Carmarthenshire's alignment across the subsequent SWR, the 1875 Act protected its owners' interests: the new line was sited east of the old. The works, including new alignments, were not inconsiderable. Attempts to engage a contractor failed, so that by 1879 abandonment seemed imminent. Quite suddenly, John Waddell of Edinburgh, from a well-known firm of contractors not hitherto active in Wales, undertook construction, eventually becoming involved in financing, building and management of the railway in association with coal mining interests in the Lliedi Valley. The L & MMR opened for local freight July 1881 and public mineral traffic 1 January 1883. By 1887, after opening of John Waddell's and son George's Great Mountain Collieries, the railway's length amounted to some thirteen miles between Llanelly and Cross Hands. In attaining in this distance an altitude of 500ft above sea level, the ruling gradient for several miles was about 1 in 40, with much severe curvature; even after the GWR took over in 1923, it was not unusual to use three steam locomotives on each train, two in front and one banking at the rear.

The L & MMR had a terminus and offices in Llanelly at Queen Victoria Street, and while not operating any public passenger service, carried some 135,000 colliers annually in a fleet of nine 'workmen's carriages', and was not above running other unofficial passenger trips on high days and holidays. At Old Castle, the L & MMR was carried over the top of the GWR main line en route to its own coal shipping stages near the North Dock, and had also a connection into the Up main line; some Stradey Estate traffic was also exchanged by this means with the GWR, especially after the close of the docks in 1951 made the level-crossing at Old Castle largely redundant; it was finally taken out in October 1963.

In 1920, three years before its absorption by the GWR, the L & MMR was carrying some 420,000 tons of coal a year down to Llanelly. In 1980 it was much in use for this purpose, although not actively since 1966 beyond the modern colliery at Cynheidre, 6¾ miles from Llanelli and authorised by the National Coal board in 1951, for the service of which considerable improvements in alignment were made to the railway during 1958–60.

In 1980 Llanelli remained important to British Railways for its industrial traffic from the Trostre, the Duport and other plants, but its days as a shipping port were long gone. Its relatively small docks, of which the North Dock of 1904 was the most modern yet accessible to ships of no more than 1,500 tons, were hampered not only by depth limitation but also by the shoaled approach of the Burry Estuary. Both Nevill's Dock and the North Dock closed in 1951, since when Llanelli has been officially a 'closed port', shipment traffic being diverted to Swansea; a close parallel with the fate of Porthcawl a half-century earlier. There were however still various industrial activities within the dock area and some minor shipments including scrap.

THE 'MOUNTAIN BRANCH'

At Cross Hands on the slopes of Mynydd Mawr, the L & MMR lay very close to the summit of the old Llanelly Railway's Great Mountain branch, extending 4¼ miles westward from Tirydail above Pantyffynon. Opened 6 May 1841, it included a ½-mile-long cable-worked balancing incline, rising at 1 in 12, beyond the top of which the traffic was moved by colliery company's locomotives. After closure of Emlyn Colliery about 1947, the upper part fell into disuse. Cross Hands goods station closed 1 November 1950 and from there down to Gulston Siding (for the private Llandebie Branch) followed in July 1951. Thence to Tirydail closed 6 March 1963. In early years the L & MMR and GWR were probably mutually accessible at their far extremities, through colliery sidings.

BURRY PORT

Four miles west of Llanelli on the main line, the title of the next local station, Pembrey & Burry Port, combines the name of the local township, Pembrey, with that of an ancient port which closed as long ago as 1942, and of a local railway company based upon it, whose short main line played an important part in the transport of coal from inland workings. In 1980 the other prominent local industry was the coal-burning Carmarthen Bay generating station established on the shore in 1954, but in its early industrial growth the area reproduced on a smaller scale the same pattern of coal, iron, copper, tinplate and brickmaking as that of its bigger neighbour, Llanelly.

In 1766 one Thomas Kymer obtained powers to make a canal inland from Kidwelly Harbour which in 1812 became the Kidwelly & Llanelly Canal & Tramroad Company; its base soon shifted to New Pembrey Harbour (first commercial harbour, incorporated 1825, opened 1832, name changed 1835 to Burry Port) whence from

1837 a tramroad ran eastward to join the (first) Carmarthenshire Railway at Llanelly. By mid century the canal-and-tramroad system was outmoded, so by Act of 5 July 1865 the company was authorised to abandon its canal and convert itself, and much of the physical canal system, into the Kidwelly & Burry Port Railway Company. Next, by Act of 30 April 1866, the harbour undertaking was dissolved and vested in the K & BPR whose title was changed, under that Act, to Burry Port & Gwendraeth Valley Railway. This statute thus resulted in one of the oldest docks passing eventually to the GWR, surviving to within five years of the latter company's demise.

The Burry Port & Gwendraeth Valley Railway comprised twenty-one route miles, all single, of which the 'main line' extended some thirteen miles from the docks. It passed under the GWR main line by a bridge having so low a clearance — as did some others originally built over the canal — as to restrict the vertical dimensions of rolling-stock. Thence turning westward to follow the former course of the canal, the railway was located parallel with the GWR before turning inland up the Gwendraeth Fawr Valley, at the foot of which two separate short branches were thrown off to Trimsaran Colliery and Kidwelly Quay (1873) respectively, the last-named having been the western terminal of the original canal and tramroad. Up into the anthracite country, the ruling grade as far as Pontyberem (reached for coal traffic in July 1869) was about 1 in 40, but between there and Cwmmawr (June 1886) the original alignment steepened in places to 1 in 32. The Kidwelly & Burry Port Railway Act of 1865 had authorised the new railway to continue beyond Cwmmawr, to terminate by a junction at Llanarthney with the Llanelly Railway's Mountain Branch, but despite extensions of time this was not carried out.

On the eastern side of Pembrey & Burry Port, the South Wales Railway encountered on its arrival yet another local line deriving its prior rights from its inception as a tramroad; this was the BP & GVR one-mile branch to Cwm Capel Colliery, which the SWR had to intersect on the level immediately on the Up side of the main-line station; this crossing lasted until 1940. Slightly further east again, the BP & GVR effected a junction into the main line, where traffic was exchanged (for a few years until the gauge conversion in 1872, a temporary transhipment station had to suffice). Through this junction, and through Dyfatty Crossing over the GWR main line, the BP & GVR continued on the course of the old tramroad and parallel with the GWR for nearly four miles towards Llanelly; if there had been a connection in Llanelly with the old Carmarthenshire line this ceased when the latter was lifted in the 1840s; only after an Act (1891) was the BP & GV able, eight years later (April 1899), to make an effective junction with the L & MMR at Sandy Gate.

   In its early years the BP & GVR was both impecunious and in its methods somewhat piratical, carrying passengers without authority, and in order to avoid the accusation of charging passenger fares, making travellers pay for bags, parcels, or snap-tins they might be carrying; coal trains frequently stopped to pick up colliers at the roadside. The company's financial trouble stemmed from the burden of inherited capital from the old canal company (£72,100), the cost of conversion (£47,900), and the slow development of the coalfield. In 1876 after the LNWR had begun working the Llandilo-Carmarthen branch and freight traffic into and out of Llanelly, it could not fail to be interested in a scheme approved by Parliament in that year for a Burry Port & North Western Junction Railway, which was to make a six-mile connecting line between the BP & GVR at Llanon and the Carmarthen Branch at Llanarthney, but nothing eventuated and the scheme was abandoned in 1889. Meanwhile the BP & GVR was twice in receivership, but with capital reconstruction, the opening of a new West Dock in 1888, and the development of the coal measures in the higher ground, things began to look up. Early in the 1900s it was recognised that complete modernisation of the railway was essential to cope with growing traffic, and with the advantage of the Light Railways Act, Lt. Col H.F. Stephens, the 'Light Railway King', was brought in as consultant. A Light Railway Order was obtained in 1909, track was relaid, signalling overhauled, and on 2 August of that year a proper passenger service was begun between the company's terminus at Burry Port (separate from that of the GWR) and Pontyberem. Owing to the need for re-alignment to avoid the gradient of 1 in 32 between the latter point and the top end of the line, it was not until 29 January 1913 that passenger trains were extended to Cwmmawr. This was the only public passenger service, but workmen's trains continued to run between Trimsaran and Tycoch Platform on the Kidwelly Branch. Beginning in the 1900s also, a relatively modern stud of 0–6–0 tank engines was introduced. Thus when the GWR took over the BP & GVR on 1 July 1922, it acquired a smart little company which from the depths of two receiverships had never failed since 1915 to pay less than ten per cent on its ordinary shares.

   In the general rundown of local passenger services, that between Burry Port and Cwmmawr was withdrawn on 21 September 1953, with the closure of ten stations and halts. Withdrawal of freight facilities, other than from private sidings, followed on 7 June, and Kidwelly–Coed Bach washery (excl) 25 October, 1965, traffic on the 'main line' being from the opencast disposal point, a substantial movement by diesel traction. With Llanelli and Burry Port docks closed, the export element went to Swansea, the rest to industry. It would not be long, however, before the former BP & GV's viability was questioned (Chapter XII). Its minor branches are gone: Tycoch Junction–Kidwelly Quay closed from 11 October 1929 and was removed in November 1933, while the Trimsaran Branch was taken out of use in June 1962. The Sandy Gate branch closed at its western end on 4 October 1962 and went out of use in December 1963 as did Sandy Sidings to Sandy Gate Junction on 2 August 1967.

GWENDRAETH VALLEYS RAILWAY

This, the last outpost of the industrial network east of Carmarthen, had an extraordinary history; it was also the smallest railway company owning rolling-stock (three miles of line and two locomotives) to be included, as a subsidiary company of the GWR, in the Railways Act of 1921. It came into existence as a physically detached promotion of the Carmarthen & Cardigan Railway Company, under the latter's powers of 1864, to make an inland railway from Kidwelly on the South Wales main line for the purpose of bringing lime into the promoting company's territory. The C & C Company being in financial difficulty, by Act of 30 July 1866 its Kidwelly Branch was incorporated separately as the Gwendraeth Valleys Railway Company, with an authorised 7½-mile line. In 1871, however, the GVR opened for just 2¼ miles, from the GWR at Kidwelly to Mynydd-y-Garreg, and the Tycoch Loop to the BP & GV, worked by one engine until about 1876 when the BP & GV supplied the power. It served silica and tinplate works at Kidwelly, in addition to the huge lime-kilns, 120ft wide and 60ft high at Mynydd-y-Garreg. Between 1892-1903 the company was in receivership, the BP & GVR working the line by arrangement until 1904, when the undertaking was sold to interests of the Kidwelly Tinplate Company, which provided two locomotives. The greatest annual volume of traffic, 123,000 tons, was hauled in 1913; by 1921 this had shrunk to 45,000 tons, and by February 1959 all traffic had ceased; the Western Region formally closed the railway as from 29 August 1960.

A FRONTIER OF CHANGE

In the roaring heyday of the South Wales coalfield and its crowded railways, few greater contrasts could be encountered in a day's train journey than that between the industrial scene of Monmouthshire and Glamorganshire, and the rural back-cloth of Western Carmarthenshire and South Pembrokeshire, now both in Dyfed. Indeed, until the Fishguard sea route to Southern Ireland was opened in 1906, there was little main line atmosphere west of Carmarthen. In this lovely country of undulating fields and woodlands, leading past the modest 1,760ft altitude of the Mynydd Precelli in the hinterland, and seaward to a superbly awesome coastline jutting pugnaciously into the Atlantic, railways and railwaymen led a more peaceful existence than in the rumbustious Rhondda or the teeming Taff Vale. Trains tended to drowse amid gentle hissings at countrified junctions – three of them in some forty miles along the main line between Carmarthen and Fishguard – while patient passengers savoured that vintage aroma of fish, milk, damp Welsh coal and warm engine-oil which some mystique made peculiarly Great Western, like the monogrammed 'GWR' gold-braided cap which on state occasions following nationalisation appeared from nowhere on the heads of senior inspectors, in silent defiance of the latest Marylebonian philippic about the 'standard uniform'.

The change from the industrial background to the rural atmosphere of the south-west corner begins when the west-bound train leaves the shores of the Burry Inlet at Burry Port and thence runs alongside the rather desolate estuary of the Towy towards Carmarthen; across the water is Laugharne, chiefly notable today for its associations with Dylan Thomas, but the objective by Act of 1866 of an abortive 5½-mile Laugharne Railway, branching from the GWR at St Clears.

CARMARTHEN

Carmarthen enjoyed a colourful history in the nineteenth century as a railway 'frontier town', being served at various times by the trains of no fewer than eight different railway companies: the South Wales, the Carmarthen & Cardigan, the Manchester & Milford, the Llanelly (Central Wales and Carmarthen Junction), the Pembroke & Tenby, and then GWR, LNWR, and LMS. The first five of these all became absorbed in the GWR except the Llanelly's link from Llandilo (completed in 1864), the initial acquisition of which by the

LNWR in 1871, in conjunction with running powers over the Carmarthen & Cardigan from Abergwili Junction into the C & C's original Carmarthen station, enabled the Euston interest to take up a strategic position on the banks of the Towy.

Neither the Carmarthen & Cardigan (which never got to Cardigan) nor the Manchester & Milford (which never got to either Manchester or Milford) form an important part of this volume in the Regional series, but it is convenient if not chronological to record at this stage the former's part in the evolution of railways at Carmarthen. As authorised in 1845, the South Wales Railway comprised a main line from the Severn to Fishguard, 288 miles from Paddington via Gloucester compared with the London & North Western's 263¾ miles from Euston to Holyhead via the Trent Valley. By the time the South Wales opened its line to Carmarthen on 11 October 1852, the extension to Fishguard was already in limbo, but Brunel had kept his eye on the ultimate objective. Carmarthen town stands on the hilltop of the ancient stronghold, and to have provided a station close to the town would have required either a very sharp loop across wet ground through 180 degrees or so, or else a stub-ended branch. So Brunel kept to his direct course to the west, and took the main line south of the town, establishing the Carmarthen station near the east bank of the Towy. The river at that time was navigable not only by the traditional coracles but also by steam packets which as late as 1851 were sailing twice weekly to and from Bristol. Brunel therefore provided two rolling drawbridge spans of 50ft clear over the waterway in his bridge of twelve spans in all; this was replaced in 1908 by a new bridge 385ft in length of five fixed spans and one 50ft bascule-type opening span constructed in steel, the opening span being electrically operated.

While Brunel was proceeding westwards, the Carmarthen & Cardigan Railway Company was incorporated by Act of 7 August 1854. It opened on 1 March 1860 from the South Wales station (soon thereafter 'Carmarthen Junction') as a one-mile broad gauge branch, diverging at Myrtle Hill Junction to a temporary Town station *en route* to its intended, but unachieved, destination. Indeed this company suffered one long, distressing saga of inadequate capital, muddle and receivership, before absorption by the GWR in 1881, by which time it had crossed the Towy by a 101yd viaduct to reach Conwil on 3 September 1860, was forced to close down between January and August 1861, and had admitted Llanelly (later LNWR) (1864 onwards), Manchester & Milford (1865–72) and

Pembroke & Tenby (1868–72) trains into Carmarthen Town station, by then in GWR ownership. Euston retained separate goods, loco-motive and traffic establishments through LMS days until nationali-sation, and discreetly embarrassed Paddington by competitive publicity. Closed on 22 February 1965, the former C & C has reopened, in stages northwards from Bronwydd Arms, as *Rheilffordd Gwili*, Gwili Railway, the first standard-gauge steam preserved line in Wales (see Volume XI).

Meanwhile the SWR had faced a major quandary. Brunel had driven on to within seven miles of Fishguard when in 1851 the works were halted. A crisis had arisen from economic collapse in Ireland following the great famine, and inability of the SWR's Irish adher-ents to continue with planned developments on their side. Paddington's guarantee (p38) depended upon completion to Fishguard – an objective now manifestly impracticable, but which Paddington was reluctant to relinquish. It had held out until November 1850 when Brunel persuaded the directors of the GWR and SWR to agree to modified terms. The latter's shareholders, however, had rejected agreement and urged pressing on to Fishguard, the works to be resumed. MacDermot, the GWR histo-rian, thought this may have brought that company's board to see reason. After negotiations, agreement was reached in March 1851 (confirmed by subsequent Act) for a working lease in perpetuity, a third of profits going to the GWR in return for stepped rent as the line was extended in stages, the new destination to be Milford Haven. The altered extension from Clarbeston Road and abandon-ment thence to Fishguard were authorised by Act of 17 June 1852. The agreement was eventually to be the basis of the absorption of the SWR under the GWR Amalgamation Act of 1863.

MILFORD HAVEN

In its choice of nearer terminus – a vast land-locked tidal sound deeply indented into the South Pembrokeshire coast – the SWR was somewhat embarrassed by the fact that its original powers provided for a branch from Whitland to Pembroke, then the most important place on the Haven and a Royal Naval Dockyard, and yet, so far from pressing on with this branch, the company was doing nothing to build it. Ostensibly the reason was legal difficulty encountered with both local landowners and the intended contractor, but more prob-ably, the company in its financial difficulties did not wish to build a branch twenty-seven miles in length when at Haverfordwest, thirty miles from Carmarthen and reached on 2 January 1854, it was already within nine miles of the town of Milford, where docks were being constructed by private enterprise.

NEYLAND

In the event, going his own way as he so often did, Brunel opted for neither Pembroke Dock to the east, nor for Milford a few miles to the west; he struck between the two at Neyland, within a short land distance from 'Old' Milford Haven on one side, and on the other by ferry to Hobbs Point, Pembroke. The extension of nine miles from Haverfordwest to Neyland was opened as a broad gauge, single-line branch on 15 April 1856. In 1859 the pontoons which Brunel had used in the building of Saltash Bridge between Devon and Cornwall were brought round by sea and used to extend a floating landing-stage, opened spring 1857, whence steam packets were run to southern Irish ports. The distance to Waterford was some forty sea miles longer than it would have been from Fishguard to Rosslare.

The SWR having put its money on Neyland, was nevertheless not quite sure what to call it, so at various times it became New Milford (Milford Haven), or just New Milford, and it finally reverted to Neyland with the opening of the Fishguard services in 1906; the latter event also witnessed the transfer from Neyland of the Waterford steamer services. Even after its maritime supersession, Neyland continued as a place of importance, both for its local originating traffic in fish and rabbits and in coal for local vessels, but also because its locomotive depot provided much of the power for both branches. Up to World War II Neyland was still the terminal of a sleeper service to and from Paddington (later transferred to Milford Haven) but eventually the Neyland branch was closed for passenger traffic on 15 June 1964, public freight traffic having ceased on 2 December the previous year.

MILFORD RAILWAYS

Meanwhile in the 1860s, the local squires had got on with building their connecting railways. The Milford Railway Company was incorporated by Act of 5 June 1856 for a broad gauge line four miles long from the town and docks of Milford Haven to the Neyland branch at Johnston; it was opened on 7 September 1863 and worked by the

GWR, with which an agreement was concluded to rent the local line. The GWR later appointed representatives to the Board, and absorbed the smaller company in 1896. This has always been a single line, with an almost continuous rising gradient towards Johnston of 1 in 60. The Neyland branch was almost equally steep, with a ruling gradient of 1 in 75. This was not the only one to include Milford in its title. The Milford Docks Company had always had its own lines in the docks area, while just to make things more complicated, a Milford Haven Dock & Railway Company was incorporated by Act of 23 July 1860 to make a 1¾-mile railway from the GWR, along the north shore of Milford Haven to a dock and pier at Noyes Point. In 1881 the company obtained powers to lease its undertaking to the contractors, Samuel Lake & Company; the line was opened on 19 January 1882 as an industrial link with ship-repairing and other plants, and was sub-let to the Milford Haven Railway & Estate Company Ltd. In 1921 it came under the control of Thos. W. Ward Ltd, by whom it is still used to serve that company's works at Castle Pill, also a fish meal factory and a government depot, motive power being borrowed from the Milford Docks Company. In 1978, a contract was let by a government agency to replace the swing-bridge over the tidal harbour by a modern structure.

Milford Haven was for long one of the country's leading fishing ports, and as late as 1947 up to three daily 'vacuum fish' expresses were being run from the port to destinations as far as Paddington. Despite the discontinuance of these fish specials as part of general railway policy, in 1972 nearly 2,000 tons of fish were forwarded from the port by ordinary services.

The line between Haverfordwest and Johnston was also notable as possessing the most westerly colliery sidings on the GWR. An anthracite colliery at Freystrop, close to Johnston station, had passed out of use by the 1920s, but Hook Colliery some miles to the east was connected not only by tramroad to a wharf on the estuary of the Western Cleddau River, but also to the GWR at Hook Colliery Siding, ¼-mile north of Johnston station. The pit was closed by the National Coal Board on 1 March 1948.

PEMBROKE & TENBY

Refusal by Parliament in 1858 of a renewal of the SWR's powers for its branch from Whitland to Tenby and Pembroke inevitably encouraged local enterprise to seek direct rail communication with the outer world. Thus the Pembroke & Tenby Railway Company was incorporated by Act of 21 July 1859, for the third rail route down to Milford Haven Sound. With a share capital of £80,000 and with powers initially to make a railway between the places named, rather more than eleven miles apart, together with a short branch from Pembroke to Hobbs Point, the latter affording ferry connection to 'New Milford' (Neyland). The company's wider intentions were from the outset made manifest by the chairman, William Owen of Haverfordwest, as being to go a good deal further eastward than Tenby, a Victorian resort of growing popularity at the time, and over the years since. A second bone of contention with the South Wales Railway, and later the Great Western, was that the Pembroke & Tenby Railway began with the standard gauge as early as 30 July 1863, when the first section was opened between Pembroke & Tenby, and when the broad gauge of its powerful neighbours was within a decade of its doom. The opening date was in itself significant as being all but a year inside the period allowed for completion under the Act of Incorporation, an achievement derived almost wholly from the energy with which the works had been driven through hilly country by the contractors, none other than the redoubtable David Davies of Llandinam, later to become the 'father' of the Barry Dock & Railways, and his partner Ezra Roberts, together holding some ⅝ths of P & T shares. They also worked the line under contract, with rolling stock imported by sea. So confident and successful were they that when the extension from Pembroke to Pembroke Dock was opened (Monday 8 August 1864) the company had secured an Act on 17 July to extend from Tenby to Whitland, while with a five per cent preference dividend under his belt, chairman Owen was able to warn the GWR that if it did not lay down 'a narrow gauge line' for the use of the Pembroke & Tenby, the latter would make its own line to Carmarthen. A 14¾-mile extension from Whitland, keeping south of the GWR until Sarnau where it crossed over and took position alongside, to join the C & C at Carmarthen, was authorised in the P & T Act of 6 August 1866, along with a half-mile branch at Pembroke Dock to Hobbs Point Pier on the south shore of Milford Haven. As to the extension, clearly implied was the further intention to join up with the LNWR when the last-named should succeed in reaching Carmarthen over the Llanelly's route from Llandilo.

In these circumstances the GWR thought it wise to come to terms with the P & T, which abandoned its projects to Carmarthen and

Milford Haven in return for the use of the GWR Up (eastbound) track between Whitland and Carmarthen Bridge, the local company contributing financially to the cost of conversion. The Pembroke & Tenby had reached Whitland on 4 September 1866, and on 1 June two years later began to work into the Carmarthen & Cardigan station at Carmarthen, over a short west-to-north 'P & T Curve', or West Loop, which took-off at 'Towy Bridge Junction' at the east end of the bridge; its powers to extend its own line to Carmarthen were surrendered under these arrangements with the GWR.

Returning to the luckless Carmarthen & Cardigan, an 1859 Bill to change to standard gauge was withdrawn after SWR opposition. Working charges demanded by the SWR could not be met and the close-down (p231) was the signal to the SWR to reimburse itself by seizure of rails. With hired stock the C & C resumed operations independently from 12 August 1861. A third rail was laid for mixed gauge between Abergwili Junction and Myrtle Hill Junction for Llanelly freight trains in 1864 (p210), and north to Pencader to permit Manchester & Milford Railway trains to reach Carmarthen from 1 November 1866 (cut back to Pencader in 1872). After fourteen years in receivership, by C & C Act of 1881 the railway vested in the GWR. The Pembroke & Tenby was to remain independent for sixteen years after this, although it had ceased to work its own passenger trains east of Whitland from 1 August 1872 following the SWR gauge conversion that May.

TIDYING-UP CARMARTHEN

The acquisition of these local companies eventually enabled the GWR to tidy-up the situation at Carmarthen in 1902, replacing the old C & C station on 1 July with a much better structure slightly to the south, at the same time restoring the former P & T West Loop to running line status, which it had lost after the Pembroke & Tenby trains ceased running east of Whitland. This enabled GWR passenger trains to run via Carmarthen station and reverse there, except (from 1906) for the Fishguard boat trains, and various express fish, cattle and other non-passenger carrying trains not requiring to call at Carmarthen. As rebuilt, on the opposite or south side of the river bridge, and further improved 1930–1, there were four platform faces, dealing (in 1939) with a basic weekday service of some thirty departures, greatly increased on summer Saturdays when, for instance, the LMS ran a through express to Liverpool.

Page 237 (*Top*) 'Stations like chapels': traditional architecture at Dowlais (Cae Harris), passenger terminus of the Taff Bargoed (GWR/Rhymney Railway) Joint Line, opened 1876, closed to passenger traffic in 1964; *(bottom)* Maximum effort manifested by LNWR/LMS 0-8-4T No 7945, hauling an Abergavenny – Brynmawr freight train up the steepest part of the old MT & A line, clinging to the narrow ledge carved for it by John Gardner along the precipitous escarpment of the Clydach Gorge. (*R. J. Doran; Oscar Elsden*)

Page 238 (Left) Former Barry Railway somersault signals at Cadoxton, 1961; *(below)* Statue of David Davies, father of the Barry Docks and Railway, outside the docks offices (the former headquarters of the company, at Barry). *(E. R. Mountford; R. C. Riley)*

The old station at Carmarthen Junction lost its passenger service on 27 September 1926 and has been demolished; freight ceased from 7 June 1965. By the early 1980s, of Carmarthen's four platforms, No 1, the bay, had been filled in, No 2 handled regular traffic with No 3 acting as occasional overflow, while No 4 was for empty stock; the engine shed, closed April 1964, had gone, as had the footbridge, leaving just the barrow crossing. Coal and freight traffic ceased in 1983, subsequent track rationalisation enabling the Welsh Water Authority to dismantle the nearby Towy Bridge in 1984 (see Chapter XII).

As eventually amalgamated with the GWR under the latter's Act of 1897, the Pembroke & Tenby comprised a system of twenty-eight route miles, all single, including the Hobbs Point Pier freight branch from Pembroke Dock (opened, after extension of time, April 1872, closed 1 January 1969). By P & T Act of 1870 a 3-furlong branch ran from near Pembroke Dock passenger station to the Admiralty Dockyard (opened 21 July 1871, out of use 15 September 1969). The 27½-mile 'main line' between Pembroke Dock and Whitland includes some heavy gradients, notably 1 in 50/52 in the first seven miles through Narberth nearly to Templeton, followed by 1 in 47/51 falling thence towards Saundersfoot. In steam days, extensive use had to be made of assisting locomotives in the summer months when through trains ran, principally on Saturdays, to and from Cardiff, Paddington, and Birmingham.

After being threatened with closure during the BR rundown era, the P & T branch not only survived the opening of the road bridge across the Cleddau between Pembroke and Neyland, but also witnessed an enterprising revival of long-distance inward excursion traffic to Tenby. Early in 1978 the government approved plans for a £4.5m ferry terminal at Pembroke Dock, to which the British & Irish Steam Packet Company transferred its services from Swansea in May 1979, with improved connections between Port Talbot or Swansea, to link with the HSTs. Mostly withdrawn in the early 1960s, surviving P & T freight ceased after 31 December 1978 (see Chapter XII).

THE SAUNDERSFOOT RAILWAY

Within the territory of the Pembroke & Tenby Railway, but by difference of gauge never physically connected with it, was the oldest statutory railway west of Carmarthen. This was the Saundersfoot Railway & Harbour, authorised by an Act of George IV (1 June

1829) for making a harbour at Saundersfoot between Tenby and Pendine, and railways or tramroads to connect it with inland collieries. The railway, which was built to an unusual gauge of fractionally over 4ft, eventually comprised two separate sections from the harbour, the westward one serving half-a-dozen or so small collieries, while the easterly arm served the Stepaside Ironworks (which used local ore) and collieries at Kilgetty and Stepaside. The railway and harbour enjoyed a fair measure of prosperity until the 1870s, when the rundown of pits and ironworks began; in its heyday the harbour had shipped nearly 40,000 tons annually. Meanwhile, the Pembroke & Tenby Railway had been opened through Saundersfoot in 1866, and after the GWR took over this line in 1897 a standard gauge connection was established to the principal colliery, Bonville's Court. Coal mining ceased entirely shortly before World War II, during which the remaining part of the Saundersfoot Railway was dismantled.

WHITLAND & CARDIGAN

The growing status of Whitland as an agricultural and dairy centre having been encouraged by its becoming also a railway junction, was further stimulated in the 1870s and 1880s by the making of a rail connection northwards into Cardiganshire. This originated with the object of serving important slate quarries at Glogue, fourteen miles from Whitland, and was incorporated 12 July 1869 as the Whitland & Taf Vale Railway Company. The River Taf concerned is not to be confused with the Glamorganshire Taff, but rises in the Mynydd Precelli above Glogue, and flows down through Whitland into its estuary at Laugharne.

The Whitland & Cardigan was very much another 'squires' railway, the directors with one exception bearing the noble Welsh names of Lewis, Davies, Evans and Owen! The exception was John Barrow of Chesterfield, who concurrently was on the boards of the Manchester & Milford and the Pembroke & Tenby companies. A notable figure and associate of David Davies to be involved in the Whitland & Taf Vale was its engineer, J.W. (later Sir James) Szlumper from Aberystwyth, who was engineer to the Manchester & Milford, became the fourth holder of the corresponding post with the Pembroke & Tenby, and eventually followed David Davies round to Barry where he became responsible for the difficult Rhondda section of the Barry Railway. There he built the 1 mile 108yd

Wenvoe Tunnel, whose now derelict portals are still inscribed with his name.

As authorised, the Whitland & Taf Vale was fourteen miles in length to Crymmych Arms, beyond Glogue. To enable it to reach its own metals, the GWR agreed to a third rail for the 2¼ miles between Whitland and the point of divergence at Taf Vale (later Cardigan) Junction. By the time the first section of the branch was open for freight, from the junction to Llanfyrnach (10½ miles) and (according to Price) probably Glogue too (11⅞) on 24 March 1873, the SWR gauge had been converted; the remainder to Crymmych Arms opened for freight by August 1874, and from Whitland throughout for passenger on 12 January 1875.

In 1877 the W & TV obtained powers to push on a further eleven miles from Crymmych Arms to Cardigan, and relevantly to change the company's name to 'Whitland & Cardigan'. The GWR took over the working of the line concurrently with the opening of the extension to Cardigan on 1 September 1886. This was a precursor to the GWR's absorbing the undertaking (and its debts) under the GWR Act of 1890, the total capital expenditure to 1882 being only £63,000 or about £4,500 per mile; the company had generally managed to earn a small surplus on revenue account, but there were substantial sums outstanding in debentures and rent charges.

Originally the line had been laid almost as a light railway. It was a very picturesque route, closely following the winding of the Taf through the vale, and climbing almost continuously at 1 in 40-50 up to Glogue, with a final pitch at 1 in 35 to the summit at Crymmych Arms. Thence it descended on a ruling grade of 1 in 40 through Kilgerran, there being three precautionary 'stop boards' in the eleven miles between Crymmych Arms and the end of the branch. Even in the context of a rural railway, the branch could never in modern terms be valid, and it was closed for passenger traffic on 10 September 1962 and for freight on 27 May of the following year.

The nineteenth-century importance of Whitland as a minor railway centre would have been further dignified had anything come of the proposed Whitland, Cronware & Pendine Railway Company, incorporated 2 August 1877 from a junction with the GWR at Whitland to Cyffic and Eglwys Cymmyn, the latter being to the west of Laugharne. The WC & P scheme was officially abandoned by Act of 20 June 1892. An oddity in this context is that a railway with the same somewhat suggestive and ill-chosen initials did in fact operate for many years as a light railway, but on the other side of the Bristol Channel in Somerset.

FREIGHT TRAFFIC IN 1980

With changed methods of marketing and distribution, and particularly with better roads and bigger and faster lorries, the agricultural traffics – especially milk and cream – which were so long the mainstay of these local railways had by 1980 partly forsaken the surviving network. Important creameries were still rail-served at Carmarthen and Whitland, but a modern note had been struck by the development of substantial flow of bulk oil and petrol traffics in trainloads from the great refineries on Milford Haven where giant tankers of up to 275,000 tons were discharged. The refinery sidings lay on the Milford side of Johnston, being reached through Waterston Junction and Herbrandston Junction, respectively 1¼ and 2¼ miles below Johnston. The Waterston connection led for another 2½ miles to the Gulf Oil installation, while the Amoco and Esso plants were one mile and 2½ miles respectively beyond Herbrandston Junction.

Involving as it did the movement of oil in tank wagons of up to 100 tons gross laden weight, this traffic had required substantial track strengthening between Carmarthen and Johnston, also in 1971 the reconstruction in steel of two bridges over the River Taf near Whitland, which had themselves replaced two of Brunel's original bridges in 1902. Colour-light signalling was put in between Carmarthen and Whitland in 1978–79. Oil train motive power was then by BR class 47 diesel-electrics (see Chapter XII).

FISHGUARD

When in 1851 the South Wales Railway Company forsook its intention of reaching Fishguard, and Brunel perforce changed course hard-a-port for Neyland, Fishguard had hitherto enjoyed as almost its only claim to fame the abortive landing nearby of a French mercenary force in 1797, the last invasion of British soil.

MAENCLOCHOG RAILWAY

Progress towards Fishguard came in stages, involving local enterprise. The first was construction, by Board of Trade Certificate of 24

June 1872 granted to Edward Cropper, of the Narberth Road & Maenclochog Railway, standard gauge, from the GWR at Clynderwen, 5¼ miles west of Whitland, to slate quarries at Rosebush. Its length was just over eight miles, and passenger service was begun on 19 September 1876; like the Whitland & Cardigan, this was a heavily-graded line into the mountains and included nearly two miles at 1 in 27 between Llanycefn and Maenclochog.

ROSEBUSH & FISHGUARD RAILWAY

As an extension of the Maenclochog Railway from Rosebush through Letterston to Fishguard, an Act of 8 August 1878 incorporated the Rosebush & Fishguard Railway Company, with powers to construct a railway nearly fourteen miles long. The R & FR Act of 11 August 1881 authorised a deviation of the line and lease or purchase of the Maenclochog. The company was soon in trouble, financially and with the contractor, delaying work on the railway and acquisition of the Maenclochog, which itself ran out of money and closed down from 1 January 1883, reopening to passengers and freight on 15 December 1884 (*Pembrokeshire Herald*, 19 December 1884). On 7 August 1884 powers were obtained by the R & FR to change the name of the company to the North Pembrokeshire & Fishguard Railway and to secure a further extension of time for land purchase and completion; two years later the process of seeking an extension of time had to be repeated, and it was not until 1893 that work was resumed.

In 1893 there entered entirely new *dramatis personae* in Joseph Rowlands and John Cartland of Birmingham, who foresaw the future of a route to Ireland via Fishguard and were prepared either to raise substantial funds towards it, or to force the GWR to resume an active interest. On 29 June that year, in association with Henry Partridge and with the support of the Waterford & Wexford Railway and other Irish interests, they obtained an Act incorporating the Fishguard Bay Railway & Pier with a capital of £120,000. The main works were to be a harbour and breakwater, and only one mile of railway was authorised, being sufficient to join up with the North Pembrokeshire's authorised extension from Letterston down into Fishguard. Concurrently, Rowlands and Cartland went on to finance the completion of the North Pembrokeshire and its acquisition of the moribund Maenclochog. The latter, relaid and improved, was re-opened in conjunction with the opening of the

North Pembrokeshire between Rosebush and Letterston, for goods traffic on 14 March 1895, and for passengers on 11 April. This 8¾-mile line was single, with heavy gradients through the Precellis nearly all against eastbound trains, including much 1/50 and a ruling inclination of 1/41.

PADDINGTON SITS UP!

Meanwhile the Great Western, which throughout the mainly chaotic history of the North Pembrokeshire had been sitting blandly on the touchline making smooth but generally unco-operative noises when approached, was being made to sit up by the vigour with which Rowlands and Cartland, both from behind the façade of the North Pembrokeshire and through their Fishguard company, were stirring the pot on both sides of St George's Channel. In the absence of GWR support, the NP & F approached the LNWR for financial help towards a proposed new line from Beag near Clynderwen to meet the LNWR at Abergwili Junction north of Carmarthen, which would have given the LNWR access to Fishguard! The Euston management had little difficulty however in deciding its strategy. It was already committed to a long line of communication through Holyhead to Ireland via the three Irish ports of Kingstown, North Wall and Greenore respectively, while in 1870 it acquired the Caernarvonshire Railway in order to protect the left flank of its route through Anglesey. There were few places in England from which an LNWR route via Fishguard could be competitive. Such meagre commercial prospects could scarcely justify a major collision with the GWR in South West Wales, so Euston politely told the NP & F that it was not interested in financing or working the latter's intended line to Carmarthen, but that if it were built, the LNWR would consider traffic facilities at and from Carmarthen

The North Pembrokeshire nevertheless went ahead, obtaining in 1895 extension of time for authorised 1878 and 1886 works, with new powers for a 5½-mile Maenclochog–Llanycefn 'Llandilo Loop', abandoning Castle Tunnel and steepest gradients, together with the 'Narberth & Carmarthen Extension Railways', linking Beag, north of Clyderwen, via Narberth, Amroth and Pendine, with the LNWR at Abergwili. In 1897 powers were got to abandon the Llandilo Loop in favour of a 12-mile 'Letterston Loop' diversion, giving an even less arduous route between Little Newcastle and Clynderwen. More audacious, but thrown out by Parliament, were clauses for extending the little railway into the heart of industrial South Wales, connecting not only with the Midland and LNWR in the Swansea area but going on to join the N & B and TVR in the Aberdare Valley! These proposals were largely aimed at diverting the substantial coal trade to Ireland through Fishguard. Rowlands and Cartland were now going great guns with this maritime project. By Act of 31 July 1894 the Waterford & Wexford Railway and the Rosslare Harbour Commission had vested in the Fishguard Bay Railway & Pier Company, with the latter's name changed to the Fishguard & Rosslare Railways & Harbours Company; a further Act of 30 May 1895, authorising the company to operate steamships, increased the capital and borrowing powers to £230,000 and £72,500 respectively.

It was time for Paddington to do more than take notice. The time was also opportune, for the Great Western had already entered the period which MacDermot has termed 'the great awakening', and which was to produce within a relatively short span of time such developments as the cut-off lines to the West of England, to Birmingham, and to South Wales via Badminton. The revival of a direct route to Southern Ireland via Fishguard was a logical if somewhat speculative complement to this programme, especially in view of the speeding-up between South Wales and London made possible by the Badminton cut-off (South Wales & Bristol Direct Railway, authorised 1896 and opened 1903, under pressure of competing projects sponsored by South Wales trading interests under cover of the Barry Railway Company).

FISHGUARD AND ROSSLARE

Rowlands' hitherto unsuccessful efforts to interest the GWR thus suddenly blossomed into fulfilment in 1898-99. In the former year, the Fishguard & Rosslare Company obtained a further Act authorising the construction of thirty-five miles of railway between Rosslare and Waterford, and enabling the Great Western and the Great Southern & Western (of Ireland) companies to subscribe £250,000 each. An agreement between the three companies provided that the Fishguard Company would complete the harbours at both Fishguard and Rosslare, and would provide the steamers (to be managed by the GWR), while the GWR would work the harbour and railways on its side of the channel, and the GSW(I)R those in Ireland.

The railways on the Irish side became quite extensive, amounting to some 104 route miles, whereas at Fishguard the mileage amounted to only sixty-four chains of track between Fishguard & Goodwick (the 'town station', GWR) and the end of the harbour lines. Thus was created the oddity of a railway in Wales partly owned by an Irish railway company. Unlike the GWR and the Great Southern of Ireland the Fishguard & Rosslare Railways & Harbours Company preserved its identity despite nationalisation in both countries, remaining (1980) jointly owned by BRB (Sealink) and Coras Iompair Eireann (but see Chapter XII). The joint companies also owned the Fishguard Bay Hotel, by the acquisition and enlargement of an existing hotel; guests enjoyed the benefit of the GWR's fishing rights on a local river, safeguarded by the company's own water bailiff. Presumably the staff department classified him as a 'miscellaneous employee', along with the twenty-five sheepdogs which the GWR maintained on its South Wales payroll in order to evict sheep from various branch lines. The hotel was eventually sold in 1968, but is still in active operation under other ownership.

Wrapped up in the Fishguard package was the long-mooted, inevitable take-over by the Great Western of the little North Pembrokeshire, whose only real value lay in the six-mile extension from Letterston to Fishguard & Goodwick. This was still under construction when the GWR assumed responsibility for the NP & F on 12 February 1898, and was not opened for traffic until 1 July 1899. This was eleven days after the NP & F as a company ceased to exist, its own Act of 20 June providing for the transfer of the company to the GWR and its formal dissolution, and the abandonment of the extension and diversion of 1895 and 1897. Including both the Maenclochog and the Fishguard extension, the NP & F had built or acquired no more than 23¼ miles of single line, yet by 1897 its capital expenditure amounted to no less than £251,767, and the capital account was in deficit by over £15,000; rarely can so small a fish have made such a splash in so big a pool.

Subsequent NP & F history was of isolated diminution. From 8 January 1917 the line closed east of Letterston station (which remained open), some track going for war material. It reopened a fortnight later, from Clynderwen to Maenclochog for freight (and passengers from Clynderwen) 12 July 1920, reaching Puncheston 14 November 1921, and Letterston, freight October 1922 and passengers 9 July 1923. Local passenger trains ceased 25 October 1937 and remaining freight (save Letterston) 16 May 1949. In September 1938 the Trecwn Branch opened from Letterston

Junction to an Admiralty Depot; busy in World War II (during which the line to the south was used for target practice), it remained in used in 1993. Letterston closed to public freight from 1 March 1965.

COMPLETION TO FISHGUARD

Now that Paddington policy was fully committed to the Atlantic venture, events began to move apace. By Act of 12 August 1898 – in which the GWR also received authority for the Castle Cary cut-off and a new harbour at Weymouth – powers were got for a direct line, 10½ miles in length, from Clarbeston Road to Letterston to join the North Pembrokeshire line down into Fishguard. Only about a mile of this cut-off was laid on Brunel's abandoned works of 1845-51, one of his bridges, left unfinished at that time, being completed after a lapse of sixty years. The main engineering work on the heavily undulating route is the 242yd Spittal Tunnel, on a westbound falling gradient of 1 in 110. The worst part of the route occurs after joining the former NP & F line at Letterston Junction, the final three miles into Fishguard falling at 1 in 50-60.

The railway engineering involved in getting into Fishguard was greatly overshadowed by that required for the breakwater and quay. All the equipment had to be carted from Letterston and lowered down the cliff-face to the working site, and two million tons of material were excavated. The Harbour station originally composed four platforms, connected across the rails by a moveable platform bridge similar to those found in East Suffolk or formerly at Malton in Yorkshire, while extensive freight sidings and cattle lairages were provided, together with a locomotive shed at Fishguard & Goodwick. Over a hundred houses were built to accommodate railway and dock staff. Three triple-screw packet steamships were ordered, the first two, bearing what would become traditional route names of *St David* and *St Patrick*, came from John Brown's Clydebank Yard, and *St George* (sold May 1913) from Cammell Laird, all in 1906; *St Andrew*, the third traditional name, arrived from Brown's in 1908.

The Fishguard-Rosslare route went into business on 30 August 1906, two days under twenty years since the opening of the Severn Tunnel. Its introduction reduced the sea passage from ninety-eight miles (New Milford-Waterford) to fifty-four miles (Fishguard-Rosslare). The former service also transferred in August 1906 to Fishguard, reducing to ninety-two miles the nautical distance to

Waterford, and New Milford reverted to its former name, Neyland. From the outset, the GWR pulled out all the stops to make the service a success: the 8.45am boat train from Paddington, advertised to call only at Cardiff, was due Fishguard at 2.20pm, and the steamer at Rosslare at 5.00pm; only 10-15 minutes were allowed for the transfer of passengers and baggage at Fishguard. Extensive advertising was launched, and cheap excursions run to the Lakes of Killarney and other attractions, souvenir postcards were issued, and the GSW(I)R sent an Irish jaunting-car to tour England, advertising the route.

THE ATLANTIC DREAM

Looming beyond the achievement of a swift new route to and from Ireland now came the prospect of Fishguard as a transatlantic bridgehead. Traditionally the operational base of the two great British liner companies, Cunard and White Star, was on the Mersey, but to meet growing competition from foreign shipping lines it was desirable both to make a brief mail-and passenger call off one of the Irish ports, and then to call at the nearest practicable UK port to disembark passengers and mails for London and other key centres. Plymouth and Southampton were already rivals in this sphere – it was from the former port that the LSWR Ocean Mails Express had crashed to disaster on the Salisbury curve in 1906 – but in terms of nautical miles Fishguard was the nearest of them all to New York, and convenient also for the Queenstown call in Ireland.

OCEAN SPECIALS

So the Great Western went all-out to capture the transatlantic trade for Fishguard. Cunard was not the first to call there, the Booth Line using it in April 1908, but in the following year the Cunard Line decided to call, beginning with the famed *Mauretania*, then only a year old, on 30 August 1909. Over 880 bags of mail were discharged into three tenders and three special trains left in close succession for Paddington, all 4–4–0 hauled: first the mail special hauled by No 3381 *Maine*, then two passenger specials hauled respectively by Nos 3402 *Halifax* plus No 4108 *Gardenia*, and No 4116 *Mignonette* plus No 4111 *Anemone*. Even this movement was eclipsed the following year, when at the end of a record-breaking round voyage to New York and back, *Mauretania* on 22 December 1910 landed at Fishguard 3,177 mail-bags and 598 passengers. First away of five connecting trains was a special train chartered by *The Daily Mail*, which reached Paddington in 271 minutes at an average speed of 57.8mph. There followed between 11.48pm and 1.15am four more specials, the first to Dover via Reading with passengers for the Continent, preceding three trains to Paddington.

Despite all this initial success there were problems. Although installation of water troughs between Carmarthen and Ferryside resolved one of them, heavy eastbound trains had either to be double-headed, or to stop for a banker from Fishguard & Goodwick up to Manorowen, and from Gowerton up to Cockett Tunnel as well. In the harbour, the big ships, unable to berth alongside, had to discharge mails and disembark passengers by tender; four of these small vessels had to be used for *Mauretania*.

The GWR had only partial success tackling the gradients. The company obtained powers in 1903 for a 'Fishguard to Letterston Up Line' of nearly 3¾ miles of easier gradients from south of Goodwick (sic) station, rejoining the existing route north of the future Letterston Junction. Work was started only to be abandoned during World War I. Though opening of the Swansea District Lines afforded easier gradients for expresses avoiding Swansea, a west-ward extension of the SDL, between Llangennech and the main line at Pembrey, avoiding Llanelly, authorised in 1914, was also deferred (below). Powers for an additional breakwater on the north side of the harbour and an 'Ocean Quay' (opened 1909) at which the largest vessels could berth, were obtained in the Fishguard & Rosslare Railways & Harbours Act of 1908.

But with World War I, the Atlantic dream faded. The turbine steamers were requisitioned as hospital ships, and the big liners ceased calling; nor, except for occasional calls such as that of *Scythia* with American visitors to the Welsh national Eisteddfod in 1926, did they come back. Shipping rationalisation began among the Atlantic lines; the proximity of Plymouth and more especially of Southampton to London and the North European shore, followed by the development of commercial air travel, left Fishguard out on a limb. In 1922-23, as the railway amalgamations came in, the Fishguard-Rosslare service was interrupted for over twelve months by the troubles in Ireland. The GWR drew in its horns by aban-doning the Llanelly Avoiding Line, together with the new Up line out of Fishguard, although part of the engineering work for the latter had already been carried out.

The steamships played an often heroic part in both World Wars. In the second of these, with her sisters on 'active service', the second (1930) *St Patrick* maintained the Irish run until her sinking by torpedo (p271) suspended operations. When services resumed post-war with the sole-surviving *St Andrew*, the route was for some years in the doldrums owing to trading difficulties, the development of air travel, and the Beeching era of railway retrenchment; indeed, at one time the withdrawal of all rail passenger service west of Swansea was seriously canvassed. Thus the rail movement of cattle by this route, once so substantial, ceased altogether. Fishguard & Goodwick motive power depot closed on 9 September 1963 and five halts/stations between Clarbeston Road and Fishguard Harbour on 6 April 1964. On 17 May 1971 the main line, mostly doubled 1906–7, was singled, Clarbeston Road–Letterston Junction, leaving the latter the only intermediate block post in some sixteen miles; the four passenger platforms at Harbour station were reduced to one in use and one spare.

Just as the Milford Haven lines took a new lease of life from oil traffic, so also were the Fishguard route and connecting rail services to be re-vitalised, especially during the 1970s with the introduction of 'roll-on, roll-off' (RoRo) services for Motorail and commercial vehicles, the development of containerised traffic via the Danygraig (Swansea) Freightliner terminal, and the generous provision of terminal facilities for these purposes.

A further stage in this growth programme was announced in November 1978, involving an expenditure of £16 million on a new multi-purpose vessel for the Rosslare service and a further extension of terminal facilities. By 1977 carryings had risen to 67,000 accompanied cars, over 200,000 motorist passengers, 16,000 lorries and 119,000 non-motorist passengers. During the summer peak a new direct Fishguard-Dun Laoghaire (Kingstown) service has been introduced – shades of the LNWR! – although the historic but outmoded Fishguard–Waterford cargo service ceased on 15 March 1978, history bowing down to progress... The quickest train service between Paddington and Fishguard, usually hauled by a Class 47 diesel-electric locomotive, then took five hours for the 261 miles, four intermediate stops included. The resurgence in fortune in the chequered career of this Irish Sea route envisaged in the early 1840s was to continue into the 1980s (Chapter XII).

RAILWAYS THAT NEVER WERE

Apart from the Homeric fantasy of the North Pembrokeshire's 'main line east' through south-west Carmarthenshire and into industrial Glamorgan, and the Pendine and Laugharne schemes already mentioned, several other abortive attempts were made to promote railways in this area. The cathedral town of St David's was a main objective. In 1898 a St David's Railway Company was formed in association with the NP & F to make a line seventeen miles long from Jordanston, between Letterston and Fishguard, to near St David's Head, but the directors quietly abandoned their powers two years later, after the NP & F had ceased to exist. Next, in 1916, a Light Railway Order was granted for a Milford & St Bride's Bay Railway, eleven miles of standard gauge, but after several extensions of time this scheme also passed into oblivion; its main objective was the prospect of additional colliery developments rather than local and holiday passenger traffic. But even as late as 1923, when the government of the day was in consultation with the railway companies about works for the relief of unemployment, Viscount Churchill, the GWR chairman, suggested to the Ministry of Transport the possibility of a branch from Mathry Road to St David's, if the government would share the cost, estimated at £350,000.

CHAPTER XI

The Twentieth Century – I
1900–1980

When the present century dawned in 1900, there were only four-teen years to Armageddon. During these intervening years, which were to witness the end of the Edwardian era with the death of King Edward VII in 1910, rail traffics continued to expand and the better-placed companies to prosper, despite temporary setbacks due to railway and coal strikes in 1911-12. The GWR in particular improved its status and its services with the opening of the South Wales Direct Line (Wootton Bassett–Patchway), the Fishguard service, and the Swansea District Lines, also by its securing control over the R & SB and Port Talbot Railways. On the debit side, efforts towards the fusion of the principal local railways serving the port of Cardiff, which would have made for greater efficiency, failed through the strength of opposition on grounds of monopoly.

THE TAFF VALE CASE

In the sphere of industrial relations, what at first appeared as a resounding victory for employers seeking damages from a trade union for losses incurred through a strike, but which was to have widespread consequences of a perhaps unexpected kind, occupied much attention during the early years of the new century. This was the famous Taff Vale Case, wherein the dismissal by the TVR of an Aberdare signalman in 1900 sparked off a fortnight's strike by TVR employees. Their real grievances were said to run much deeper, however, being directed against several broader aspects of the Taff's feudal attitude to its servants under the autocratic but often paternal management of Ammon Beasley. The strike was supported by the Amalgamated Society of Railway Servants, against which the company sought an injunction in the High Court, the case mainly turning on legal points as to whether or not a trade union could be sued for damages. Mr Justice Farwell's judgment in favour of the company was overturned by the Court of Appeal, but the TVR carried its case to the House of Lords, where under the presidency of the Lord Chancellor, Lord Halsbury, the Law Lords unanimously found in favour of the company and upheld the judgment given in the High Court. The Taff Vale accordingly sued for damages, and upon the jury finding in its favour, these were agreed at £23,000 against the ASRS. This was regarded as a great triumph for the railways and for Beasley personally, but it was to lead the trades unions generally to align themselves more closely with the Socialist movement, thus indirectly to the formation of the Labour Party, and to the Trade Union Act of 1906 with its provision to protect trades unions against certain types of action at law. In 1913, the ASRS joined with two other unions to form the National Union of Railwaymen.

WORLD WAR I

The year 1913, the last before World War I, was also the last of the traditional supremacy of coal movement by rail to the South Wales ports for export or bunkering, with a record total for the six principal ports of 38.7 million tons in twelve months, Barry Docks with nearly 11m tons narrowly heading Cardiff (10.5 million tons). With the outbreak of war in August 1914, nearly all the railways (except, so far as South Wales was concerned, the little Gwendraeth Valleys) came under Government control through the Railway Executive Committee. Despite heavy loss of manpower to the armed forces, the South Wales collieries sustained an output which from the 53.8 million tons of 1914 never fell below 46.7 million tons during the subsequent war years, but the movement requirement changed dramatically; many export markets were automatically cut off, and coastwise shipping was progressively reduced.

COAL FOR THE GRAND FLEET

The paramount requirement became the movement of South Wales steam coal to the northern bases of the Royal Navy, by far the largest single such movement being for the Grand Fleet based on Scapa Flow. Before the war, the Admiralty had already taken a hire option on 4,000 wagons for this traffic, the total number eventually required being 16,000. Movement of the 'Jellicoe Specials', as the special trains came to be known after the Grand Fleet's Commander-in-Chief, Admiral Lord Jellicoe, began on 27 August 1914. The departure point for traffic from the Rhondda and Aberdare districts and from the Rhymney line was Pontypool Road, and onwards to Warrington LNWR, and thence mostly over the West Coast Route to the Fleet coaling base at Grangemouth in Central Scotland, a total distance of 375 miles. This was one of the great railway achievements of all time, to quote Edwin Pratt's *British Railways and the Great War* (Selwyn & Blount, 1921):

> The total number of special trains run from South Wales with Admiralty coal between 27th August 1914 and December 31st 1918 was 13,631. Taking an average of forty wagons per train, this was equal to 545,240 wagons, and allowing an average of ten tons per wagon, an approximate total of 5,452,400 tons of coal... On several occasions the number of coal specials sent from South Wales to Grangemouth in a single week was 114. There were days when 19 special trains, conveying approximately 7,600 tons of coal, were run; but in November 1918 the consignments dispatched on a single day attained a total of over 14,000 tons. The largest quantity of coal dispatched from South Wales to Grangemouth in any one week was just over 56,000 tons. During the period from March 11-20th 1918, the consignments of coal from South Wales to all points on Admiralty account amounted to 115,652 tons... generally the time taken from Pontypool Road to Grangemouth was less than 48 hours.

To this great effort the GWR committed nearly the whole of its fleet of 2–8–0 tender locomotives, while in the latter part of the war the line capacity of the North and West route became fully taken-up. Recourse therefore was had to a supplementary and difficult line of communication, over the mountainous single line of the little Brecon & Merthyr Railway (which, astonishingly, had handled no less than four million tons of coal and other minerals in 1913, compared with the Taff Vale's nineteen million) to Talyllyn, and thence over the Cambrian Railways to Gobowen, where the GWR took over. It had taken a world crisis to consummate, temporarily at least, Sir Edward Watkin's dream of this long, straggling thread of Welsh single lines becoming a trunk route.

Page 255 (Top)   A British Rail Penarth-bound diesel multiple-unit leaving the southern end of Caerphilly Tunnel at Cefn On, Rhymney line; (bottom) Standard Class 7 Britannia 4-6-2 No 70026 *Polar Star* on the Up 'Red Dragon' at Coalpit Heath on the GWR Wootton Bassett–Patchway cut-off in 1955. (H. J. Ashman; R. C. Riley)

Page 256 Prestige passenger past, GWR: Ocean Liner Express about to leave Fishguard for Paddington with passengers from RMS Mauretania in 1909, in the charge of 4–4–0s Nos 4116 *Mignonette* and 4111 *Anemone*; Prestige passenger present, BR: HST InterCity 125 at Cardiff Central, with power car 43124 heading the 07.45 from Milford Haven to Paddington, February 1990. *(British Rail; Peter E. Baughan)*

The effect of the wartime change-over in South Wales from predominantly short-distance movement of coal to long-distance inland haulage was exemplified at the Rogerstone yards, north of Newport, which pre-war had dealt with ninety per cent shipbound coal, and the rest locally or inland; under war conditions this balance was completely reversed. Shunting and marshalling facilities were enlarged to deal with the extra traffic at Quakers' Yard, Pontypool Road, and Stormstown (TVR).

The great increase in freight traffic to and from South Wales, initially from trade expansion and later from wartime traffics, led to remarkable growth in the numbers of freight trains passing annually through the Severn Tunnel: 1907 7,776; 1913 18,099; 1917 24,027.

The South Wales ports and railways played an immense part in the war effort; typical was that of the Barry Railway and docks, 6,700 ships being loaded for the Service departments, and 6,000 Admiralty transports being bunkered; in 1916 a record 3,990 ships with an aggregate registered tonnage of over five million tons entered the port. At Cardiff alone, over 200 ambulance trains were handled.

More than 3,700 employees of ten 'independent' railway companies joined the armed forces, of whom over one thousand went from the TVR alone; in three of the companies the numbers joining-up exceeded 30 per cent of their manpower at the outbreak of war. No separate figure is available for the great numbers of railwaymen and women of the three main line companies enlisting from South Wales, but the GWR's all-line total was over 25,000, or 32.6 per cent of the pre-war staff.

THE GROUPING

World War I was not yet over before the Government of the day began to consider the future of the railways. Mr Winston Churchill, as he then was, talked about nationalisation, but the scheme eventually put forward by the newly-formed Ministry of Transport under Sir Eric Geddes envisaged the formation of large groups of companies as the basis of a more compact system, which it was suggested would obtain the advantages known today as 'the economies of scale'. Other features of the Government Bill introduced in 1921 and rushed through to Royal Assent on 19 August of that year were a large degree of authority reserved to the Minister of Transport, an entirely new system of control of rates and charges through a

Railway Rates Tribunal, and compensation to the companies for the inadequate financial basis on which their costs had been met during the war. Some 120 railway companies were swept into the four new groups, even the little Gwendraeth Valleys failing this time to escape the net which had omitted to encompass it in 1914, when it was for some reason left out of Government control (perhaps they did not then know it was there...). So all the South Wales independent railways, except semi-private lines like the Milford Haven and the Nevill's Dock & Railway system at Llanelly, were allocated to the proposed Western Group, of which the GWR was necessarily the largest dominant unit.

During the to-ing and fro-ing over the scheme, no positive proposal for a separate Welsh Group appears to have materialised as was to be the case two decades later at nationalisation, when both the British Transport Commission and the Railway Executive toyed with the idea of forming a separate Welsh Region, but quietly left it aside. South Wales commercial interests which for a century had been obsessed with their aversion to monopoly, did however canvass the idea of putting the Rhymney Railway into the proposed London Midland and Scottish group, which would give a competitive route from England into Cardiff, but nothing came of that. Meanwhile the powerful Paddington lobby had persuaded the Ministry that the GWR should be the only constituent company within the Western Group, all the Welsh companies to be merely subsidiaries. This evoked a violent reaction in South Wales, notably from the directors of the Barry, who could point to their having paid a ten per cent dividend on ordinary stock in 1920, whereas the GWR paid only 7¼ per cent. In the event, it was agreed that the title of the company forming the Western Group should be 'The Great Western Railway' – the only one of the main line companies so to retain its title – while the Barry, Cambrian, Cardiff, Rhymney, Taff Vale and the Alexandra (Newport & South Wales) became constituent companies of the GWR, the remainder becoming subsidiaries. So the GWR was free to continue carrying into the Principality its armorial device embodying parts of the arms of London and Bristol only; had the grouping taken place in the 1970s, even Paddington would surely have been forced to seek a new version incorporating the Welsh Dragon!

Amalgamation of the constituent companies with the GWR, planned for 1 January 1922, was delayed by the Amalgamation Tribunal until 25 March 1922. Dates for the subsidiary companies were:

On and from 1 January 1922 –
   Penarth Harbour, Port Talbot, R & SB.
On and from 1 July 1922 –
   B & M, BP & GVR, N & B, Vale of Glamorgan.
On and from 1 January 1923 –
   Gwendraeth Valleys, L & MM, Penarth Extension, SWMR.

The former LNWR and Midland lines in South Wales went to the LMS Railway and so remained (leaving the LMS access to Newport, Cardiff and Swansea) until after nationalisation in 1948. Joint lines between the LNWR or MR and GWR or companies taken-over by the latter similarly remained as joint GWR/LMS lines until 1948. Each of the constituent companies was empowered to nominate one director to the GWR Board, which in January 1923 included in its membership eleven gentlemen of title.

   Some of the South Wales companies' senior officials who stayed on after the amalgamation achieved important status within the new hierarchy, this being especially the case in the docks department. From having been little involved in major docks activities prior to the grouping, and in the light both of its limited experiences at Porthcawl and Briton Ferry, and its knowledge of the difficult financial history of the Bute Docks making it perhaps somewhat sceptical of the future outlook in this field, the GWR found itself the owner of one of the two largest docks groups in the country, the other being the LNER. Fortunately the absorbed companies brought with them plenty of managerial expertise in this specialist activity, and the GWR was able to fill the new post of chief docks manager by appointments from within South Wales: successively J.H. Vickery, the Alexandra's last general manager; Edward Lowther (formerly general manager of the Port Talbot, who had earlier become the GWR's chief goods manager on amalgamation); and C.S. Page from the Cardiff. Additionally, the Barry's last general manager, Edward Waddell (having as a young man helped to build both dock and railway for that company) became docks assistant to the chief (civil) engineer, while John Auld, the last locomotive superintendent of the Barry, became docks and personal assistant to the CME at Swindon.

   In statistical terms, the GWR acquired from its new components (excluding the Cambrian Railways, which became a constituent but which barely penetrated the northern fringe of the region) some

528 route miles of railway, including joint lines; some of this mileage, on the TV and ex-RR lines especially, was four-tracked, while both on its Rhondda line and on the Vale of Glamorgan, the Barry had platform loops at some intermediate stations to enable goods trains to be overtaken. The largest owned route mileage, 112, belonged to the TVR, while surprisingly the straggling 'little' B & M came third (after the Barry) with nearly sixty miles. The total route mileage thus acquired by the GWR was notable for its shortness relative to the intensity of traffic dealt with. Signalling was generally mechanical, large signal-boxes including Pontypridd (230 levers), Caerphilly (162), and Barry Island Junction (90), while signals on many of the amalgamated railways were of the somersault type, thanks to energetic selling by McKenzie & Holland, and in the case of the Barry Railway, Evans & O'Donnell. On some of the steeper LNWR branches, distant signals were to be regarded either as stop signals, equivalent to outer homes, or as stop-and-proceed at caution. One or two of the somersault signals survived into the 1970s. The GWR continued and extended the practice of some South Wales companies in identifying valley freight trains by the use of coded target boards on the locomotives.

Statistics in the sections following are based on the returns of the companies concerned, as at 31 December 1921, but minor discrepancies occurred in this classification.

LOCOMOTIVES

The South Wales companies handed-over to the GWR a very mixed bag of some 760 locomotives, the largest stocks being those of the TVR (274), the Barry (148) and the RR (123); a further twenty-three dock shunters from the Swansea Harbour Trustees and their sub-contractors, Powlesland & Mason, were acquired in 1924, following the separate absorption of the SHT in 1923. Going back in history, the earliest locomotives used by the local systems included four-coupled tender designs. As the coal traffic developed it became desirable to have an increasing proportion of multi-purpose locomotives suitable for access to both colliery sidings and dock roads, which could work main line and branch coal trains, and could preferably also take a passenger turn if required; hence the total fleet of 760 included nearly 200 0–6–0Ts and some 450 0–6–2Ts. The latter type had the advantage of affording greater coal and water capacity, plus better adhesion, and was introduced into South

Wales by the TV and R & SB Railways almost simultaneously, within a few years of the type being pioneered by the Lancashire & Yorkshire Railway in 1879. The final examples of the 0-6-2T type built in the present century, for the TVR, RR, B & M and N & B Railways were both handsome and powerful.

Although six-coupled tank engines thus latterly predominated, there were in all fourteen different wheel arrangements represented within the fleet which the GWR took over. On the Taff Vale some 0–6–0 tender locomotives survived into grouping days; tank engines of the 2–4–0, 2–4–2, 0–4–4, 4–4–0 and 4–4–2 types were all in use for passenger work, while 0–4–0Ts were used as dock shunters at Newport, Cardiff and Swansea; indeed the GWR perpetuated the last-named variety after amalgamation. There were also locomotives of various GWR designs which had been acquired second-hand from that company, and which were received back (but not necessarily always welcomed) into GWR stock at grouping.

Among other locomotives acquired second-hand from railway companies, two noteworthy series, which the ADR obtained in time for taking over the Pontypridd-Newport coal trains from the TVR in 1906, comprised seven 2–6–2Ts and three 0–6–4Ts, which had been rendered redundant by the electrification of the Mersey Railway. The outside-cylindered 2–6–2Ts proved so successful that the design was subsequently repeated in two more, supplied in 1920 by Hawthorn, Leslie, the last locomotives to enter ADR stock.

Apart from the ADR, the only other South Wales railway to bring the 0–6–4T wheel arrangement into the amalgamated stock was the Barry, which obtained ten new locomotives of this type from Hawthorn, Leslie in 1914. These powerful machines seemed to be overborne by misfortune as were some of the same wheel arrangement on other railways, through their propensity to derailment when working on secondary trackwork off the main line, and although the GWR went to the expense of fitting four of them with new boilers, the whole series was summarily withdrawn in 1926.

The Barry Railway having expanded during a period when British locomotive manufacturers were fully occupied with both home and foreign orders, had to shop around for new locomotives in a sellers' market. Hence its resort at various times to the purchase in 1889 and 1897 of four 0–8–0 tender locomotives built by Sharp, Stewart for a Swedish railway which could not pay for them; of five 0–6–2Ts from the American Cooke Locomotive Company in 1899; and of five 0–6–2Ts from the Franco-Belge concern in the following year. The Barry also favoured the 0–8–2T wheel type with seven locomotives, the first of this type in Great Britain, delivered by Sharp, Stewart in 1896; two examples of the same wheel arrangement, but of United States design were built by Cooke's for the Port Talbot Railway in 1899. The rebuilding of these 'Yankees' by the GWR in 1908, with Swindon boilers and fittings atop the existing bar frames, produced what can only be described as a swollen bullfrog of a locomotive.

Following the amalgamation, the GWR reboilered many of the acquired South Wales locomotives with Swindon boiler fittings and cabs. One of the most striking rebuilds was that of some of the Rhymney Railway's Class 57 0–6–2Ts. Like many other classes of RR engines, these reflected the preference of the Grand Old Man, Cornelius Lundie, for outside frames and saddle tanks, the extra adhesion weight afforded by the latter being regarded as over-ruling the risk of unsteadiness, having regard to the generally low speeds. But six of this class as rebuilt at Caerphilly Works by the GWR would have made Cornelius turn in his grave, because they emerged as pannier tanks with GWR fittings and cabs, retaining the double frames and outside bearings; in the event, to the writer they always looked a neat job. The RR was also the only absorbed company to use the Westinghouse brake.

Before leaving this necessarily brief reference to locomotives, it should be recorded that prior to amalgamation the GWR itself had introduced several types of locomotive which were for the special purpose of meeting its own South Wales traffic requirements, notably the 26XX or 'Aberdare' class of double-framed 2–6–0s, designed at the turn of the century and subsequently multiplied to over eighty locomotives which were used, as their class name implied, for working coal trains from the Aberdare district to Newport, Pontypool Road, or beyond. Two other GWR types which were introduced for both main line and valleys freight traffic, were G.J. Churchward's 42XX series of 2–8–0Ts in 1910, and C. B. Collett's rebuild version of some of these as 72XX 2–8–2Ts beginning in 1934; altogether there were 151 of the former class and 54 of the converts, both series lasting well into the nationalised regime. Finally in 1924, Collett introduced his 56XX class of 0–6–2Ts, which reproduced many of the characteristics and much of the general appearance of the more modern examples of this wheel arrangement inherited from the absorbed companies, the rebuilt versions of which they closely resembled; they were equally at home on passenger or freight work in South Wales.

STEAM RAILMOTORS

After the fashion of the period, six of the South Wales companies (the ADR, Barry, Cardiff, Port Talbot, Rhymney and Taff Vale) had from 1903 onwards introduced steam railmotors having a small motive unit built integral with a passenger coach. The TVR was the largest user of these machines, in conjunction with numerous halts or 'platforms'; in 1906 twelve of the TVR cars aggregated nearly 200 trips, 1,200 miles and a payload of 6,000 passengers per day. In general these cars suffered from limited power on steep gradients, from mechanical limitations (the Barry was reputed to have to employ bar-boys of specially small physique to enable them to get into the fireboxes), but most importantly from their inability to meet the extra traffic which they generated, as on Saturdays, when ordinary trains had often to be turned-out. All had therefore disappeared in their original form by 1920, either by withdrawal or by conversion of the passenger units to the more flexible pattern of autotrain (push-and-pull) working, in which form some of the vehicles passed into GWR ownership.

CARRIAGES AND WAGONS

The absorbed South Wales companies brought to the GWR more than 900 coaching vehicles, 1,100 service vehicles, and about 7,150 goods wagons. The small number of freight units in relation to the huge total traffic came about because practically the whole of the coal and coke business was carried in wagons belonging variously to the colliery companies, coal factors, and wagon hiring firms. Passenger stock ranged downward in standard from modern bogie vehicles, steam-heated and electrically lit (but without passengers' emergency communication, Board of Trade regulations not requiring this unless non-stop runs exceeded twelve miles), to small four- and six-wheeled coaches, including many provided for workmen's trains, though some colliery companies possessed their own. The South Wales railways had been substantial buyers of other companies' cast-offs, including the Metropolitan, Mersey and Metropolitan District when these systems were electrified and the LSWR. There were also some highly individualistic oddities, such as the American type bogie vehicles built for the British tour by

Barnum & Bailey's circus, which came into the possession of the ADR; the B & M had a 'picnic saloon', and the Barry a 'pay clerk's van' which at one time was powered, somewhat unsuccessfully, by a small petrol motor. Failures of this last unit were not infrequent, and one wonders whether in such circumstances the pay clerk went back with detonators 'to protect the train', or whether he sat still clutching the money until help arrived...

Where there was any doubt in the Great Western's mind as to whether vehicles were to be retained or not, they were ordered to Swindon. In some cases where passenger coaches had been laid aside for some time out of use they were non-runners, so the bodies were taken off the frames and loaded in wagons to Swindon; but this journey was not necessarily their last, for some of them finished up on the ground as huts for various staff purposes. One of the Alexandra's Barnum & Bailey coaches, which may in its time have had the great Buffalo Bill as a passenger (I still have the medal which my father won in one of his shooting competitions in 1902) ended up as a staff office at Pill locomotive shed in my home town of Newport. After grouping, coaches of GWR origin appeared in increasing numbers on the absorbed lines, and as late as 1939 the company built at Swindon a small batch of bogie coaches with specially low roofs for the restricted clearances on the BP & GV section.

WORKSHOPS

The locomotive, carriage and wagon workshops of the South Wales railways also ranged from the efficient and impressive to small establishments, usually allied with the locomotive running sheds, where only light repairs were performed, sometimes in the open. The TVR had its locomotive works in the Cardiff docks area at West Yard, where locomotives entering and leaving the shops had to be shunted across the street leading to the dock entrance; a small proportion of new locomotives was built in these works until near the end of the last century. The TVR carriage and wagon shops were at Cathays Yard, which adjoined the TVR main line about one mile north of Queen Street, and passenger coaches were built there until about 1905. West Yard Works quietly disappeared in the GWR regime, but Cathays continued as a British Rail wagon repair and engineering works, celebrating 'TVR 150' in 1991 (but see p298).

The Rhymney Railway also had its original rolling stock establishment in the Cardiff docks area, but in 1901 completed a move to an excellent site on vacant land to the east of Caerphilly station, where it established what was to become, over a period of some sixty-two years, the premier establishment in South Wales. The RR rebuilt locomotives and had constructed coaches at Caerphilly, which after the amalgamation absorbed the work of West Yard, of the ancient B & M shops at Machen – which from the age of the buildings might well have been the workshops of the historic Rumney Railway – and other small depots; the GWR added a new erecting and carriage shop at Caerphilly. The GWR also continued until after grouping heavy locomotive repairs at Maesglas (Ebbw Junction) shops on the western outskirts of Newport, but this work was transferred to Caerphilly in 1927, whereafter those Ebbw Junction men who elected to follow the work to Caerphilly enjoyed a daily private train in each direction. Sadly, with the introduction of diesel traction on British Railways, the end came for Caerphilly Works in 1963, and one more chapter in Welsh railway history thus ended. (See Chapter XII.)

THE TROUBLOUS YEARS

The GWR had very little time or opportunity to do more than carry out some changes in divisional organisation, and some mundane tidying-up of its South Wales inheritance – the abolition in 1923 of second class on those local systems which had provided it, and the renaming of some seventy-five stations and halts by 1924 – before it became engrossed with the basic economic changes which overtook South Wales in the aftermath of World War I; very much the same sort of fate was to beset British Railways a quarter of a century later. Although there was a short industrial honeymoon in the early 1920s, and a few individually good years thereafter, it soon became clear that the great days of the native coal industry were over. The combatant and merchant navies of the world were turning to oil fuel; alternative sources of energy, oil and electricity, were becoming more freely available for both industrial and domestic use, while fierce competition developed from other coal-producing countries. Between 1923–39, coal shipments from Bristol Channel ports, including coastwise and bunkers, declined from 36.7 million tons to 19.3 million tons, the latter figure being just half that of the peak year, 1913, while during the great coal strike and the brief general strike of 1926, the South Wales ports began importing foreign coal.

In the same period other heavy industries fell on evil days, too. The great steelworks at Dowlais and Ebbw Vale both closed – the latter albeit temporarily – while in their wake iron, copper, tinplate, fireclay, pitwood and other ancillary and supporting industries all suffered grievously. By the 1930s, South Wales was in the grip of the great depression, whereby places such as Merthyr, Dowlais and Blaenavon became like ghost towns. In this grim period, with its concomitant hardship and misery for the working population, of whom up to sixty per cent were unemployed in some places, it is perhaps enough to record that through reluctant migration, the population of the region fell by nearly half-a-million, and that of the Rhondda Valleys alone by 30,000 over two decades.

The GWR faced up to its resultant problems by economies in working, and by forward looking and development. In the first category, powers were obtained in 1929 to abandon the Old Town Dock at Newport, which the Alexandra Company had acquired in 1884. Penarth Dock was closed to trade on 6 July 1936 when its shipments of coal had fallen from the 1913 peak of 4.5 million tons to 635,000 tons; it was to re-open temporarily in World War II, only to close for commercial use finally in 1962. The North and South Docks at Swansea were also closed about 1928. Should modern students of transport think that 'rationalisation' began with Beeching, some fifty stations and halts in the region were closed to passenger traffic during the Great Western's period of responsibility, 1922-47; by 1936, the company had reduced its staff in South Wales by some 5,000. But the Great Western management deserves, in retrospect, all credit for positive steps taken to modernise dock equipment, to reduce rates (1923), and to campaign for new types of cargoes for the South Wales ports, particularly liner traffic and imports for the Midlands and the North West. A special effort was also made to improve the loadability of coal traffic by the introduction of 20-ton wagons in substitution for some of the 116,000 privately-owned 10-ton and 12-ton wagons which had been extant in South Wales in 1918; the GWR pointed out that a train of fifty ten-ton wagons occupied some 1,000ft for a payload of 500 tons, whereas a similar number of 20-tonners occupied 1,225ft of track but carried 1,000 tons payload. The company therefore offered a rebate for the use of the larger wagons, the first trainload of which was tipped at Port Talbot on 27 August 1924, with a saving of 35 per cent in dock siding space; by 1925 there were over 1,000 of these larger wagons in use, but the hoped-for scale of adoption was never realised because in a falling market, many coalowners could not afford to convert their loading equipment.

MERCHANDISE LOSSES

Traffic losses following World War I were by no means confined to coal. Until the early 1920s, railways had long enjoyed a monopoly of general merchandise carryings, mostly finished products outward from South Wales, and consumer goods inwards. Until the amalgamation, for instance, traffic for the Midlands and North West could be loaded at four different railway companies' depots in Cardiff. This situation was exemplified by the TVR's 6.55pm express goods from Cardiff to Merthyr, which had to be marshalled 'with traffic for the L & NW Railway next to the engine and in front of traffic for the B & M, Cambrian and Midland Railways'. (The Barry Railway made every effort to exchange such traffic with the GWR at its tranship shed at St Fagan's, in order to avoid tolls to the Taff Vale). As instancing the wide range of traffics passing by rail at that time, the aforesaid 6.55pm express goods stopped at Abercynon to attach priority van traffic in 'hides, skins and pelts' for some unspecified but clearly important destination!

All this began to change in the aftermath of World War I, which had not only imparted a great technical stimulus to the development of road motor transport, but had led also to the acquisition by a new generation of 'hire and reward' hauliers of large numbers of surplus War Department lorries, and free at that time of almost any restraint on their operations, whereas the railways were still tied by the obligations to provide 'reasonable facilities' and to publish their rates. It was not surprising that by 1931, the GWR chairman Viscount Churchill had to report that notwithstanding the introduction of zonal railheads with road distribution, eighty-two per cent of the company's total loss in general merchandise traffic had taken place in South Wales.

Nevertheless, the GWR made progress despite its troubles. Various government measures aimed at the reduction of unemployment helped the company to modernise its passenger stations at Newport, Cardiff and Swansea, together with several goods stations and motive power depots in South Wales. Government aid also led to the setting-up of trading estates at Treforest, Hirwaun, and elsewhere, the former being rail-connected to the ex-TVR main line in 1937, an arrangement which lasted until 1974. But the wagon-load or container traffic generated at these trading estates, or at new factories established at Merthyr, Pontypool and other places, was no substitute in volume or profitability for the lost business of the heavy industries, and was particularly susceptible to road competition, notably by the C-licence operations of firms carrying their own traffic in their own lorries. Meanwhile principal LMS goods depots in South Wales, at Swansea (ex-MR) and Cardiff (ex-LNWR) had been closed in 1929 and 1933 respectively, their traffic being transferred to GWR depots, although Swansea's Victoria goods, ex-LNWR, lasted until 1965.

Another important development of the period was the acquisition by the main line companies, under powers granted by Parliament in 1928, of shareholdings in road passenger transport undertakings, with the right to make co-ordination agreements, appoint directors and so on. In South Wales the GWR came to such an agreement leading to the formation of the Western Welsh Omnibus Company, in which its shareholding amounted by 1938 to £203,000, with earnings of £23,000. As part of this agreement, the GWR's own bus operations in South Wales, which had continued to expand until the late 1920s, were handed over to the associated company. It perhaps reads a little oddly in view of such alliances, that between 1928 and 1932 the GWR had opened over the system as a whole fifty-one new halts, and had built in 1931–2 two series of 0–4–2T and 0–6–0PT engines for auto-train operation on light passenger lines.

CHANGE IN THE VALLEYS

Following the amalgamation the GWR made some useful changes in its newly-acquired passenger services. Some of these, such as the switch of the Rhymney Valley services to Queen Street, and the diversion of the ADR and Barry services into Pontypridd ex-TVR station, have been recorded in earlier chapters. The GWR also developed the use of the valley lines for holiday relief and excursion trains, starting some of them from Treherbert or Aberdare and using the Pontypridd-Caerphilly–Bassaleg route into Newport so as to ease the main line working at Cardiff; summer trains to South West Wales were similarly run in the reverse direction to Carmarthen via Pontypridd, Treherbert, the R & SB and Swansea District Lines to rejoin the main line at Llanelly. The TVR had run a seasonal train to Llandrindod Wells via Merthyr, the B & M and Cambrian Railways, and beginning in 1923 this was started back from Barry. In 1906 the GWR had begun in conjunction with the Barry and the Great Central Railways a through 'Ports to Ports Express' between Cardiff and Newcastle via Cheltenham, Kingham and Banbury, using GC and GW stock on alternate days; in the pre-grouping period the Barry Company insisted on using its own locomotives between there and Cardiff, express lights and all, and entering the General Station with much elan, panache, and *hwl*. Barry's favourite driver for this job was known, from the manner of his approach to Cardiff, as 'Ianto Full Pelt'. After the amalgamation the GWR further extended the service to Swansea via the Vale of Glamorgan line, using Great Western 4–4–0 or 2–6–0 tender engines.

Meanwhile communication between South Wales and London had improved rather slowly, apart from the dashing Ocean Mail Specials from Fishguard. Corridor trains had been introduced on the Swansea route in 1894 and sleeping cars in 1907, but between 1913 and 1939 the quickest journey time between Paddington and Cardiff or vice-versa had improved only from two hours fifty minutes, including a Newport stop, to two hours thirty-one minutes, partly because of pathing problems through the Severn Tunnel, and partly because the loading of the more popular business trains tended to be heavier than those on the Paddington-Bristol route.

DIESELS AND AEROPLANES

The GWR has often been accused of ultra-conservatism, but in fact it was in some directions highly enterprising. Beginning 9 July 1934 the company introduced diesel railcars with buffet service on the Cardiff-Birmingham express service. Capable of speeds up to 80mph, they proved highly successful when traffic was light, but had to be replaced by conventional trains at weekends; some units were also used on South Wales branch services. Some survived on these services until after World War II, having afforded valuable data as to both the capabilities and the limitations of the principle they represented.

Another direction in which the GWR was to evince its pioneering spirit was in the development of air services, demonstrating the advantage of this medium over land transport where, for instance, there was a watergap, as between Cardiff and Weston-super-Mare or the Devonshire resorts. The first rail-air service in which the company was interested began between Cardiff and Plymouth on 12

April 1933, the GWR becoming a participant in the establishment, in conjunction with Imperial Airways, of Railway Air Services Ltd in March 1934, one of the first directors being Mr Keith Grand of the GWR. Its activities went into suspense during World War II, whereafter the Transport Act, 1947, debarred British Railways from further direct participation in air transport.

WORLD WAR II

Beginning with re-armament in 1938, the South Wales railways again became active in the national effort for successful prosecution of a world war, but this time were to suffer from air attacks, especially those on Swansea and Cardiff between 1941 and 1943. Of those desperate, heroic years, the *Great Western Magazine* recorded that since the war began the company's South Wales docks dealt with 262,000 troops, and loaded or discharged more than 100,000 vessels with 90 million tons of cargo. In the preparation for the 'Overlord' operation for invasion of Normandy on 6 June 1944, 33,000 tons of steelwork were conveyed to South Wales ports for the assembly of prefabricated 'Mulberry Harbours', while over 50,000 wagons conveyed petrol to the ports; at the same time not a single colliery was stopped for wagons. The concentrated pre-invasion loading programme alone involved 158 vessels, 90,000 tons of cargo, 6,000 vehicles and 42,000 troops. By VE-Day, loadings since D-Day had risen to 753 vessels carrying 1.4 million tons of war materials. During 1943–44 Newport Ebbw Junction was principal USA Transportation Corps depot for the British Isles, some 500 USA locomotives, mainly 2–8–0s, but also 0–6–0Ts and 0–4–4–0 diesels, being tested and serviced by the USA 756th Railway Shop Battalion, and GWR footplatemen, the 2–8–0s being stored at Tonteg (p151), Penrhos and Cadoxton before and after D-Day while awaiting shipment overseas. South Wales was also the location of works for manufacturing war materials, notably the Royal Ordnance Factory at Glascoed on the Pontypool Road–Monmouth Branch, and at Bridgend, with its Tremains Platform for workers' trains sited on platform loops to the main line, east of the station.

Meanwhile, the company struggled to maintain a public service, with 'Castles' loaded to as much as 500 tons on ordinary Paddington–Swansea expresses. One line was assigned to military purposes (p247). There was tragedy too: among the steamships *St Patrick* was twice attacked while on normal passage and finally sunk, with loss of life, on 13 June 1941; *St David* was also sunk off Anzio while requisitioned as a hospital carrier. Ordinary services between Fishguard and Rosslare were not resumed until after the war.

NATIONALISATION

The end of World War II found the railways of Britain in an even more run-down condition than they were after World War I, thanks to their great war effort, serious arrears of maintenance and new construction, and damage by enemy action. With the advent to power in 1945 of a political party committed to the doctrine of public ownership, it was to be expected that the nationalisation of transport would follow that of the coal mines under the National Coal Board (NCB) in 1946. Thus the Transport Act, 1947, which took effect on the following New Year's Day, provided for the dissolution of the four grouped railway companies and London Transport, and the vesting of their assets in the British Transport Commission (BTC), whose management agent for railways (other than LT) was the Railway Executive, directing a railway system divided into six 'regions'.

Although it ceased to function as a management body, the GWR as a company continued until its formal dissolution on 23 December 1950, after 115 years' continuity, the longest life of any main line British railway company. It is no part of this book to dwell upon the political, emotional and controversial overtones which this and successive transport reorganisations have evoked, so let a plain record suffice.

All the railways in South Wales, with the exceptions of the Swansea & Mumbles, the domestic lines of the NCB and the private dock-area railways at Llanelly and Milford Haven, became part of the Western Region, which by and large represented the GWR system under a less prestigious and less popular title. The Fishguard & Rosslare Company also retained its joint status – the only joint railway to survive as such in Wales – but with the GWR's share ownership taken over by the BTC. The ex-LMS lines, including the Central Wales route from Craven Arms, were absorbed into the Western Region in 1948–49, and the LMS local management headquarters at Swansea and Abergavenny (the latter by this time a district engineer's headquarters only) were closed.

The Act of 1947 provided the BTC with other Executives to manage respectively Docks & Inland Waterways, and Hotels, removing these functions (also railway catering) from direct railway control, so that what had long been regarded as integral functions of the railway companies, became the subject of liaison arrangements, and sometimes of differences which theoretically could only be resolved by the BTC. Thus after a long period of railway ownership and management, the South Wales Docks were transferred to the control of the Docks & Inland Waterways Executive on 1 August 1948. If this represented a major loss of activity in which the GWR had evinced both energy and pride, there could have been no regrets at the transfer to the D & IWE in May 1949 of the seventy miles or so of now moribund canals which the GWR had acquired in South Wales at various times. These comprised the Monmouthshire, the Brecon & Abergavenny and the Swansea Canals, none of which had any future except as water-feeders, and some pleasure boating on the B & A. Indeed, the GWR had thought so little of its waterway inheritance that in 1922 it had bought six barges for five shillings (25p) each from a colliery company on the Swansea Canal, in order to get the traffic on to rail!

One other early consequence of the 1948 re-organisation was the transfer in 1949 of the management of the Fishguard–Rosslare and Waterford shipping services to the London Midland Region, the object being to group all British Railways steamer services between Great Britain and Ireland (Fishguard, Holyhead, Heysham, Larne, etc) under one maritime control. From 1968 these services were put under the control of what became Sealink (UK) Ltd., a BRB subsidiary (see Chapter XII).

WAGON FLEET TAKEN-OVER

Another significant feature of the 1947 nationalisation was the transfer into BTC ownership of almost the whole of the privately-owned wagon fleet, excluding a few special types and those required by NCB for internal colliery use. In order to avoid the traditional process of having to sort out and return to loading points the varied array of wagons owned by colliery companies, wagon hirers and others – a task to which the South Wales railways had necessarily devoted specialised attention – the wagon fleet had been included in the government control of the railways during World War II. By nationalisation, many of them required heavy repair or replacement, so that British Railways had to undertake a construction programme which eventually embraced some 400,000 wagons,

Page 273 (Top) Bridgend, looking west, with up passenger train, early 1850s; (centre) Nantymoel, looking north, with saddletank on three coach train, postcard c1919; (bottom) Barry Railway paddle steamer *Gwalia*, operating as Furness Railway's *Lady Moyra* c1911, sunk Dunkirk as *Brighton Queen*, May 1940. (Courtesy Railway Magazine, top; Peter E. Baughan collection)

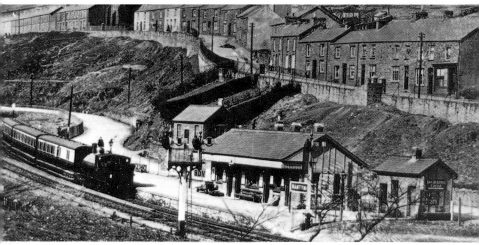

Page 274 *(Top)* Talybont-on-Usk, Brecon and Dowlais Line, looking south to start of infamous 7-mile 1 in 38 climb to Torpantau, probably 1930s; *(centre)* Carmarthen, looking north c1910; *(bottom)* Saundersfoot Railway 'Miners' Express' hauled by 0–4–0 Manning, Wardle saddletank, c1914 *(Peter E. Baughan collection)*

mostly all-steel mineral carriers, but including many four-wheeled box vans. The virtual monopoly of wagon ownership thus vested in the BTC by legislation had a reverse side to its medal, because while traders had retained a vested interest in rail movement so long as they owned their wagons, this tended to diminish when they not only had to depend upon BR for wagon provision, but were also subject to demurrage charges for not promptly unloading them.

During the early years of nationalisation, British Railways was not only pre-occupied with major organisational changes and with the effects of wartime arrears on performance, but was suffering from shortages of manpower and steam coal, due to the financial need to conserve coal for export. During one of the periodic energy crises, some South Wales services had to be worked by locomotives temporarily converted to oil-burning, while coal was being imported from foreign countries; the latter had also happened in Consequence of the General Strike, and the more prolonged miners' strike, in 1926.

IMPORTED COAL

Much later, and again arising from yet another energy crisis, the largest coal trains to operate in South Wales began in October 1979 to run between Cardiff or Newport with American or Australian imported coal for Didcot power station in Oxfordshire, which lies alongside the London-South Wales main line. Each train, hauled by a Class 56 diesel-electric locomotive, comprised forty-five automatic-discharge wagons with a total payload of 1,350 tonnes. What 'Dai Davies yr Ocean' would have thought – or most likely pungently said – of bringing coal from abroad into South Wales for use in England remains to be conjectured, but it should also be recorded that in 1978 the British Transport Docks Board brought into use at Barry a new coal and coke conveyor loading installation at a cost of £420,000, which by the end of that year was expected to have exported some 100,000 tonnes, mostly from rail. In 1978 the total outward shipments of coal and coke from South Wales ports were 969,000 tonnes, compared with 807,000 tonnes in 1977.

THE ACT OF 1953

With the advent of a government of different political complexion, the line of direction from the centre to the railway regions was

shortened through the abolition, provided for under the Transport
Act, 1953, of the Railway Executive and the establishment of a direct
line of policy command from the BTC to the regions. In respect of
the co-ordination of freight traffic between rail and road, however,
the new set-up was scarcely encouraging to the railways. The
Transport Act of 1947 had provided for a substantial measure of
public control over the road haulage industry by the establishment
of a Road Haulage Executive (trading as British Road Services),
together with stringent licensing powers. The latter was substantially
abolished by the Act of 1953, while the size of BRS was greatly
reduced; the author as a former railwayman found himself involved
in the process of advertising for re-sale to private enterprise road
haulage units which had been nationalised since 1947!

MORE REORGANISATION

Under the next major Transport Act (1962) the Commission itself
was abolished; separate boards were established for railways (BRB),
docks (BTDB), waterways, and a Transport Holding Company
which acquired responsibility for the shipping services and BRS,
though BRB obtained control of British Transport Hotels Ltd.
Meanwhile, railway freight traffic was going downhill; although
nationalisation of both mines and railways had produced a simpler
and more direct relationship for planning and movement control,
coal traffic was falling through disappointing production in the face
of diminishing markets and rising costs. Penarth Dock had already
closed, coal exports from Newport ceased in 1964, in which year the
Bute West Dock at Cardiff closed for trade, and the East Dock six
years later. Meanwhile, much wagon-load general goods traffic had
dwindled away through the growth of road transport and the
closure of small stations and many private sidings under the
Beeching Plan.

The ensuing Transport Act of 1968 (here we go again!) set up the
road-orientated National Freight Corporation, to which there was
required to be offered the right of handling all freight originating
on road, other than that tendered to the railway initiated
Freightliner Company, in which in any case NFC had a controlling
interest – more recently, one is glad to say, the Freightliner
Company has been handed back to BRB. The agreement that all
'smalls' consignments other than parcels should be offered to NFC
also seems to have resulted in the admittedly unprofitable railway

sundries business having been virtually handed over to NFC : in South Wales, all railway tracks leading to Cardiff's once paramount goods station at Newtown have been severed, but in September 1979, a new modern freight handling depot operated by Corylink and costing £250,000 was opened on the former site of Canton Milk Sidings, Cardiff, which was expected to handle up to 250,000 tons of rail freight annually, hitherto roadborne.

FREIGHT IN THE 1970s

While some traditional freight traffics have declined during the present century, the 1960s and 1970s nevertheless witnessed in the Cardiff Division – which was Britain's busiest for freight, handling 24 million tons a year – a vigorously-developed transition into the basic pattern of the modern freight railway; the rapid movement of bulk commodities, eighty per cent in trainloads, between production plants and specialist terminals (over ninety per cent was in fact to or from private terminals, with no road involvement whatever). Coal and coke traffic amounted to twelve million tons a year to power stations, to industrial plants, to Barry or Swansea for shipment, or to power stations such as Aberthaw, normally served by fifteen, 28-wagon merry-go-round (mgr) trains daily. Including the bulk iron-ore movement to Llanwern already mentioned, steel traffic amounted to six million tons annually, some of this later being carried by Freightliner and by the new Speedlink service of express goods trains comprised of high-capacity wagons. Other major bulk traffics included oil, as described in the previous chapter, chemicals, cars and car components, cement and fertilisers.

Three other developments contributed to the growth and efficiency of South Wales freight traffic: the expansion of the private owners' fleets of high-capacity wagons, the 'TOPS' system, and government grants to present or intending rail customers under Section 8 of the Railways Act, 1974. TOPS (Total Operations Processing System) was BR's own computerised method of monitoring the movement and utilisation of every BR and privately-owned wagon in the system. Following successful pilot schemes launched in the Radyr and Aberdare districts in 1973, covering at that time sixty-three terminals in an area of 600 square miles, the system was soon extended to the entire Cardiff Division, operated through fourteen Area Freight Centres, from Severn Tunnel

Junction to Llanelli. As regards the 1974 powers under which the Welsh Office, subject to the support of BR and of local authorities, may make grants to industry of up to fifty per cent of the capital cost of terminal and other facilities for the purpose of retaining or diverting suitable traffics to rail, ten such grants totalling some £5 million were shortly to be approved on behalf of industries located at Aberthaw, Baglan Bay, Cardiff, Llanelli, Bridgend, Swansea and Cwmbargoed. A late example was a fifty per cent grant to NCB towards the cost of a new railway at Crynant, to link Treforgan Colliery with BR's Dulais Valley (ex-N & B) line, thus enabling over 500,000 tonnes of coal annually to be moved by rail, instead of by lorry, to Aberpergwm washery in the adjacent Neath Valley.

Major industrial bulk traffics were not without their problems, however, as witness the closure in 1978 of the East Moors Steelworks at Cardiff, and the doubts raised as to the long-term future of other BSC plants. Again, although BR benefits from inter-plant coal movements for washing or blending, the NCB policy of leading coal underground from one colliery to be wound through the shaft of another nearby, led directly to the closure of railway branches, eg the ex-RR Aber Branch and the Pontypool–Hafodyrynys connection at the eastern end of the old NA & H Railway's Taff Vale Extension.

PASSENGER SERVICES

Progress in the recovery of passenger services to and from South Wales was particularly slow after World War II and in the first decade of nationalisation, due to heavy loadings, numerous permanent way slacks for arrears of track maintenance, heavy line occupation through and west of the Severn Tunnel, locomotive fuel problems, and ministerial edicts to save coal. In 1949 the fastest journey time between Paddington and Cardiff was still twenty-three minutes slower than it had been in 1939, while two years later a short-lived Paddington-Cardiff non-stop averaged only 54mph between the two capitals. By 1955 the WR had introduced a shop-window, fastest-yet 62.5mph schedule between Paddington and Newport by *The Pembroke Coast Express*, covering the 133½ miles in 128 minutes. On 13 June of the same year, a steam-hauled Pullman service was begun between London and Swansea, but taking twenty-one minutes longer to Newport than *The Pembroke Coast*, albeit with a slightly heavier load. For years the indefatigable Castle class 4–6–0s of GWR design bore the brunt of the South Wales expresses, but in the latter years of steam the heavier trains became the responsibility of Britannia Class Pacifics, and of the King Class 4–6–0s (between Paddington and Cardiff only).

By the late 1950s, diesel traction was entering the scene, Swindon-built diesel multiple-units taking-over the Swansea–Birmingham express service, and beginning to move into the valleys, where an intensive regular-interval steam-worked service had been introduced in the Cardiff area in 1953.

The 1960s witnessed the progressive introduction of diesel main line locomotives on the South Wales trunk route, together with more modern coaching stock, a more frequent and more effectively grouped service pattern, and hence a growth in patronage. Locomotive types involved initially were the two Western Region classes of diesel-hydraulics: the moderately-powered Hymeks and the 2,700hp Westerns, but eventually the Class 47 Brush diesel-electrics, initially rated at 2,750hp, became the dominant class, later forming with the English Electric 1,750hp Class 37 (for a time used in pairs on some South Wales expresses) the backbone of heavy freight haulage in the Cardiff Division Even earlier, the steam-hauled Pullman trains had been superseded in September 1961 by the 'Blue Pullman' diesel-electric multiple-units, which initially reduced the journey time between Swansea and Paddington to just over 3½ hours, including a then fastest-ever time between Cardiff and Paddington of two hours seven minutes. By the autumn of 1965, there were nearly twenty start-to-stop schedules at 60mph or over by trains originating or terminating in South Wales, the fastest being Paddington–Newport at nearly 71 mph.

Passenger traffic was also stimulated during this period by the restoration in 1964 of day sailings via Fishguard and Rosslare, after an interval of more than twenty years. In the following summer a car-carrier service, precursor of the Motorail trains, was inaugurated between London and Fishguard.

THE END OF STEAM

Meanwhile, conversion to diesel haulage had led to the elimination of steam on regular public services between London and South Wales in 1962. At nationalisation, the GWR had handed over to British Railways some 1,400 steam locomotives in South Wales alone, based at thirty depots in the area. Nearly one hundred more had been transferred to the Western Region through the absorption of ex-LMS lines. The steam stock diminished only gradually until the rundown of small goods stations and private sidings, coupled with the more intensive user of diesel traction, began to bite. But by 1965 BR steam traction had finally died in South Wales, although for years to come, the unforgettable exhaust thunder of hard-worked steam engines was still to echo through the valleys on the colliery lines of the NCB. In 1980 the total number of diesel locomotives stationed at the five main depots of Cardiff (Canton), Swansea (Landore), Margam, Newport (Ebbw Junction) and Severn Tunnel Junction was rather less than 300, with some units within this total outstabled at signing-on points like Radyr and Llanelli; in addition there were fifty-four diesel multiple-unit sets within the Cardiff Division.

THE HST ERA

The passenger accelerations already described formed the prologue to the introduction, partially in 1976 and fully in 1977, of the High Speed Train (HST) service between London and South Wales, a powerful riposte to the completion of the M4 Motorway and of the Severn Road Bridge. Perhaps the most remarkable aspects of the HST service are that even with regular-interval HSTs all making standard intermediate calls at Bridgend, Port Talbot and Neath, the running time between Cardiff and Swansea was not only still quicker than anything achieved by non-stop steam trains, but the entire journey between London and Swansea, 191 miles was scheduled in two hours forty minutes at fractionally over 71mph, five stops included. The HSTs reduced the quickest times between London and Newport to eighty-four minutes (over 95mph), and to Cardiff, including the Newport stop, one hour thirty-three minutes (average 84.5mph), representing in the latter case a saving of thirty-three minutes on the fastest time before the HST service. The HST accelerations could not have been achieved, to the extent described, by traction alone. There had been massive investment on the whole main line in track engineering, with major easement of speed restrictions, together with the progressive introduction of centralised power signalling through installations at Newport, Cardiff and Port Talbot; the last-named covered the main line through Swansea to Pembrey (exclusive) beyond Llanelli.

LOCAL SERVICE GRANTS

As in many localities elsewhere, local passenger services in South Wales are fundamentally unprofitable. Prior to the Railways Act of 1974, Government grants towards such losses were itemised in the BRB annual accounts. In 1974, they aggregated £4.6 million for the area's services, comprising £1,928,000 for the Cardiff Valleys, £1,138,000 for the Crewe-South Wales group, including the Central Wales line; £582,000 for the Severnside Group (Cardiff-Bristol and Cardiff-Gloucester), and £817,000 for the West Wales Group. From 1974, these grants were not itemised in the published accounts, being comprehended within the total grant provided by central government against Public Service Obligation.

Although the Transport Act, 1968, provided for the establishment in appropriate conurbations of Passenger Transport Authorities and Executives, no such bodies were set up in South Wales. But under provisions of the same Act, all three Glamorgan County Councils financed park-and-ride car parks mainly at commuter stations – ten on the local lines radiating from Cardiff, one at Gowerton on the western outskirts of Swansea, with another planned for Neath, while contributions to improved passenger facilities at Port Talbot and Llanelli were made by the West Glamorgan and the Dyfed County Councils respectively.

POSITION IN 1979–80

In 1913 there were in South Wales some 600 rail-connected collieries; nearly seven decades later there was only about one-tenth that number of coal loading points, including opencast sites, washeries, fuel preparation points, and so on.

The South Wales system then (1913) comprised over 1,200 route miles of railway, and more than 450 passenger stations and halts open for traffic. In 1980, the BR Cardiff Division's activities in Wales (but excluding for comparative purposes its responsibilities across the border, which extend into parts of England) embraced 656 route miles, 109 passenger stations – including Knighton on the Central Wales line, where the town is in England but the station in Wales – and 183 freight depots and sidings. A staff of some 8,300 administered, operated and maintained 345 passenger trains originating daily in the division, and 275 originating freight trains, nearly 80,000 tons of freight traffic. The change in scale was notable, but this was a different railway performing its task in a world which industrially, socially and indeed politically, had greatly changed.

To a greater degree perhaps than most other regions within the British Isles, South Wales had displayed within a compact framework, over some two hundred years, every facet of transport, except main line electrification, from the horse-worked tramroad to the High Speed Train. Its railways derived their origins, strength and prosperity from the Industrial Revolution, of which they became one of the most influential adjuncts. After a long summer of continuous expansion, two World Wars and the stresses of economic, social, political and industrial change had reduced their physical scale, but not the importance of their role relative to a much altered industrial pattern, which they still served effectively and progressively: different railways in a different world. *Cymru a fu a Chymru a fydd.*

CHAPTER XII

The Twentieth Century – II
Towards the New Millennium

THE EIGHTIES – DECADE OF CHANGE

This decade witnessed arguably a greater number and variety of changes in South Wales than any other 'region' of BR. It began in recession. Passenger traffic was down, with HST InterCity 125 (IC125) takings badly hit. The mid eighties saw reorganisation of management and operation of the former Cardiff Division, mirroring what was taking place on British Rail as a whole and fully described elsewhere.* Concurrently, resurgence brought higher speeds, improved long-distance connections, reopenings of passenger routes, additional stations, a massive investment in Cardiff's 'Valley Lines', and reconstruction/renovation of many stations. 'Sectorisation' resulted in new liveries for locomotives and rolling stock, while passengers ('customers' since 1988) in modern, bright coaches had smoother rides in less comfortable but ergonomically correct seats. On the freight side changed operating procedures, altered traffic flows, and increasing use of air-braked stock brought rationalisation with closure of large 'hump' marshalling yards in favour of smaller sorting yards. In the early nineties county councils continued to campaign for 25kV electrification to maximise Channel Tunnel opportunities for South Wales.

In 1983 motorway coach competition between Cardiff and London, soon extending to Haverfordwest, was countered with fare reductions and an early morning IC125 from Haverfordwest to Paddington. That October two Swansea–Paddington IC125s were upgraded to 'Executive' status and named 'Red Dragon' and 'Saint

* *BR in the Eighties* David St John Thomas & Patrick Whitehouse (1990)

David', becoming 'Super Executive' in 1986, and 'Red Dragon' a Pullman in 1988. By mid decade through services extended to Scotland, the North-East, North and West Wales, and the South Coast. Some trains remained locomotive-hauled by classes 40, 45 and 47, with 50s becoming common by 1984. By 1987 Paddington–Swansea was third most profitable InterCity route, with London–Cardiff timings about 100 minutes – appreciated by Mr John Evans of Fforestfach, Swansea who in August, at age 110, was BR's guest on his *first* visit to London! From 1988 Super Sprinters began taking over many provincial services. 'Extra-mural' activities included special steam workings in 1985–87, some VSOE promotions, and the 'Travelling College' – a unique peripatetic twelve-coach educational experiment, with classrooms and all on-board facilities, which took its inaugural trip in May 1989 but sadly ended in receivership. Supported by local government, Cardiff's 'Valley Lines' received an injection of capital and hope. The 'Valley Train/Tren-y-Cwm' image was launched at Pontypridd on 2 February 1985. Effective marketing and fares reductions generated a million more passenger journeys than in 1984; by December 1986 there were five thousand more passengers daily than in 1982. Though following the full local introduction of Sprinters there were problems leading to protests by passengers, press and local authorities (p293), the 1991–2 financial year showed a five per cent increase in Valley Lines revenue. On freight, 1980 saw reduced demand for coal and steel; cheaper, subsidised coal was imported while exports declined; Welsh coal swelled growing stockpiles. Though movement continued of domestic coal – itself a shrinking market – to local coalyards (superseded by mechanical concentration depots at Newport and Swansea in 1984), declining traffic led to some network pruning. More pits closed, stockpiles taking time to clear. By the early nineties most colliery branches had gone, replaced by slow greening of tips and slopes, where once busy, humming wheels proclaimed the cutting of coal far below. At the start of the decade there was a handful of Speedlink trains in South Wales, carrying varieties of wagonload freight. The service developed rapidly, with a separate 'Network Coal' operation using hopper wagons based successively at Pantyffynon, Radyr, Briton Ferry, Radyr again, and East Usk yards. In 1988 Speedlink merged with Freightliner under Railfreight Distribution (RfD), while bulk-load workings merged under Trainload Freight, with sub-sectors of Coal, Construction, Metals and Petroleum. Speedlink ceased operating from 8 July 1991, seventy per cent of its traffic staying with RfD. As to metals, in 1980 British Steel was laying-off employees; October saw the ore trains (p44) cut to three daily. At Llanelli the Duport steelworks closed in March 1981. When, six years later, British Steel was buoyant, it was Metals traffic which required reconstruction of Margam Yard (p294) and upgrading of Cardiff Tidal Yard to eighteen double-ended sidings shared with Coal, Petroleum and Speedlink (for Petroleum, see p301). Freight trains generally were hauled by class 37 and 47 locomotives, but single class 60s started working ore trains from 1991.

EASTERN AND WESTERN MONMOUTHSHIRE (GWENT)

South Wales main line. Severn Tunnel Junction marshalling yard and diesel depot closed 10/11 October 1987. East Usk and three other Newport yards at Alexandra Dock Junction, Ebbw Junction and Godfrey Road took on an increased role, as did Cardiff Tidal Yard. (Ebbw Junction diesel depot closed October 1982.) Speedlink services which had used STJ 'Undy' Yard until November 1983 and 'Bristol' Yard thereafter, transferred to East Usk, Cardiff Tidal, and Briton Ferry (soon superseded by Margam). Bi-directional signalling was introduced in the Severn Tunnel area in January 1990. Within the tunnel, on 7 December 1991, a Portsmouth Harbour–Cardiff Sprinter ran into a Paddington–Cardiff IC125. Over a hundred passengers were injured; the tunnel reopened on 10 December. Though at the time of writing (May 1993) the cause of the accident remained uncertain, £5.5m had been pledged by BR for additional safety measures. Up to 1987 East Usk Yard held coal trains to and from Uskmouth power station at the end of the East Usk Branch. The branch was singled in November 1983. Deliveries to the power station ceased by 1988, coal going instead to Newport Docks for blending before being delivered by road. A spur was opened on 19 August 1988 from East Usk Junction to a new Isis Link terminal in connection with BSC Orb Works and a further length of the branch reopened on 23 March 1989 to Alpha Steelworks. At this time Newport Docks was receiving imported coal for Aberthaw power station and (until December 1989) for Chinnor cement works in Oxfordshire. East Usk Yard ceased to be a Speedlink marshalling point in July 1990. Newport Dock Street (Gwent Coal Distribution Centre) saw its last rail delivery on 11 September 1990, the branch beyond Courtybella Crossing closing officially from 26

January 1991; part reopened in the spring, however, to serve the AS & W Whitehead plant.

The Newport–Hereford line, or 'North and West Route'. Abergavenny Monmouth Road goods closed April 1981. On 11 May 1986 a new station officially opened to serve Cwmbran – sixth largest town in Wales, first Welsh new town, and Gwent's administrative centre; 26 weekday and six Sunday trains called starting 12 May. Within a week passengers were double those expected. January 1991 saw the end of regular locomotive-hauled passenger trains on the route, though shortages in 158s in February 1993 resulted in a class 37/4 diagram on Cardiff–Liverpool services. On the closed Llantarnam Junction–Talywain Junction–Blaenavon line (p67), the Pontypool & Blaenavon Railway hoped to preserve Pontypool Crane Street–Blaenavon High Level/Furnace Sidings, adjacent to the Big Pit Colliery Museum and the latter's own railway system, to which the P & BR would operate steam;tourist trains over the scenic route including Horseshoe Bend and Garndiffaith Viaduct. From January 1983 removal of Pontrhydyrun Bridge at Pontnewydd severed the line from BR. The 1983 summer Bank Holiday witnessed opening of ½-mile of the former LNWR line from Furnace Sidings to Garn-yr-Eirw. Over the next few years weekend passenger services operated seasonally. Platforms and run-round loops were constructed, 'Whistle Platform' opening 30 April 1988. Unable to extend northwards to Waunavon, the P & BR turned south towards Forgeside Road. In 1991 Pontypool Crane Street station was dismantled for rebuilding at Furnace Sidings. Nevertheless, by 1992 unresolved differences with Torfaen Borough Council meant that the railway might have to move elsewhere, though reprieve became possible following a European Regional Development Fund Grant in 1993.

On the Western Valleys line, a 1¼-mile single track deviation was opened on 24 November 1981 to accommodate the Rogerstone–Risca by-pass; it was the last of three alterations that autumn: from 31 October Park Junction–Courtybella Junction closed, ending two hundred years of railway history; Gaer Junction–Park Junction and Park Junction–Lime Kiln Junction were singled on 2 November. The 'Western Valley Railway' – in BR press release parlance – carried yearly traffic of over ½ million tons of steel coil to Ebbw Vale for coating, with finished tinplate outwards, and almost 1½ million tons of coking coal for BSC and for coke ovens, the domestic market, and electricity generation – all equivalent to four hundred loaded lorry movements daily. South Celynen

Colliery closed in September and Rose Heyworth Colliery in October, 1985. Coal stocks at Rose Heyworth, last remaining colliery on the Western Valleys line proper, were cleared by 29 November, and after a railtour on 5 April 1986 the branch down to Aberbeeg went out of use; Aberbeeg Junction was removed in December 1988. On the Ebbw Vale Branch Aberbeeg–Waunllwyd (Ebbw Vale Works) was singled in August 1981. In 1985 Marine Colliery scrapped screen loading in favour of a concrete pad and mechanical shovels – a method increasingly adopted. The last train left Marine on 2 March 1989, after which the rail link to the Ebbw Vale Branch closed. At Ebbw Vale, on 3 January 1989 guests were carried by BSC train over a viaduct and extension, gained after a climbing zig-zag movement, to new sidings, replacing the Waunllwyd Sidings which closed 28 January 1989 to become part of the 1992 Garden Festival site. BSC's tinplate works sidings were maintained and operated by Hunslet Barclay. The Garden Festival was open between 1 May and 4 October 1992, served by buses from Newport station. It included a funicular railway, passengers being carried in 96-seater 'toast-rack' vehicles in two three-car trains hauled by endless cable. Unique features included 3ft 6in gauge which widened to 4ft, and loop points with no moveable parts. On the Hall's Road/Penar Branch Markham Colliery closed September 1985. Some three miles to the south, the last train left Oakdale Colliery on 26 August 1989, track being lifted down to Lime Kiln Junction in 1990. On the stump of the Bassaleg Junction–Rhymney line Bedwas Colliery closed in 1985, the last train running on 8 April. The smokeless fuels plant and British Benzole sidings at Trethomas also having closed, the line went out of use west of Machen Quarry, track going in 1987. Machen Quarry remained one of the main ballast suppliers to the Western Region.

CARDIFF AND ITS VALLEYS

Cardiff Central station received a facelift, with a modernised concourse, opened by Viscount Tonypandy on 16 January 1984. A nice touch was to retain 'GREAT WESTERN RAILWAY' on the front elevation, revealed after years behind a hoarding. Planned for 1993 were road improvements south of Central, sweeping away the GWR parcels depot and two Riverside platforms and embankment. Queen Street was modernised in 1988–89; from 24 September 1990 platform 3 became a through road linking with the Bute Road

Branch. Tyndall Field Goods closed in 1981, and Gabalfa and Roath coalyards in 1984. In Cardiff Docks the swing bridge between Roath Basin and Dock was abolished after a new runround loop in May 1991 at Splott Junction allowed movement to continue from the Cardiff rod mill to Queen Alexandra Dock Sidings. In 1989 Pengam Freightliner depot was chosen as the site for the South Wales Channel Tunnel RfD terminal. From spring 1993 operations at Cardiff Tidal Yard were taken on by locomotives and staff of the adjacent Allied Steel & Wire Company. BR shared Bute Road platform with Butetown Historic Railway Society, housed in the Grade II listed station building and adjacent yard, in 1989 becoming the nucleus of the Wales Railway Centre. Though the BR track was slewed to the disused west platform in 1987, providing a running line on the east side for the Centre, the Cardiff Bay Development will require its relocation.

From Queen Street, where the old Parade buildings were demolished in 1989, the Rhymney Branch passes beneath the A48 (on the site of the Roath Branch) before reaching Heath Junction for the single track Coryton Branch. On 20 November 1984 the junction was moved 300yd north, controlled by new colour-light signalling. On 29 April 1987 a branch station opened at Ty Glas, the other five branch stations being refurbished to match the new arrival's 'Valley Lines' image. Continuing towards Rhymney, on 4 November 1986 a new Lisvane & Thornhill station replaced the nearby, little used Cefn-onn, originally a golfing halt, closed 27 September. In Caerphilly Tunnel a brickwork collapse led to single line working and a short-lived closure in February 1992. At Caerphilly the Ness Tar Distillation Works connection went in April, and goods facilities in June, 1982; the coalyard closed October 1983. Station improvements, a new Up side waiting room with ramp access to the street, a new footbridge, and enlarged car park, were completed in October 1990. A thriving railway society – inspired by the locomotive works history – had steam open days and undertook restoration, one locomotive being ex-Taff Vale No 28 of the National Railway Museum collection, last surviving Welsh-built standard gauge example. To see if reduced freight traffic could be re-routed, Walnut Tree Junction–Aber Junction ('The Big Hill') was closed 21 June 1982, though the last train was a special on 23 October. The experiment proved capacity was sufficient via Caerphilly and Queen Street. Track lifting started in 1984, but ¼ mile of Down line remained at Walnut Tree for an engineers' headshunt until 1987. Aber Junction

Yard also closed. From May 1987 Aber Junction box closed following resignalling with colour-light, Heath Junction becoming the control point up to the section under the ex-RR box at Ystrad Mynach. A new crossover, installed in March 1987 at Caerphilly, allowed some trains to terminate there instead of at Aber, though from May some services continued to Ystrad Mynach, the main park-and-ride station. Bargoed Colliery Branch saw its last train on 13 May 1982, though the junction remained until October 1983. After rationalisation Rhymney consisted of single line and platform; the coalyard closed May 1983. From Ystrad Mynach South Junction the Taff Bargoed Branch climbed to the head of Cwm Bargoed, throwing off, at Nelson & Llancaiach Junction, the short 'Ocean' Branch which divided to serve Deep Navigation and Taff Merthyr Collieries and Trelewis Drift Mine. Nelson & Llancaiach closed to freight April 1981. In October 1983 Cwmbargoed–Dowlais Furnace Top went out of use. Trelewis closed in 1989 when British Coal invested in its opencast site at Cwmbargoed. A landslip between Cwmbargoed and Taff Merthyr branches closed them both from 7 February 1990, Taff Merthyr reopening on 18 February and Cwmbargoed on 9 March. British Coal and Ryans at Cwmbargoed were sufficiently profitable to warrant track renewal north of Nelson in 1990, with resignalling and a passing loop at Trodomen, opened by May 1991. Deep Navigation closed March 1991, coal stock removal continuing until January 1992, followed that October by closure of Taff Merthyr Colliery. Based at Rhymney, South Wales' first woman train driver qualified in March 1993.

Cardiff–Merthyr. A new station – first in Cardiff for over forty years – opened at Cathays on 3 October 1983. With reduced demand for maintenance of Valley Lines rolling stock Cathays Works formally closed, except for some departmental wagon maintenance, on 18 March 1993; that month Radyr Yard was also to close. At Taff's Well the attractive TVR buildings were replaced by a shelter in 1982. The Nantgarw Branch (stub-end of the Cardiff Railway, joined by a spur to the Taff main line when Coryton Halt–Nantgarw New Spur Junction closed 16 June 1952) served Nantgarw Colliery and coke ovens. Mining ceased November 1986. The branch went out of use in April 1987, the first ¼ mile remaining as a reversing siding for passenger trains at Taff's Well; track was lifted in 1991. Trefforest, station for a suburb of Pontypridd and the Polytechnic of Wales (now University of Glamorgan), closed to goods December 1981 and coal September 1982. Pontypridd, down to one platform (pp145–6) lost its freight facilities in May 1981. The buffet, last in the Valleys, closed May 1983. Its approaches reduced to single track, reintroduction of Cynon Valley services (below) strained capacity at the station, and the Up side goods lines became relief roads at which a new four-car Up platform opened on 16 (officially 25) September 1991. From Stormstown Junction a short length of the Ynysbwl Branch served Lady Windsor Colliery, closed March 1988, the final train being a railtour that October. Following closure of Merthyr Tydfil goods and coal yards in April 1981 and May 1982 respectively, freight workings ceased beyond Merthyr Vale, where colliery and washery closed in August and November 1989. Subsequent removal of the loop adversely affected operation of passenger trains, ending the half-hourly peak service after May 1992. The 3¼ miles from Abercynon to the loop henceforth operated by NSKT working (see p298). North of Merthyr, the Brecon Mountain Railway (p168), Pant–Pontsticill, opened 8 June 1980 and prospered throughout the decade. Additional working stock was introduced and a three-storey station, with restaurant, shops and parking was built at Pant.

On the Cynon Valley Branch, Aberdare closed to goods in May 1982 and coal May 1984. The private Hirwaun–Penderyn Quarry Branch closed December 1982 when BR's ballast contract with Amey Roadstone ended. It reopened June 1983, ballast going to roadworks in West Wales and closed in 1985, becoming a cycle track for Brecon Beacons National Park. Penrhiwceiber Colliery closed October 1985 and the Abercwmboi phurnacite plant in March 1990. Following countrywide 1992–93 closures, Tower Colliery at Hirwaun looked likely to become the sole surviving South Wales pit. Christmas 1984 saw 'Merrymaker' shopper specials to Cardiff Queen Street and Central from Aberdare, Mountain Ash and Pontypridd. Successful repetition led to a regular Saturday service from 5 October 1985, with temporary platforms at Cwmbach and Penrhiwceiber that November. On 27 September 1988 the branch formally reopened to passenger traffic. A free service operated on 2 October, regular trains starting next day. There was a new platform at Aberdare, south of the 'High Level' site, new stations at Cwmbach, Fernhill, Mountain Ash and Penrhiwceiber, and an 'Abercynon North' – cheaper than moving back into the old Abercynon where the main line platforms assumed the suffix 'South'. Colour-light signalling and an hourly Sprinter service operated from November 1989; a week later Abercwmboi box closed, the

Page 291 (Top) Pembroke Dock, looking west, with DMU C807, August 1986; (centre) Haverfordwest, looking north-east, with DMU C803 leaving for Milford Haven, August 1986; (bottom) Newport (Gwent), with eastbound steel coil train headed by 37711 *Tremorfa Steel Works*, February 1989. (Peter E. Baughan)

Page 292 (*Top*) Pontypridd, looking north-west, with Sprinter 150273 on City Line service to Coryton, February 1989; *(centre)* Cardiff Queen Street, looking north, with 37887 on coal train, February 1990; *(bottom)* Derek Barrie: 'Men were and are the lifeblood' – Great Western staff at Ogmore Vale. *(Peter E. Baughan, top and centre; Peter E. Baughan collection)*

Up line becoming bi-directional with the Down as a loop. At the time of writing consideration was being given to extending the passenger service to Hirwaun.

On the Treherbert Branch March 1981 saw Porth–Cwmparc singled (existing single track continuing to Treherbert), Rhondda Fach Junction South and Cwmparc boxes closed, and a new box at Porth controlled the branch by NSKT signalling. Treorchy closed to freight April 1981 and to coal (Cwmparc) December 1982. Tymawr Colliery closed July 1983, the last coal being cleared in June 1984. New stations, at Ynyswen, between Treherbert and Treorchy, and a double-platformed Ystrad Rhondda, with loop, at Gelligaled Park, between the existing Ystrad Rhondda (renamed Ton Pentre) and Llwynpia stations, opened formally on 28 September 1986, and for public use the following day. In 1989 Dinas and Llwynpia received park-and-ride facilities. Maerdy Colliery on the Rhondda Fach Branch closed June 1986, the pit by then being connected by underground conveyor belt to Tower Colliery, Hirwaun; the final working was of a clearance train on 22 August. Tracklifting left a reversing siding at Porth.

From May 1985 Radyr Junction–Penarth Curve North Junction–Cardiff Central joined the passenger network, permitting extension of a Merthyr–Cardiff train to Bristol, and forming part of a new 'City Line' service, Merthyr–Radyr–Cardiff–Coryton, as part of the Valley Lines network. A half-hourly service started on 5 October 1987 – first new passenger service in Wales for 75 years – with intermediate stations at Danescourt, Fairwater and a refurbished Ninian Park (closed since September 1939 but used for football specials). Waungron Park station opened 2 November. As in other 'reopenings', this service was popular initially, but suffered delays from Sprinters developing door faults, and being incapable of rescue except by another Sprinter. There was severe overcrowding. Sufficient passengers returned to their original transport to threaten viability of that section of the City Line; by spring 1990, contrary to results elsewhere, it attracted half the expected number of passengers. Other problems were vandalism – Police being spread more thinly as stations opened, revenue lost from an 'open stations' policy introduced 1985–9 (ie no barriers) and, since the issue of 'Portis' ticket machines to Valley Lines guards starting July 1986, difficulty in collecting short-journey fares on crowded trains. From March 1993 some redeployment of Cardiff suburban station staff to city stations and partial return to station ticket machines and barriers produced significant additional excess fare revenue.

At Penarth North Curve, Sloper Road Sidings closed September 1982 and Virgil Street coal depot May 1984. On the Ferry Road Branch, by 1981 the final ½ mile to the Esso Siding was out of use; Taff Wagon Engineering Works closed April 1987, and BP traffic ceased early in 1990. That year the superseded 1888 Penarth station was demolished, the Penarth Branch having been reduced to the former Up line since February 1967. The Barry and Penarth branches were busy with Valley Lines services and carried heavy freight, serving Barry Docks and Aberthaw power station and cement works. A new station opened at Eastbrook on 24 November 1986. Barry closed to goods in September and coal in October, 1983. The docks dealt with coal, steel, grain and chemicals. Nearby was Woodham Bros' scrapyard from which, by the foresight of David Woodham MBE, who thoughtfully scrapped wagons before locomotives, from September 1968 over two hundred of the three hundred or so ex-BR steam locomotives now preserved, were rescued. The final engine left in November 1989; one of the last, 27 years on site, was presented by Dai Woodham for display at Barry. Most of Woodham's Yard was lifted by mid 1990.

WESTWARD FROM CARDIFF

Between Cardiff and Court Sart Junction there were in 1980 two stations, Bridgend and Port Talbot; by the early nineties two had been added and five proposed (two being between Neath and Swansea). Pencoed, with a platform either side of the level crossing, and Pontyclun, coinciding with reopening to Maesteg (p296), opened 11 May and 28 September 1992 respectively. The five proposals, Pyle, Baglan, Briton Ferry, Skewen and Llansamlet, served a Swansea–Bridgend local service for which West Glamorgan CC received a grant in 1993. Llantrisant coalyard closed November 1983; the goods yard closed February 1988, thereafter hosting engineers' trains. In 1979 Brunel's Italianate Bridgend station gained new facilities; the goods yard closed September 1983. In 1992 the Up bay was extended for the Maesteg service. To attract motorists to the trains, Port Talbot received an enlarged car park, becoming Port Talbot Parkway from 3 December 1984; the goods yard closed April 1981 and the coalyard May 1984. The 52-siding Margam 'hump' marshalling yard closed on 31 October 1987; on the following day Railfreight opened the rebuilt, adjacent 'Knuckle'

Yard, with eighteen sidings and colour-light signalling to process 85 trains weekly, conveying coal and lime, and hot and cold reduced coil and steel slab to and from BSC's Margam plant sidings with which eleven Knuckle sidings were linked, BSC's diesels tripping wagons between yard and plant. Three sidings were dedicated to Speedlink trains.

On the Vale of Glamorgan line the branch authorised by BR Act of 1978 to the Ford Motor Works (p178), saw cylinder block castings arriving and half-a-million completed engines leaving annually to Dagenham, Halewood, and Saarlouis (West Germany) via the Dover–Dunkerque train ferry. Aberthaw cement works installed MGR facilities to receive coal, following the power station's example which in 1981 required twenty MGR trains daily compared to seven in 1980. Bridgend Coity coalyard closed November 1983. Though Bridgend East Junction–Barry was used for diversion of all traffic from the South Wales main line, despite lobbying, BR refused to reopen the route for regular passenger traffic. A proposed service to Rhoose for Cardiff–Wales Airport was rejected as 'not remotely profitable'. In 1990 a development project allowed for a 1¼-mile spur from the eastern end of Porthkerry Viaduct to an airport station, with a large car park for Vale commuters. The question of reopening to passengers remained live in 1993. North of Llantrisant, the final coal train to Coed Ely coke works arrived on 29 September and the last wagon left the branch on 4 October, 1983. Mwyndy Junction closed 2 April 1984. Cwm Colliery closed November 1986; stockpile removal lasted two months. Llantrisant (Cowbridge Road Crossing)–Cwm went out of use on 2 October 1989. Nevertheless, the branch was partly realigned in 1990 for construction of Talbot Green by-pass; in May 1993 Coal Products and Trainload Coal were discussing possible reopening to Cwm. Out of use since 1978, the Creigiau Quarry Branch (p175) officially closed 1 January 1981.

From 8 October 1983 the Tondu Middle Junction–Ynysawdre Junction double track became two single lines, one to Nantymoel on the Ogmore Branch, the other to Blaengarw on the Garw Branch. After closure of Wyndham Western Colliery the Ogmore Branch above Caedu Crossing went out of regular use. Ogmore washery closed July 1986, when Nantymoel–Caedu tracklifting started. Attempts to preserve Ogmore Vale station for use by the Travelling College failed when it was bulldozed in March 1987. The last train ran on 23 April 1989, after which the branch was severed when the westerly end was slewed into the Garw Branch at Brynmenyn, rendering superfluous the northerly of the two tracks into Tondu. On the Ogmore Vale Extension the 1983 changes included closure of Cefn passing loop and Cefn Junction box which became a Heritage Centre. Mill Pit opencast mine closed in 1989. At Garw, mining ceased in December 1985. Coal continued travelling to Tondu for reversal up to Ogmore washery to clear the stockpile until 15 May 1986 when the branch went out of use. It reopened on 23 September 1991 for a British Coal scheme to remove a million tons of coal from tips from the Garw and Ffaldau Collieries, the work being inaugurated on 26 November with a 23-wagon train from a loading pad north of the former Pontycymmer station. Extracted shale was used to landscape abandoned railway and mine workings towards Blaengarw. In April 1981 Maesteg closed to goods, coal remaining. Maesteg washery was reached by a run-round loop and reversal from Llynfi Junction. Coal from St John's Colliery reached the washery via Cwmdu and reversal up to Maesteg. St John's ceased production in November 1985 with the last rail movement on 21 March 1986. The washery closed October 1989, remaining stock removal taking until 23 February 1993. In 1985 BR considered reintroduction of branch passenger services, approval being given in 1990. Cardiff–Maesteg passenger trains started operating on 28 September 1992. Apart from new main line stations (p294), branch stations were Windmill, at Coity; Sarn; Tondu; Maesteg (Ewenny Road), south of the town, opened 26 October; and Maesteg (Gateway), 100yd south of the former GWR station site. At Cardiff trains took the Leckwith loop (formerly freight) and 'City Line' via Ninian Park. Official reopening was by the Duke of Gloucester on 30 October 1992. Results exceeded previous successful reopenings, stranded Saturday passengers being carried forward by bus. Farcically, Windmill, opened 16 November, closed immediately as its shelter was too near the platform edge, allegedly by *one inch*! It 'reopened' on 12 December 1992.

From Briton Ferry Yard, south of Court Sart Junction, the Port Wallaroo Dock line served the north side of Briton Ferry Dock, closed 1950. From it, along the east bank of the River Neath, the Giant's Grave Branch served Ward's scrapyard until sold to North British Maritime Shipping in 1983. As Norbrit Wharf Siding it dealt with general import/export traffic, later becoming Neath Cargo Terminal for intermittent export of steel into the nineties. Briton Ferry Yard also sorted Speedlink workings, and traffic to and from

Baglan Bay chemical works, Llandarcy refinery, Clydach aluminium and West Wales coal.

NEATH AND SWANSEA

The Swansea Avoiding Line (Landore Junction–Swansea Loop West Junction) was singled 22/23 February 1986, and from a mile west of Cockett Tunnel – using the Up line, slewed to serve Gowerton Down platform – to the west of Duffryn Crossing on 11/12 October 1986. Loughor Viaduct was strengthened in 1980. Neath closed to goods April 1981, and to coal May 1984. In January 1984 Swansea Loop East Junction became a single lead into the Up main line, thereafter being bi-directional down to the station, which, virtually unchanged since the thirties (p202), underwent a £350,000 modernisation opened in August 1984, including an enlarged concourse (by shortening tracks 30ft in May 1983), bigger travel centre and improved ticket collection – all more fitting to the terminus of the IC125 Paddington–South Wales service. On the Vale of Neath, Blaengwrach and Aberpergwm Collieries closed July 1983 and October 1985 respectively; the line north of Neath N & B Junction went out of general use from 4 March 1986, though remained for BR staff training on ballast tamping machines. In 1992 Ryan Mining gained a Freight Facilities Grant to expand opencast working, reopening Pentreclwydau anthracite mine, coal to be conveyed to the V of N at Cwmgwrach. Onllwyn–Craigynos on the Dulais Valley line went out of use in 1977, full closure being on 28 November 1981, abandoning Dame Adelina's station (p209) to the elements, and Onllwyn–Banwen went by 1989. Blaenant Colliery closed May 1990, and the loops in 1991, N & B Junction–Onllwyn washery becoming 'one train working'. Though the R & SB trackbed in the Afan Valley returned to nature, Court Sart Junction–Dynevor Junction was part of the Swansea District route, while at Jersey Marine Junction South the R & SB joined the former V of N into Swansea Docks. Eastern Depot closed 15 May 1983, and February 1987 saw last use of the dock coal hoists – shippers sending coal instead by container, via Ellesmere Port – followed in April by closure of the coal concentration depot. The 88-lever ex-GWR Burrows Sidings box closed December 1990, access to the sidings being controlled by Port Talbot power box. Danygraig Freightliner terminal closed February 1988 (postponed from April 1987). Upper Bank Junction–Six Pit Junction reopened 1978–79 for ballast trains for embankment reconstruction near Landore Viaduct. Disused again in 1980 it was adopted by the Lower Swansea Vale Railway Preservation Society as a first step to restoring part of the Swansea–Brynamman line. Eastern Depot Junction–Morriston, serving scrapyards and BSC Duffryn, closed by March 1983; from 24 May 1983 a stop block on the V of N effectively closed Eastern Depot–Morriston, isolating the preservation society. The latter, with Light Railway Order granted in 1985, and renamed in 1986 as the Swansea Vale Railway, operated steam trips from May 1987, converting a disused foundry at Upper Bank into a restoration works.

Court Sart Junction–Llandeilo Junction, avoiding Swansea and the gradients west of Cockett Tunnel, was refurbished in 1991, including viaduct repairs. By 1983 Jersey Marine South Yard was reduced to allowing reversal of trains between Aberthaw/Margam and Blaenant/Onllwyn. On the Pontardawe/Clydach-on-Tawe Branch, despite the connection (p220), Felin Fran Junction to the end of the branch was closed for some time, being latterly used by occasional trains conveying butane and naphtha gas, before full closure on 26 September 1992. Felin Fran Yard went in 1989. That August the BSC Velindre tinplate plant closed, stock movement continuing until 17 October. On the Llanelly Railway, Gorseinon closed to goods and minerals after May 1982; when the coal depot went two years later the line to Brynlliw went too. Though Brynlliw Colliery closed July 1983, intermittent stockpile clearance kept the northern end in use until 19 October 1989. As to Llanelli–Llandeilo, in 1980 the railway north of Morlais Junction was in poor shape. The May timetable showed five passenger trains each way daily between Swansea and Shrewsbury via Llanelli. Economies on maintenance from January 1981 limited traffic to DMUs, though a lightweight diesel worked the twice-weekly Llandeilo (Margam from October 1982) to Llandovery freight. Main line diesels were banned, but returned from June 1983. Details of changes made to the 'Heart of Wales' line which rescued it from closure are recounted in Volume 11. At the southern end of the line, Llandeilo and Llandovery closed to goods and coal by April 1983, and Ammanford in May (coal, May 1988 when Wernos washery sidings were cleared). The novel 'No Signalman Key Token' (NSKT) working was introduced between Craven Arms and Pantyffynnon (reached August 1986), where the controlling signalman was located, trains passing at loops controlled by hydropneumatic trailing points with semaphores removed. At loop platforms drivers obtained telephone permission from Pantyffynnon to deposit and withdraw metal tokens from platform instruments enabling them to proceed through the next single line section. Coal distribution ceased from Pantyffynnon from 20 January 1989. Though a Sprinter appeared in 1986, full introduction came with the advent of class 153s replacing 'Heritage' DMUs from May 1992 (the inaugural 153 on the line appearing in February that year). The line celebrated its 125th anniversary with steam specials in May–June 1993. After closure of Wernos washery and Abernant Colliery in March 1988, and the Wernos Branch in June 1990, Abernant washery operated until March 1991; the final train ran on 9 April when the branch went out of use, as did the Betws Branch following closure of Betws Colliery on 25 March 1991. The branch to Gwaun-cae-Gurwen opencast disposal point closed November 1987 but reopened March 1988 for MGR working.

THE SOUTH-WEST CORNER

Llanelli station, modernised in 1979, was reversal point for the Swansea–Shrewsbury service. Goods depots at Pembrey & Burry Port and Whitland closed June 1982, and Llandeilo Junction hump yard that October, the Down side remaining for local Llanelli traffic. Coalyards mostly closed in 1983: Llanelli, Carmarthen and Whitland in May; Pembrey & Burry Port in October. Carmarthen Bay power station, fuelled with coal from Brynlliw, closed October 1983. At Carmarthen, closure on 8 October 1983 of the goods yard north of the River Tywi was followed by removal of the rail bridge over the river. A scheme for moving the station south to the main line did not proceed; instead, the junction Down main loop closed 6 January 1985, the main line being slewed to the south on 19/20 January, following which Carmarthen Junction and Carmarthen Bridge Junction curves to Carmarthen P & T Junction were singled, the junction box controlling new colour-light signalling, linking to Carmarthen–Whitland resignalling inaugurated in 1979. Carmarthen closed to coal in 1983; the south yard remained open, latterly for fertiliser traffic. Container trains to Fishguard (p250) ceased in 1978. The motorail service, started in June 1965, was withdrawn after the 1980 season. At Fishguard Harbour station the single main line was slewed to the westerly boundary between 13 June and 4 July 1982, during which Fishguard & Goodwick station reopened; it closed to freight May 1982 and coal a year later. From June 1983 Letterston–Fishguard Harbour was converted to NSKT working. A BR subsidiary, Sealink owned the railway and Harbour station beyond 287 miles 52 chains: in July 1984 BR's interest was sold to Sea Containers. From 7 January 1986 there were two daily Fishguard–Rosslare ferry services, operated jointly by Sealink and B & I (below). That May the summer boat train became an HST, 'The Hibernian', dep Paddington 09.30, arr Fishguard 13.32, the afternoon return including a 101 minute Cardiff–Paddington timing. From May 1989, when the midday stopping train was withdrawn, boat trains, and freights serving MOD Trecwyn, comprised the only traffic west of Clarbeston Road. There were advertised buses between Fishguard, Goodwick and connecting trains at Haverfordwest.

Returning to Llanelli, Cynheidre Colliery closed in 1989, rail movement ceased after 24 March, and Llanelli West Junction–Cynheidre was 'mothballed' three days later. Strangely, the last train matched the very first – a passenger working – on 14 October 1989 when a railtour traversed the branch. On the Cwmmawr Branch, BR took powers in 1981 to close Burry Port–Trimsaran and replace a mile of track, Coedbach washery–Kidwelly, closed 1965 (p229), allowing trains between main line and washery to be drawn by class 37 diesels, eight times more powerful than the class 03s which, even in multiples of three, hauled only 35 wagons on the former Burry Port & Gwendraeth Valley line, itself plagued by low bridges – the reason for using cutdown 03s. Last working over the Burry Port section was on 17 September 1983. The first revenue train over the new line, carrying domestic anthracite, ran two days later, with official opening on 27 October. Access to the main line was by reversal and run-round loop. The 03s were replaced north of the washery by 08s, given the historic names *Gwendraeth*, *Kidwelly* and *Ashburnham*. Containerised coal to Ireland, via Ellesmere Port, started with a trial run of Cawood containers from Coedbach in December 1986.

Whitland–Pembroke Dock. The B & I shipping line started a Pembroke–Cork service in May 1979. The Grade II listed Pembroke Dock station was renovated by May 1980 when B & I introduced a Rosslare service, and there were more trains and improved timings. The Cork service was withdrawn in 1983, and though B & I at Pembroke Dock and Sealink at Fishguard tried to rationalise Rosslare sailings, B & I transferred to shared facilities at Fishguard from January 1986. In 1988 the Pembroke Dock Branch was resignalled, Tenby box closing in December on introduction of NSKT working. Local traffic was now predominantly passenger, worked by Heritage DMUs, with extra holiday trains in season. A summer Saturdays ex Pembroke (*not* Dock) to Paddington IC125, calling at Tenby, started in 1983, being an extension of the earliest of two Up morning HSTs introduced that May from Carmarthen to Paddington, neither return trip reaching Pembroke, though a non-HST from Paddington arrived at Pembroke in mid afternoon. The Pembroke IC125 did not survive into 1984, but form 1985 a regular summer Saturdays InterCity 'Pembroke Coast Holiday Express' (later omitting 'Holiday'), ran between Paddington and Pembroke Dock. The summer Saturdays train between Tenby (a 'Golden Rail' resort) and York (later Leeds and Newcastle), became an HST from 1985, continuing into the nineties. Hitherto connecting at Whitland with main line services, from mid decade branch trains ran to Swansea, uniting with/splitting from Milford services at Carmarthen. Branch takings ended with a marked upturn: in 1988–89, some 39 per cent over the previous year and 62 per cent over 1986–87. Much credit went to the Pembrokeshire Rail Travellers Association for active support in publicising West Wales railways. On 5 October 1991 passengers escaped injury when a DMU coach was gutted by fire at Narberth.

At Milford Haven the goods yard closed June 1982, and the coalyards there and at Haverfordwest in May 1983. As to Milford freight branches, the Royal Naval Armaments Depot (Newton Noyes) Branch received a replacement swing bridge over the Pill in 1980, but a decade later the depot was up for sale; the Herbrandston Branch (opened 1960) went out of use from Amoco Junction in January 1984 following closure of the Esso refinery; the Waterston Branch (1968) continued to serve the Gulf Oil refinery; and the Robeston Branch (1974, from Amoco Junction) the Amoco refinery. Destinations ranged from North Wales and Lancashire to Southern England, 1990 also seeing increased traffic from the Minimet (late Texaco) terminal at Cardiff Docks. September 1983 saw a through Haverfordwest–Paddington service (p283), the gain from which was offset by loss from 3 October of the night sleeping car service from Milford Haven. Johnston (incl)–Milford Haven was singled, and colour-light signalling introduced, from June 1984, and Johnston–Clarbeston Road, similarly, from September 1988. At Haverfordwest trains used the bi-directional Up side unless passing by the Down loop extending from north of the station to the south of the bridge over the Western Cleddau. DMUs in West Wales were mostly replaced by class 153 Sprinters from February 1992, 10 May being the last Heritage working. That month class 158s started operating, and to mark their successful introduction September witnessed civic leaders entertained by Regional Railways to a luncheon cruise on the Cleddau as a mark of appreciation for local support for the railway. And long may it be so!

Author's Acknowledgements

The author's half-century of research into and writing about railway history, especially that of his native country, was sparked-off around 1927 when his news editor dumped some books on his desk, saying, 'Get some bright reviews out of this lot for the Bristol paper'. The books included the first volume of E. T. MacDermot's massive and fascinating *History of The Great Western Railway*. Although MacDermot gave excellent coverage of the railways built or acquired by the GWR in South Wales down to 1921 his remit necessarily excluded, except as incidental to the GWR's own story, both the numerous independent companies which did not join the Paddington fold until 1922–23, and the South Wales lines which became components of the LMS Railway during the latter period. Moreover, with the exception of the packet port of Fishguard and some minor dock facilities acquired through the years at Cardiff, Porthcawl, Briton Ferry and Llanelly (now Llanelli) the GWR did not until 1922 become the owner of one of the two largest dock groups in Great Britain. So there has been a lot to be told, subsequent to MacDermot, about the South Wales railways as a whole, although until just before World War II, this seems to have been a somewhat neglected field among railway historians. To present a bibliography of this railway region, and to acknowledge all those organisations and individuals who have helped the author to build up his reference library over so many years, is therefore both a massive task and an invidious one, should I offend through inadvertent omission. Firstly my gratitude for information and advice is due to many past and present officers of the GWR/Western Region, beginning for instance with the late Mr H. H. Philips, who, as a junior clerk in the personal office of the formidable TVR general manager, E. A. Prosser, and who when last we met was assistant general manager at Paddington. Gratitude next to my former colleagues at BR Headquarters, and prior thereto on the LMS Railway. Officers of the British Transport Docks Board (especially Mr G. W. Cansdale), of the British Waterways and their statutory predecessors, also of Sealink (UK) Ltd, which is now responsible for the Fishguard services, have also been helpful, while successive BR Divisional Managers at Cardiff WR and their Public Relations Officer Mr Neil W. Sprinks, have ensured that my information on recent developments is up to date to the end of 1979.

Other organisations and companies who have either provided or corrected information include the National Coal Board (especially Mr Islwyn Evans); Messrs Cory's; Nevill, Druce & Co Ltd. and Batchelor Robinson & Co Ltd. (both of Llanelli), and Thos. W. Ward, Ltd, Briton Ferry. Municipal authorities who have helped are Newport and Cardiff (Librarians), Bridgend, Port Talbot, and Llanelli.

Facilities for research have kindly been afforded by the National Railway Museum, York, (Mr T. J. Edgington, Technical Information Officer); the former Archivists BTC/BRB, and the Curator (Historical Relics), BTC/BRB.

My indebtedness is also due to many friends and correspondents, including Dr A. L. Barnett, Messrs G. J. Aston, W. A. Camwell, C. R. Clinker, F. K. Davies, R. J. Doran, John Drayton, Charles Hadfield, CMG (particularly for use of information from his invaluable canal histories), Charles E. Lee, R. M. Robbins, T. B. Sands, B. G. Wilson, and the late Messrs D. E. Cameron, M. D. Greville, V. Stewart Haram, and R. E. Thomas. Other acknowledgements are in the ensuing bibliography.

Finally, my special thanks are due to my friend and fellow historian, Mr E. R. Mountford of Caerphilly, for patiently reading, correcting and making valuable suggestions in regard to the manuscript; to Miss M. Micklethwaite for interpreting my handwriting and Welsh spelling and for typing the whole of the manuscript; and by no means least to Professor J. Allan Patmore, co-editor of the *Regional History* series, for his wise guidance and unfailing patience.

Bibliography

GEOGRAPHY AND ECONOMICS

Chappell, Edgar L. *History of the Port of Cardiff* (Priory Press, Cardiff, 1939)

Edwards, A. Trystan. *Merthyr, Rhondda & The Valleys* (Robert Hale, 1938).

Gale, W.K.V. *The British Iron & Steel Industry* (Newton Abbot, 1967).

Galloway, Robert L. *A History of Coal Mining in Great Britain, 1882* (reprinted with new introduction, etc, Baron F. Duckham, Newton Abbot, 1962).

Howells, C.S. *Transport Facilities in South Wales & Monmouthshire* (University Press, Cardiff, 1911).

Hughes & James. *Wales, A Physical, Social & Economic Geography* (University of London Press, 1960).

Jenkins, Gwyn. *Wales* (B. T. Batsford, 1975).

Lewis, E.D. *The Rhondda Valleys* (Phoenix House, 1959).

Lewis, H. Harry. *Gwent Panorama* (Griffin Press, Pontypool, 1975).

Matthews, James. *Historic Newport* (published privately, 1910).

Pannell, J.P.M. *An Illustrated History of Civil Engineering,* (Thames & Hudson, 1964).

Piehler, H.A. *Wales for Everyone* (Dent, 1963).

Pritchard, A.J. *Griffithstown* (Griffin Press, Pontypool, 1957).

Rees, J.F. *The Story of Milford* (University of Wales Press, 1957).

Senior, Michael. *Portrait of South Wales* (Robert Hale, 1974).

Vaughan Thomas & Llewellyn. *The Shell Guide to Wales* (Michael Joseph, 1969).

Williams, W.E. *Transit & Commerce* (South Wales Daily Post, Swansea, 1907).

PRIMARY SOURCES

Prospectus, Parliamentary Bills, Committee proceedings, Acts minute books, half-yearly reports, etc, public and working timetables and appendices, rule books, etc, of the various companies concerned, for access to certain of which I am grateful to the Archivists (Historical Records) of the British Transport Commission and the British Railways Board. Also to the late Mr John de Winton of Brecon (a great-grandson of the first chairman of the B & M Railway Company), for access to family papers and legal records. Similarly my late mother's papers relating to the former family business of Southwood Jones & Co. Ltd have been of value in relation to railways in the Ebbw and Sirhowy Valleys.

For use of maps, junction diagrams, and schedules of running powers, etc, thanks are due to the Railway Clearing House, especially Mr T.J. Lynch, former secretary.

Reports of inquiries into accidents (Board of Trade and Ministry of Transport); Board of Trade and South Wales Ports Shipping returns.

CANALS AND TRAMROADS

Baxter, B. *Industrial Archaeology, Stone Blocks & Iron Rails* (Newton Abbot, 1966).

Hadfield, Charles. *The Canals of South Wales & the Border* (Phoenix House, 1957).

Lewis, M.J.T. *Steam on the Penydarren* (Industrial Railway Record Journal No 59, April 1975).

Priestley, Joseph. *Historical Account of the Navigable Rivers, Canals & Railways Throughout Great Britain* (Longmans and others, 1831).

RAILWAYS, EARLY

Dendy Marshall, C.F. *A History of British Railways Down to the Year 1830.* (Oxford University Press, 1938).

Lee, Charles E. *The Evolution of Railways* (2nd Revised Edition, The Railway Gazette, 1943).

Lewin, H.G. *Early British Railways, 1801-44* (Locomotive Publishing Co); *The British Railway System* (to 1844), (G. Bell & Sons, 1914) *The Railway Mania & its Aftermath, 1845–52* (Railway Gazette, 1936).

GREAT WESTERN RAILWAY

Ahrons, E.L. *Locomotive & Train Working in the Latter Part of the Nineteenth Century* (GWR and the Cambrian, B & M, TV, Rhymney and Barry Railways); Vol. 4 of articles originally published serially in *The Railway Magazine* (Edited in book form by E. L. Asher, W. Heffer, Cambridge, 1953).

Booker, Frank. *The Great Western Railway, A New History* (Newton Abbot, 1977)

Clinker, C.R. *Great Western Railway: A Register of Halts and Platforms, 1903–1975.* (Published by the author, 1975).

MacDermot, E.T. *Official History,* published by the Company in two volumes, 1927 and 1931. Re-published as revised by C.R. Clinker, 1964 (Ian Allan) with additional volume (to 1948), by O.S. Nock, 1967.

LOCAL RAILWAY HISTORIES

Barrie, D.S.M. *The Taff Vale Railway (* 1939, reprinted and updated 1969); *The Rhymney Railway* (1952, reprinted and updated 1973); *The Brecon & Merthyr Railway* (1957, reprinted and up-dated 1975); *The Barry Railway* (1962, reprinted and up-dated 1978).

Lee, Charles E. *The First Passenger Railway* (Railway Publishing Co., 1942, revised and re-published under title *The Swansea & Mumbles Railway,* 1970).

Morris, J.P. *The North Pembroke* [sic] *& Fishguard Railway(1969).*

Price, M.R.C. *The Saundersfoot Railway,* 1964.

Pritchard, A.J. *The Railways of S. E. Monmouthshire,* (1939, reprinted with addenda 1962).

Tasker, W.W. *Railways in the Sirhowy Valley (* 1978).

(All the above in the Oakwood Press Series).

Barrie, D.S.M., and Lee, Charles E. *The Sirhowy Valley & its Railways* (Railway Publishing Co., 1940, a reprint of articles in The Railway Magazine).

Bowen, Raymond E. *The Burry Port and Gwendraeth Valley Railway* (reprint from The Carmarthenshire Antiquary, 1976).

Gasquoine, C.P. *The Story of the Cambrian* (Caxton Press, Oswestry, 1922).

Rimell, R.J. *History of the Barry Railway,* 1884–1921 (company official history, 1923).

Smith D.J. *Shrewsbury to Swansea* (history of the Central Wales route, Town & Country Press, 1971).

ROLLING STOCK, WORKSHOPS.

Ahrons, E.L. *The British Steam Locomotive, 1825–1925* (Locomotive Publishing Company, 1925).

Dendy Marshall, C.F. A *History of Railway Locomotives Down to the End of l931.* (Locomotive Publishing Company, 1953).

Mountford, E.R. *Caerphilly Works, 1901–64* (Roundhouse Books, 1965).

Mountford, E.R. *A Register of GWR Absorbed Coaching Stock,* 1922-23 (Oakwood Press, 1978).

Railway Correspondence & Travel Society. *The Locomotives of the Great Western Railway* (Series). Parts Three (Absorbed Engines, 1854-1921, published 1956); Ten (Absorbed Engines, 1922-47, published 1966) and Eleven (The Rail Motor Vehicles and Internal Combustion Locomotives, published 1952, 2nd edition 1956).

CLOSURES

Clinker, C.R. *Clinker's Register of Closed Passenger Stations and Goods Depots in England, Scotland and Wales, 1830–1977* (Avon Anglia Publications, 1978).

Hill, N.J. and McDougall, A.O. *A Guide to Closed Railways in Britain, 1948–75* (Branch Line Society, 1977).

Page, James. *Forgotten Railways – South Wales* (Newton Abbot, 1979).

PROCEEDINGS OF HISTORICAL, ETC. SOCIETIES

Cardiff Scientific Society (paper by the author, 22 February 1950).

South Wales & Monmouthshire Railways & Docks Lecture & Debating Society (papers by the author 2 January 1951, and by R. H. Edwards (docks aspect), 5 March 1957).

Merthyr Tydfil Historical Society. Merthyr Historian Vols. I (1976) and II (1978) – lectures of local railway interest, notably on Dowlais industrial lines.

Gwent (formerly Monmouthshire) Local History Council. Gwent Local History (previous title Presenting Monmouthshire), numerous articles and references. The author is grateful to Professor S.H. Beaver, MA, FRGS, formerly Head of the Department of Geography at the University of Keele, for being able to peruse, and in some cases to take facts from, a valuable but hitherto unpublished manuscript, *Transport & Industry in*

South Wales, 1750–1950: A Study in Railway Geography. This formed the basis of two addresses given by Professor Beaver to meetings of The British Association at Cardiff in 1962 and at Swansea, 1971.

Also to Mr T.B. Sands for permission to use some of the results of his original and extensive research into the railways of Swansea Vale, published in The Railway & Canal Historical Society Journal, July 1973.

BIOGRAPHICAL

Addis, John P. *The Crawshay Dynasty* (University of Wales Press, 1957).

Bessborough, the Earl of (as Editor). *Lady Charlotte Guest: Extracts from her Journal 1833-52* (John Murray, 1950).

Thomas, Ivor. *Top Sawyer, a Biography of David Davies of Llandinam* (Longmans, Green, 1938).

REMINISCENCES, PERSONAL

Drayton, John. *On the Footplate, Memoirs of a GWR Engineman* (Bradford Barton, Truro, 1976).

Gooch, Sir Daniel. *Memoirs & Diary,* edited by Roger Burdett Wilson (Newton Abbot, 1972).

Morgan, Bryan, & Meyrick, Bette. *Behind the Steam* (Hutchinson, 1973).

Neele, G.P. *Railway Reminiscences* (McCorquodale, 1904). Mostly the recollections of an LNWR Chief Officer. I am grateful to my cousins, the late Mrs Henty Thorne and Miss F. V. Neele, granddaughters of G. P. Neele, for access to his manuscript diaries.

NEWSPAPERS

Abergavenny Chronicle, Brecon & Radnor Express, The Cambrian, Cardiff & Merthyr Guardian, Merthyr Telegraph, South Wales Argus (Newport), South Wales Daily News, South Wales Daily Post, South Wales Echo, Western Mail, West Wales Guardian.

PERIODICALS

Herapath's Journal, The Railway Gazette (notably historical supplements for GWR 30 August 1935, and LMSR 16 September 1938), Railway Magazine, Railway Review, The Railway Observer (RCTS), Railway Times, Journal of the Stephenson Locomotive Society, Branch Line News (Branch Line Society), Powell Duffryn Review, etc.

Outstanding as a source of this kind is the GWR Magazine, 1889-1947. The Journal of Transport History, New Series Vol III No 2, included a notable article by M. J. Daunton under title *Aristocrat and Traders:* The Bute Docks 1839-1914, on the relationship between the Bute Estate and the dock and railway undertakings (Leicester University Press, September 1975).

Bradshaw's Guide. Bradshaw's Railway Manual. The Railway Year Book.

FURTHER BIBLIOGRAPHY 1976–1992

Baker, S.K. *Rail Atlas Great Britain & Ireland* (Oxford Publishing Co., various edns 1977–92).

Barry, D.S.M rev. Kidner, R.W. *The Brecon & Merthyr Railway* (The Oakwood Press, 1991).

Body, Geoffrey *PSL Field Guide: Railways of the Western Region* (Patrick Stephens, 1983).

Butcher, Alan (edit.) *Railways Restored* (Ian Allan, various edns 1980–93).

Chapman, Colin. *The Cowbridge Railway* (Oxford Publishing Co, 1984).

Cooke, R.A. *Atlas of the Great Western Railway* (Wild Swan Publications, 1988); *Track Diagrams* for South Wales as published by R.A. Cooke to date).

Cummings, John. *Railway Motor Buses and Bus Services in the British Isles 1902–1933* (Oxford Publishing Co, 1980).

Gladwin, D.D. & J.M. *The Canals of the Welsh Valleys and their Tramroads* (The Oakwood Press, 1991).

Hawkins, Chris & Reeve, George. *LMS Engine Sheds Volume One* The LNWR (Wild Swan Publications, 1981).

Hurst, Geoffrey. *Register of Closed Railways 1948–1991* (Milepost Publications, 1992).

Lee, Charles E. *The Swansea & Mumbles Railway* (The Oakwood Press, 1988).

Morgan, H. *South Wales Branch Lines* (Ian Allan, 1984).

Mountford, Eric. *The Cardiff Railway* (1987); *The USA 756th RSB at*

Newport (Ebbw Junction) (1989). (Both The Oakwood Press).

Page, James. *Rails in the Valleys* (David & Charles, 1989).

Price, M.R.C. *The Whitland and Cardigan Railway* (1976); *The Pembroke and Tenby Railway* (1986); *The Llanelly & Mynydd Mawr Railway* (1992). (All The Oakwood Press).

Quail Map Company. *British Rail Track Diagrams 3 Western Region* (1989).

Rhodes, Michael. *Diesels in South Wales* (Oxford Publishing Co, 1984).

Rhodes, Michael & Shannon, Paul. *Freight Only Vol 3 Wales and Scotland* (1988); *Freight Only Yearbook Nos 1 and 2* (1990 and 1991). (All Silver Link Publishing).

Tasker, W.W. *The Merthyr Tredegar & Abergavenny Railway and Branches* (Oxford Publishing Co, 1986); *Railways in the Sirhowy Valley* (The Oakwood Press, 1992).

Thomas, David St John & Whitehouse, Patrick, *BR in the Eighties* (David & Charles, 1990).

The author of chapter XII acknowledges drawing heavily on the files of *Branch Line News, Modern Railways, Rail Enthusiast* and *Rail; Railway Magazine, Railway Observer* and *Railway World.*

Index

Illustrations are in *italic type*.